16095
15 99

D0308185

46.99
B!

WITHDRAWN
FROM STOCK

# Fashioning London

## CLOTHING AND
## THE MODERN METROPOLIS

**Christopher Breward** is Professor in Historical and Cultural Studies at London College of Fashion, The London Institute. He has taught art and design history at Manchester Metropolitan University and the Royal College of Art, London, and has lectured widely in Great Britain, the United States, Australia and Europe. He has also served on the executive committees of the Design History Society and the Costume Society. He sits on the editorial board of the international research journal *Fashion Theory* and has contributed to the *Journal of Design History*, *Parallax*, *Gender and History*, *New Formations* and the *London Journal*. His publications include *The Culture of Fashion* (Manchester University Press 1995), *The Hidden Consumer* (Manchester University Press 1999), *Fashion* (Oxford University Press 2003), and co-edited collections *Material Memories* (Berg 1999) and *The Englishness of English Dress* (Berg 2002).

# Fashioning London

## CLOTHING AND THE MODERN METROPOLIS

## CHRISTOPHER BREWARD

❀ BERG
OXFORD • NEW YORK

391.
009421
BRE

First published in 2004 by

**Berg**

Editorial offices:

1st Floor, Angel Court, 81 St Clements Street, Oxford, OX4 1AW, UK

838 Broadway, Third Floor, New York, NY 10003-4812, USA

© Christopher Breward 2004

All rights reserved.

No part of this publication may be reproduced in any form

or by any means without the written permission of Berg.

Berg is the imprint of Oxford International Publishers Ltd.


**Library of Congress Cataloguing-in-Publication Data**

A catalogue record for this book is available from the Library of Congress.


**British Library Cataloguing-in-Publication Data**

A catalogue record for this book is available from the British Library.


ISBN 1 85973 787 0 (Cloth)
      1 85973 792 7 (Paper)




Designed and Typeset by Oroon Das

Printed in the United Kingdom by Biddles Ltd, Guildford and Kings Lynn




www.bergpublishers.com

# CONTENTS

# ACKNOWLEDGEMENTS

First I should like to thank Edwina Ehrman and Oriole Cullen of the Museum of London for their unflagging interest in this project. Along with my wonderful colleague Caroline Evans, Edwina has also been the most patient and perceptive of readers. Their commentary on every draft has shaped the final form of the book in a profound sense. Others have been spared the labour of reading the whole in its unedited versions, but I am very grateful for the insights of John Styles, Lynn Nead, Frank Mort, Barbara Burman, Carole Turbin, David Green, Elizabeth McKellar, Elizabeth Wilson, Adam Briggs and Alistair O'Neill. Their expertise ensured that individual chapters are reasonably free of mistakes (any that remain are entirely my responsibility) and benefit from the broader perspective generally denied the lone author.

In the wider academic community I must credit those who invited me to air early ideas at seminars and conferences and offered their ideas in return, or who simply exchanged views over a coffee or a glass of wine at the British Library and elsewhere. Michael Hatt, Andrew Stephenson, Reina Lewis, Marcia Pointon, Cheryl Buckley, Malcolm Baker, Sean Nixon, Deborah Ryan, Mica Nava, David Gilbert, Simona Segre, Miles Ogborn, Juliet Ash, Lesley Miller, Ulrich Lehman, Dana Arnold, Tim Barringer, Susan Kaiser, Joe Kerr, Bo Lonquist, Lou Taylor, Jude Freeman, Gerda Buxbaum, Adrian Rifkin, Judith Walcowitz, Madeleine Ginsberg, Margaret Maynard, John Marriott, Carol Tulloch, Aileen Ribeiro, Valerie Steele, Amanda Vickery and Djurdja Bartlett have all contributed in this respect.

At my own institution Becky Conekin, Pamela Church Gibson, Sandy Black, Andrew Tucker, Sue Chowles, Elizabeth Rouse, Katherine Baird, Caroline Cox, Justin Lorenzen, Kitty Hauser, Andrew Hill, Jamie Brassett, Judith Watt, Andrea Stewart, Agnes Rocamora, Norma Starszakowna, Graeme Evans, Alan Canon Jones, Sonia Ashmore, Toshio Watanabe, Orianna Baddeley, Janice Hart, Jane Holt, Sandra Holtby, Roy Peach, Ann Priest, Julia Gaimster, Maggie Nordern, Francis Geesin, Tim Jackson, Robert Lutton, Amy de la Haye, Heather Lambert, Bill Stubbs, Linda Sandino, Caroline Dakers, Rebecca Arnold and Lorraine Gamman proved to be supportive colleagues in many different ways. Furthermore, the enthusiasm and interests of the postgraduate student community at the London College of Fashion and the London Institute has played a major role in directing the concerns of the book. In this respect I owe a special debt of gratitude to Bronwen Edwards, Clare Lomas, Ann Bailey, Jessica Bugg, Nicholas Cambridge, Valerie Wilson Trower, Jane Tynan, Hilary McCool, Kevin Willoughby, Janice Miller and Alice Cicolini.

Time and resources for researching *Fashioning London* were greatly augmented by funding from several external bodies. I am therefore grateful for the award of a Visiting Fellowship to the Centre for British Art, Yale University in 2000 and a period of Research Leave supported by the Arts and Humanities Research Board in 2001. Picture Research for the book was ably provided by Marketa Uhlirova as part of the 'Fashion and Modernity Project' based at Central Saint Martins and London College of Fashion. Her time together with substantial copyright and reproduction costs were also funded by the Arts and Humanities Research Board. Many copyright owners were similarly very generous in agreeing free use of images or reduced rates. Kathryn Earle and her colleagues at Berg Publishers showed great faith in sticking with the book long after the first deadline had passed and were always ready with useful advice and reassurances.

Finally, beyond the professional sphere I am aware that this is a book which reflects an ongoing relationship with London itself. I have lived in this extraordinary place for almost all of my adult life and it has come to represent a home whose unique comforts and daily stresses have been shared with a close family of friends. For sustaining me in the city over twenty years and sharing my passion for its sublime character I thank fellow Londoners Daniel Scott, Rachel North, Josephine Matthews, Rupert Thomas and especially James Brook.

Every effort has been made to trace copyright holders of images reproduced in this book. If any copyright holders have not been properly credited, please contact the publishers, who will be happy to rectify the omission in future editions.

# ILLUSTRATIONS

# INTRODUCTION

This is a book about fashion and the city. More specifically it is a book about fashion and its role in the lives of Londoners during the modern period. Unsurprisingly it derives its theoretical underpinnings from the exciting work that has been completed over recent years by scholars in the disciplines of cultural studies, art and design history, architectural criticism and theory, human and cultural geography and social and economic history.[1] Yet while several ground-breaking texts emerging from these fields of study have acknowledged the important connections to be made between histories of place, sartorial cultures and defining moments of modernity, the crucial status of fashion as a motor for urban change and the formation of metropolitan identities has so far been rather overlooked, or taken for granted.[2]

Such academic myopia is partly due to the ubiquitous presence of fashion in the day-to-day rhythms of city life and to its tantalizing ephemerality. This has perhaps had the effect of setting fashionable clothing beyond the sights of historians with more 'serious' political concerns or a scrupulously empirical bent. A relative paucity of published work in this field is also a result of the tendency of many scholars to dismiss fashion as a superficial symptom of modernity rather than seeing it as an active agent of progress in the manner of other creative practices such as architecture, film or fine art. Furthermore, like the metropolis itself, fashion is marked by the complexity of its many-layered meanings, which makes any attempted analysis an especially fraught endeavour. It is a bounded thing, fixed and experienced in space - an amalgamation of seams and textiles, an interface between the body and its environment. It is a practice, a fulcrum for the display of taste and status, a site for the production and consumption of objects and beliefs; and it is an event, both spectacular and routine, cyclical in its adherence to the natural and commercial seasons, innovatory in its bursts of avant-gardism, and sequential in its guise as a palimpsest of memories and traditions. These shared characteristics endow both cities and clothes with a vital energy that begs further explanation and helps to define the structure and focus of what follows.

In the absence of a discrete literature of urban fashionability, I want to open this study by isolating just three statements on method from the richness of general theoretical works dealing with the nature of urban culture. Though they represent only a partial approach to the practice of constructing a sartorial history of the city, in their different ways these texts have guided me toward a useful working framework for studying fashion in its spatial and temporal contexts; one that moves beyond the frustrations imposed by disciplinary boundaries and recognizes the very special circumstances that endow London fashion with its unique emotional, economic and aesthetic imprint. First, working in an arena that initially seems very remote from the concerns of the fashion historian, literary theorist Julian Wolfreys is interested in the representation of London in nineteenth-century literature, as a terrifying and unfathomable spectre. He is critical of the way in which many historians have attempted to use the writings of authors such as William Blake or Charles Dickens as a key to understanding the 'real'

❶　Map of London, 1851 (Corporation of London)

London because in his view the written and the material city are both fugitive experiences, contingent only on the particular position of the beholder. In this sense the city exists for Wolfreys almost as a form of filmic representation, in constant flux, knowable only through traces and chance recollections. In effect the written city is not so far removed from the circumstances pertaining in fashion culture, where representations of fashionability are bound into a system of periodic renewal and retrievable in fragments, never as a coherent whole:

Attempts to write the city's sites and spaces carry in them an understanding, at the level of grammar, syntax, rhetoric and enunciation - in short at all levels of form - of the excess beyond comprehension which is the modern city.... It hovers beyond the possibility of simple representation, but is never yet reducible to a series of simulacra. 'London' does not name a location or base. Instead it names a multiplicity of events, chance occurrences and fields of opportunities... In assigning a city a history we overwrite a past on to what has always been a city in the act of becoming, a city always in the process of self- transformation. Such an overwriting erases the transformative becoming-modern, the city's constant movement towards a future which is yet to arrive.[3]

Geographer Nigel Thrift works against interpretations of urban culture based around theories of representation in his plea for a theory of the city which prioritizes its haptic properties, as a phenomenon which is felt, heard, smelt and tasted as much as it is seen, as a place situated in the concrete world of the here and now rather than residing solely in the imagination or as a figment of purely scopic regimes. In this request he echoes the demands of recent fashion theorists for a study of clothing which acknowledges its proper relationship to the body, and opens up a space in which fashion, as much as architecture and planning, can be interpreted as a visceral part of the metropolitan experience[4]:

The linguistic turn in the social sciences and humanities has too often cut us off from much that is most interesting about human practices, most especially their embodied and situated nature, by stressing certain aspects of the visual-cum-verbal as 'the only home of social knowledge' at the expense of the haptic, the acoustic, the kinesthetic and the iconic.... Non-representational thinking argues that practices constitute our sense of the real... it is concerned with thought in action, with presentation rather than representation... it is concerned with thinking with the entire body. In turn, this means that non-representational models valorise all the senses, and not just the visual, and their procedures are not modelled solely on the act of looking.[5]

The influential work of sociologist Michel de Certeau bridges the disparate positions of Wolfreys and Thrift by upholding the status of the city as an archive of many competing pasts, which are nevertheless 'embodied'. He acknowledges its mysterious and subjective character but locates this in the sensate sphere of demotic actions, offering the silent stories of everyday life as a means of uncovering the obscured significance of metropolitan space. This combination of the mythic and the material which typifies de

Certeau's account of the urban experience offers a fascinating model for extending the study of the metropolitan to an examination of dress; for the defining features of fashion, both as a concrete object produced and consumed in metropolitan situations, and as an ephemeral and unstable cipher for shifting desires and attitudes, would seem to hold as much, if not more potential than other elements of material culture for tracing the interplay of time and space which identifies the city as a cradle for modernity:

Gestures and narratives... are both characterised as chains of operations done on and with the lexicon of things. Gestures are the true archives of the city... they remake the urban landscape every day. They sculpt a thousand pasts that are perhaps no longer namable and that structure no less their experience of the city... The wordless histories of walking, dress, housing or cooking shape neighbourhoods on behalf of absences; they trace out memories that no longer have a place. Such is the 'work' of urban narratives as well. They insinuate different spaces into cafes, offices and buildings... With the vocabulary of objects and well known words, they create another dimension, in turn fantastical and delinquent, fearful and legitimating. For this reason they render the city 'believable', affect it with unknown depth to be inventoried, and open it up to journeys. They are the keys to the city; they give access to what it is: mythical.[6]

Other authors have of course already utilized such methods as those noted above and produced sophisticated accounts of the city and its myths. Richard Sennett for one has traced a fascinating history of city planning, urban experiences and their relationship to modernity through a careful deconstruction of the developing symbolism of the body in Western culture. His bodies, though, are generally abstracted or naked, or both; their veins, nerves and sinews adapted to the development of circulatory transport systems, receptive to the neurosis of the faceless urban crowd, or flexed in defense of political regimes and metropolitan institutions. But the body clothed and fashioned, as a signifier of the commercial, social and leisure spheres of the city, is largely absent from Sennett's reading.[7]

A handful of exemplary texts have positioned the idea of fashionability as a central concept of urban culture more emphatically, but I think it would be fair to suggest that these authors have been concerned primarily with other agendas than that of plotting the story of a city through the sartorial habits of its inhabitants: Valerie Steele with establishing a material history of the Paris fashion industries and their global dominance; Elizabeth Wilson with tracing the experiences of women in urban landscapes which have generally been defined as dangerous or constricting - where fashion is only one of several phenomena which have marked that experience as pleasurable or compromising; and Mark Wigley with uncovering the guilty and ambivalent debt owed by those modernist architects who planned the cities of the early twentieth century to the feminized sphere of fashion.[8] So, the productive identification of the relationship between fashion, space, time and place as a tool for the examination of metropolitan culture or the construction of urban histories has not thus far been directly approached as a meaningful project in its own right.

Geographer David Gilbert has, however, provided an appropriate template for the task ahead.[9] He suggests five historical themes which might be considered in any attempt to chart 'the long-term development of the geography of fashion's world cities', and these certainly underpin the case-studies which form the substance of this volume. First Gilbert identifies the emergence of 'modern' urban forms of retailing and consumption from the eighteenth century onward as a prerequisite for the rise of the fashion city. Such innovatory practices of commerce and display were concentrated in different and competing sites across the globe, but their development was marked at different stages in Paris and London, then Berlin and New York and finally in the twentieth-century Milan and Tokyo. Secondly he notes the economic and symbolic systems of European imperialism introduced during the eighteenth and nineteenth centuries, in which the ordering of the fashion industry was shaped around the international networks of trade and labour established as part of the colonial project. This coincided with the increased circulation of stylistic codes for the exotic and the luxurious which placed European capitals at the centre of this real and imagined geography. Thirdly, and deriving from this same mobilization of imperial power, fashion emerged as a currency that encouraged cities and nations to compete, its value equivalent to the promotion of state architecture, exhibition culture, grand street plans and organized tourism.

Gilbert also considers the influence of an American engagement with European fashion in the twentieth century as a defining factor in a popular, global understanding of the generic fashion city. In this conflation of influences, Hollywood imagery branded an understanding of Paris as world fashion capital on the Western consciousness, while New York developed as a particularly concentrated example of the promotion of a city as a spectacle of commercial culture. London, in this vision, featured either as a bastion of tradition and conservatism or as a gothic formation of fog-shrouded alleyways, the frightening home to high fashion's 'other'. Finally Gilbert positions the development of a symbolic ordering of cities within the fashion media as a key influence on the ways in which fashion is currently understood in an urban context and vice versa - noting the growing tendency of stylists, photographers and advertisers to conflate urban culture itself with the consumption and experience of fashion . As he suggests 'if fashion culture enjoys inventing and re-inventing its urban geography, it retains a certain conservatism about its world centres'. For Paris, New York, Milan or London 'the rhetoric is sometimes one of newness and dynamism, but more often it is of an almost organic sense of fashionability growing out of the rich culture of metropolitan life'.[10] This tension between longer histories and future projections situated in fashion's status as a phenomenon of the present is perhaps what lends clothing and its representation such potency as a measure of city life and its development.

Taking the suggestions of Gilbert on board, this book therefore aims to examine the relationship of London's spaces and their inhabitants to the production and consumption of fashionable clothing from the late eighteenth century to the present. In researching a series of discrete case studies spread across two hundred years of change and stasis I have endeavoured to pull together sources and methods that in combination shed new light on the developing material culture of the capital. In practice this has meant using the Museum of London's extensive dress, ephemera and other visual collections, drawing on items that are unfamiliar, or which when considered together with more 'traditional' evidence provide new insights into the status of fashion as an important aspect of London's social, cultural and economic history.[11] This approach presents fashionable clothing as a further resource through which the story of a city might be written, and demonstrates how the production, retailing and wearing of dress in London has contributed toward the shaping of different locales, informing the material, emotional and spatial experience of city life across all levels of society.

The remainder of the book is divided into distinct chapters, each centering on particular areas of London and the iconic figures associated with them. Its organization pays light-hearted homage to the picturesque tradition of categorizing the city's teeming streets under the headings of a colourful gallery of characters, such as Laroon's *Cryes of London Drawne after the Life* of 1687, or the later investigations of Mayhew and Dickens.[12] In this way I hope to illustrate the rise and mediation of identifiable 'London styles' across different sectors of the clothing and retail trades and the population at large, and tell the story of the city through its garments, with fashion joining architecture and other material artefacts as a form of urban biography.[13] While individual chapters concentrate on a specific time and place, the design of the whole also aims to suggest linkages and overlaps between moments, locales and styles. The majority of chapters include a close analysis of one or more garments, chosen either because of their links with the geographical area under study (generally they were made, worn or sold in the vicinity) or to suggest the broader social and aesthetic concerns of the local population during the relevant period. From a consideration of the material object, chapters develop to incorporate discussion of the representation of fashionability in space, linking clothed bodies to the built environment, the life of the street and the wider dissemination of a 'London style'.

In this manner *Fashioning London* sets out to reposition London's own clothing cultures as an important influence on the development of global fashions. It focuses on Londoners as arbiters of a distinctive and compelling sense of style. And it shows how the production and consumption of clothing has echoed and influenced London's economic fortunes, cultural status and demographic health during the modern period. However, while it provides some evidence for the ways in which fashion ideas have been developed, made concrete and disseminated in London at key moments, this book makes no pretence at offering a smooth and all-encompassing fashion history. Rather it foregrounds fashion as a 'memorializing' practice which underpins our comprehension of space and time as vividly as the built environment or the social, economic and cultural infrastructures through which its forms and shifting meanings are manifested.[14] In this sense its content is as subjective as any remembered event, and as fragile as the state of any discarded garment.

The first chapter concentrates on the development of Savile Row, Bond Street and the district around St James's Palace as a locus for one of the most influential and long-lived London styles - that of the gentleman dandy. The juxtaposition of the tailor's workshop and the dandy's dressing room links issues of production and consumption, while contemporary accounts and examples of dress illustrate the extensive nature of the male wardrobe and show how London manufacturers and retailers established themselves as the originators of the typical dandy's look. Visual and textual material focus on those personalities and pastimes associated with the dandy lifestyle, drawing out the connections to be made between high- and low-life in the formation of a modern fashionable style. The emergence of the West End as a centre for leisure and retailing concerns focused on aristocratic patronage provides the architectural and economic background for this chapter. The visual register of a neo-classical architectural grammar and the concomitant organization of streets, parks and squares during the period offers a spatial context for considering issues pertinent to the public display of masculine tastes and desires.

Chapter 2 broadens out the theme of contrast in geographical and racial terms, presenting the elite dressmaker's showroom and the sweatshop as prime sites for the construction of fashion-related identities in the mid-nineteenth century. Beyond these specific spaces the section will also consider the importance of the 'urban exotic' in fixing London as a centre for imaginative explorations in metropolitan fashion cultures. The elaborate artifice on display in Regent Street is linked here with the aestheticization of poverty and 'otherness' by journalists writing on the East End. The second-hand clothes trade and growth of immigrant communities in Whitechapel, Wapping and Bermondsey offered an ideal opportunity for showcasing the sublime confusion of clothing worn by the London poor alongside the opulent choices of the wealthy, while the figures of the foreigner and the middle-class shopper were elided in a potentially dangerous manner. This was a period where the contrasting textures and colours of clothes lent themselves to authors who were attempting to describe the feel and atmosphere of the Victorian metropolis.

Chapter 3 concentrates on fashion as an important component in the development of London's mass-leisure industries in the late nineteenth and early twentieth centuries. Orientating itself around the Strand, it aims to show how ordinary Londoners engaged with an idea of their city that was both cosmopolitan, bohemian, fun-loving, modern and seemingly democratic. The extravagant dress worn by actresses and music-hall performers established a pattern of accessible 'glamour' that linked the risque attractions of burlesque to the promotional techniques of London's new garment industries. Supporting ephemera and visual material is used to consider the role played by the city's burgeoning culture of theatre and fashion promotion in both fixing and circulating a fashionable style of London dress. Despite the local prominence of designers such as Lucile and style-leaders such as Marie Tempest, this was also a period when fashionable Londoners looked out toward other centres for their stylistic cues - to Paris, Berlin, and New York - while the developing touristic and official culture of their city increasingly embraced a repertoire of city-types whose clothing and context announced a forward-looking version of London that prioritized the spectacular, the innovative and the unashamedly sentimental aspects of urban living. Thus the dapper guardsman, the chorus girl and the newly emancipated working woman were as representative of a London version of style as the gaudy attractions of a frenetic Oxford Street.

In the inter-war figures of the Society hostess and the suburban housewife, Chapter 4 traces the divergent strands of conspicuous pleasure and conservative respectability which typified London fashion culture after the First World War. Elite provision continued along the lines established in the late nineteenth century, with Mayfair and Kensington emporia offering aristocratic women bespoke service in opulent surroundings. At the same time the reorganization of the ready-made garment industry along Fordist lines provided middle-class women with the well-made suits and frocks which became a staple of suburban good form. These conflicting worlds met at intersections engineered by London's transformation into a modern twentieth-century city. At the cinema, in the dancehall and on the underground the democratic potential of metropolitan fashion was refined for a new generation.

Reconstruction and transition provide the major themes for Chapter 5, which looks to Mayfair and Belgravia, the working-class districts of South London and the no man's land of Soho as the districts which established themselves in the minds of consumers, visitors and commentators as the cradles for a distinctive London style in the post-war period. The contribution of elite London designers including Digby Morton, Victor Stieble, Hardy Amies and Norman Hartnell to the creation of a refined form of English elegance in women's wear forms the background to a more sustained analysis of the concurrent rise of New-Edwardian dressing for men in the 1940s and early 1950s. Men's wear in this period takes on a particular prominence due to its London roots and its links through to subcultural forms of dressing in the following decades. The terrain is perhaps a familiar one, but the chapter endeavours to show how these enduring styles interweave with the geography and changing social fabric of London's 'bohemian' and subaltern quarters, mirroring those patterns of gentrification and redevelopment that in their different ways went on to transform areas such as Brixton and Hackney, Islington and Covent Garden.

Chapter 6 unpacks the most famous period in London's development as a fashion city. In the youthful figure of the Dolly Bird, the world's media found an icon for Swinging London, and on the surface her emancipated lifestyle and challenging dress sense symbolized all that was progressive about the capital in the 1960s. Looking to the King's Road as the main artery of London's fashion renaissance, this study also charts the more reactionary currents that flowed beneath the Swinging city, noting its elitist tendencies, sexist assumptions, amateurism and nostalgic sentimentality. In the end, the heady excitement of 1965 seems to have been captured most effectively in the mirage-like output of the image-makers. Beyond the puffery of the lifestyle magazines and 'experimental' films, however, the real legacy of the Dolly Bird was the emergence of the nihilistic Punk in the following decade.

The last chapter presents late twentieth-century London as a fashion city defined through its long-standing culture of innovative entrepreneurship and a corresponding sense of confusion and decay which have perversely encouraged creativity. This is illustrated through examples of progressive design and retailing which blurred the boundaries of fashion while drawing on London's extraordinarily rich cultural fabric. The roots of this phenomenon can be traced through the fashion training provided by London Art Schools and in an older tradition of small-scale workshop production which has always dominated the London fashion trades. But the continuing attraction of London to global brands and international consumers is here considered through an examination of the thriving network of counter-cultural street markets unique to the city, such as Camden. Both trends can be seen to relate back to what could be described as one of the major themes of the book (of the tension between individualism and commodification which has continually generated new versions of urban fashionability) and to an ongoing emphasis on the diversity, contingency and mystery of London as expressed through its clothing.

This sense of contingency and wonder brings me finally to a quotation by the architectural theorist Ignasi De Sola-Morales. Cited by Julian Wolfreys in his work on the nineteenth-century urban text, I think it reinforces how close the fugitive experience of the city and the fleeting meanings of fashion are, suggesting not least through its evocative idea of the 'fold' how one might be constitutive of the other. Ultimately it provides an eloquent motto for anyone seeking inspiration in London's sartorial past:

The city is comprehensible only as a culture of the event : a culture that in the moment of fluidity and decomposition leading toward chaos, is capable of generating instants of energy that from certain chaotic elements construct... a new fold in multiple reality... The event is a vibration... a point of encounter, a conjunction whereby the lines of a limitless itinerary cross with others to create modal points of outstanding intensity... It is a subjective action, producing a moment of pleasure and fragile plenitude.[15]

**2** *Alfred, Count D'Orsay* by Daniel Maclise, c.1840 (National Portrait Gallery)

# *The* **D**andy:

## LONDON'S NEW WEST END 1790-1830

**A**pril 13th 1845, - To-day, oddly enough, while I was engaged in re-reading Carlyle's 'Philosophy of Clothes', Count d'Orsay walked in. I had not seen him for four or five years. Last time he was as gay in his colours as a humming bird - blue satin cravat, blue velvet waistcoat, cream coloured coat lined with velvet of the same hue, trousers also of a bright colour, I forget what; white French gloves, two glorious breast-pins attached by a chain, and length enough of gold watch-guard to have hanged himself in. To-day, in compliment to his five more years, he was all in black and brown - a black satin cravat, a brown velvet waistcoat, a brown coat some shades darker than the waistcoat, lined with velvet of its own shade, and almost black trousers, one breast pin, a large pear shaped pearl set into a little cup of diamonds, and only one fold of gold chain round his neck tucked together right on the centre of his spacious breast with one magnificent turquoise. Well ! that man understood his trade; if it be but that of dandy, nobody can deny that he is a perfect master of it, that he dresses himself with consummate skill ![1]

Jane Carlyle, wife of the great sage Thomas, was in a better position than most to form a critical opinion on the trade of the dandy. When the maturing Count d'Orsay called at her Chelsea residence on a Spring day in 1845, he stood before her as the epitome of 'the clothes-wearing man' who had formed the focus of 'Sartor Resartus', her husband's recent treatise on morality and modern masculinity. By this date D'Orsay's famously athletic figure, the beetle-like brilliance of his costume, and his witty repartee had lost that glossy sheen which had so distinguished the Count as the revolutionary inheritor of the dandy's crown on his proper arrival in London in 1830.[2] However, the softer tones of his later wardrobe, his insistence on the quiet layering of a monochrome palette and avoidance of extravagant accesorization, positioned the ageing peacock more firmly within a sartorial genealogy which since the late eighteenth century had identified the West End of London as the pre-eminent global site for a distinctive mode of masculine self-fashioning. D'Orsay's youthful persona drew its news-worthiness from a deliberate and rather gallic rejection of the restraint which had characterized the 'London style' since the glory days of Beau Brummell in the first two decades of the new century. Yet the underlying philosophies of dress that linked both champions of the tailor's art relied equally on the spaces and services of the capital to furnish the appropriate context for their displays of narcissistic posturing. Lord Lamington remembered the alien glamour that attended D'Orsay's earlier sorties from his (then rural) Kensington home to the salons of the metropolis or the aristocratic retreats of Richmond:

I have frequently ridden… with Count D'Orsay. A striking figure he was in his blue coat with gilt buttons, thrown well back to show the wide expanse of snowy white shirt-front and buff waistcoat; his tight leathers and polished boots; his well curled whiskers and handsome countenance; a wide-brimmed, glossy hat, spotless white gloves. He was the very beau-ideal of a leader of fashion… I was greatly interested in noticing the admiration with which he was regarded… they stared at him as at a superior being.[3]

This is the flashy image that posterity has come to associate with the practice of dandyism; the heroic romantic whose total self-possession, communicated through the perfection of his clothing, elevated him above the humdrum concerns of the masses. As this chapter will go on to suggest, it is a 'look' whose co-ordinates, far from residing solely in the interior realm and private tastes of the dandy individual, extended outward into the shops and streets of London's evolving 'menswear' quarter; and an attitude toward life which drew on the complex material relationship between the city and its elite male consumers. The careers of Brummell and D'Orsay, respectively a déclassé social climber and a continental sexual adventurer, bracketed the development of an urbane commercial milieu in which London itself emerged as 'King of the Dandies', above and beyond the narrower aspirations of those two compromised 'outsiders' yet also somehow described by their actions and tastes. Without the tools and props, the roles and opportunities which the 'World City' provided, the dandy's trade would have been of little use to these self-obsessed men in their short rise to celebrity and longer notoriety as ciphers for the triumph of style over substance. Their activities may well have helped to fix the enduring reputation of London as the centre for a particular mode of masculine display, but it was in the broader physical framework of the metropolis itself that the essence of dandyism lay.

# FITTING OUT THE DANDY WARDROBE

Four items in the dress collection of the Museum of London attest to the skill of London's tailors and consumers in constructing a fitting carapace for the performance of a dandy sensibility during the years of the Regency. A single-breasted dark-green cloth coat of about 1800-1810, cut away at the front, with a stand collar and finished with cut steel buttons, and the black silk jersey breeches with which the coat was probably worn, once belonged to a Sir Gilbert Heathcote (possibly the descendant of his namesake, founder of the Bank of England and late seventeenth-century Lord Mayor of the City of London).[4] They look back to the formal magnificence of eighteenth-century Court ceremonial (indeed they may have constituted court dress), while also

**❸** Sir Gilbert Heathcote's Coat, *c.* 1800-1810 (Museum of London)

reflecting the rise to prominence of a more secular and patrician celebration of the homosocial pleasures of urban society. The dark and sober palette would have thrown the accompanying white linen and probable white waistcoat into high relief, the only concession to surface decoration consisting of the sparkling buttons and the addition of a chain of gold seals at the hip. In terms of their construction, the garments do not vary so drastically from the make-up of the embroidered-silk coat and breeches which would have constituted formal dress for the previous generation. The residual deep cuffs pay clear homage to an older style. But in the detail, a subtle realignment away from the role of clothing as a foil and frame for hierarchical surface decoration toward a tendency for revealing (or enhancing) the corporeal individuality of the wearer is clearly evident. When unbuttoned and opened, the coat offers up the secrets of the tailor's art, its cream-silk lining padded out across the tightly fitting shoulders and upper chest to resemble finely toned musculature, the small of the back gracefully tapered to accentuate narrow hips. This is a garment designed to fit a body trained in the rules of deportment, a wearer well-used to framing his identity as public spectacle through posture and a discerning attitude toward dress.

The breeches extend this sense of a restrained perfection in affairs of the wardrobe. Here the maker has favoured the dark covered buttons advertised as the preferred choice of fastening of the Prince of Wales in an 1808 edition of the fashion magazine *The Beau Monde*.[5] Four of them pull the cloth close to the calves, drawing attention to suitably sculpted and shapely leg muscles, while a further set attach the fall front of the breeches to the body of the garment at the waist. Inside, the top of the breeches have been lined with a tough brown cloth which betrays the functional nature of the opening, and in a further concession to elegance the back seam is inset with laces so that the fabric can be drawn tightly across the buttocks, enhancing the curved sweep of the spine. As far as elegance was concerned, the shirt which would have sat underneath these two garments provides the strongest evidence of the time and care lavished on this new presentation of the male body. The museum holds a fine example from the following decade which gives a good sense of the desired effect.[6] Constructed of fine linen with a transparent linen ruffle at the neck, it boasts a high collar fastened by two exquisite Dorset thread buttons. Plain cuffs finish very long sleeves which would have protruded, a concession to excess, from the sleeve of the coat. Wrapped in a complicated manner around the throat and tucked decoratively down the gap between the shirt-front frills, a linen stock of the same or a contrasting shade would have completed the pouter-pigeon effect. This element of the wardrobe offered most potential for the display of individual taste and while Brummell's sartorial philosophy was strictly opposed to any form of extrovert fashion, his mastery of the necktie attained the currency of a folk-legend. Captain Jesse recounted Brummell's method in the most authoritative of the Beau's several biographies:

**4** Fine Linen Shirt, *c.*1800-1820 (Museum of London)

Brummell was one of the first who revived and improved a taste for dress amongst gentlemen; and his great innovation was effected upon neckcloths : they were then worn without stiffening of any kind, and bagged out in front, rucking up to the chin in a roll; to remedy this obvious awkwardness and inconvenience he used to have his slightly starched… The collar, which was always fixed to his shirt, was so large that before being folded down, it completely hid his head and face, and the white neckcloth was at least a foot in height. The first coup d'archet was made with the shirt collar, which he folded down to its proper size; and Brummell then standing before the glass with his chin poked up to the ceiling, by the gentle and gradual declension of his lower jaw, creased the cravat to reasonable dimensions, the form of each succeeding crease being perfected with the shirt.[7]

A final piece from the museum's collection moves out from the dressing-room, equipping the dandy for the inclement London streets. A double-breasted greatcoat of dark-blue facecloth was tailored by John Weston of 34 Old Bond Street sometime between 1803 and 1810.[8] It was deposited soon after its manufacture at Coutts Bank by Weston for an unnamed client whose order had been handled by Coutts account

**❺** Coat by John Weston, c.1803-1810 (Museum of London)

holder Jonathan Gordon. An accompanying letter from the tailor to Gordon states that 'I have sent an exceedg. good blue cloth Great Coat for your Friend, made in ev'ry respect in the best manner, which I hope in point of fitting & c. will give satisfaction.'⁹ The coat conforms well to expectations of suitable attire for 'rambling' in the shopping streets of Mayfair and St James or taking control of a carriage in Hyde Park, and Weston's reputation as tailor and draper to The Prince of Wales and the Dukes of Cambridge, Sussex and Gloucester adds to its cachet. A high-fastening dark-blue velvet collar, a figure-hugging cut in which the fine cloth closely caresses the shoulders and torso, and six pairs of large gilt buttons (made by the London-based metal worker Charles Jennens), lend the coat the requisite military associations; for this was a period (dominated by war with France) during which the trappings of martial swagger borrowed from an army tailor's pattern book could suggest the requisite degree of patriotic bravado. As Aileen Ribeiro comments with reference to the allied fashion for frogging and braid : 'Hussar regiments wore some of the most dashing uniforms during the Napoleonic period and it was inevitable that some of this glamour rubbed off onto civilian clothing.'¹⁰

'Glamour' was the key factor which placed stylish young men in early nineteenth-century London at the forefront of fashionable life for the first time, establishing the West End, their dressing-box and playground, as a rival to Paris in its role as global forcing-house for new sartorial trends. Roy Porter describes how Regency bucks 'forged an aesthetic of the urban, a worship of town as a temple of pleasure that culminated in the image of the dandy. The emergence of the West End gave urban lifestyles a glamour that became the envy, or amusement of the rest of the nation'.[11] Thus the rise to pre-eminence of the clothing and lifestyle of the wealthy Englishman and the development of London as an international centre rivalled in size only by Peking and Edo and unchallenged in terms of its cultural diversity and economic clout by any other European City, go some way toward explaining Porter's claim that by 1800 Londoners had become 'city watchers, self-referential… in love with themselves'.[12] Clearly earlier groups of fashion-conscious young men (especially the Macaronis of the 1770s) had also fostered a self-love and an infatuation with the possibilities of ultra-fashionable living which drew on the resources of London. But their urban performances were more subcultural in nature, engineered to challenge the status quo and often dismissed by commentators as unpatriotic.[13] The significance of this later generation was that their masquerading was taken to the heart of the establishment, setting up a mode of behaviour and appearance that functioned as a badge of belonging rather than one of resistance. The legend of Beau Brummell illustrates this development most clearly. Forty years after Brummell's fall from grace as a debtor and exile, Captain Gronow, a former grenadier guard, one time neighbour of the famous dandy, and Member of Parliament for Stafford, recalled in his reminiscences how Brummell's emergence on the social scene coincided precisely with London's transformation as a city of shimmering facades and vistas, whose seeming insubstantiality actually represented a massive enhancement of the city's formidable reserves of social, political and economic power :

Amongst the curious freaks of fortune there is none more remarkable in my memory than the sudden appearance, in the highest and best society in London, of a young man whose antecedents warranted a much less conspicuous career… there are comparatively few examples of men obtaining a similarly elevated position simply from their attractive personal appearance and fascinating manners.[14]

Through careful connections and judicious introductions Brummell managed to insinuate himself into, indeed made himself synonymous with, London's newly fashionable and seriously wealthy residential, retail and leisure sectors. As a later biographer, Roger Boutet de Monvel, attested 'London was the chief attraction for Brummell with its sumptuous clubs and its aristocratic parks, with its proud and splendid mansions, the doors of which were beginning to open before him, with its streets and promenades.'[15] His apartments in Chesterfield Street and Chapel Street sat at the centre of a golden triangle which boasted the shops of St James's and Old Bond Streets, the driveways of Hyde Park, the reception rooms of Carlton House Palace and the libraries and refreshments of Clubland at its perimeters; all within a relaxed twenty-minute stroll. The opulence of such a milieu caused the normal boundaries between public and private to dissolve. Brummell's own dressing room functioned in exactly the same way as the fenestration of his favourite St James's Street Club, as a necessary stage for the enactment of an exemplary and voluptuous manner of existence. Renaissance notions of princely magnificence paled beside Brummell's audacious aping of ancien regime spectacle :

In the zenith of his popularity he might be seen at the bay window of White's club, surrounded by the lions of the day, laying down the law, and occasionally indulging in those witty remarks for which he was famous. His house in Chapel Street corresponded with his personal 'get up'; the furniture was in excellent taste, and the library contained the best works of the best authors of every period and of every country. His canes, his snuff boxes, his sevres china, were exquisite; his horses and carriage were conspicuous for their excellence; and, in fact, the superior taste of a Brummell was discoverable in everything that belonged to him.[16]

Yet despite the manner in which Brummell placed his environment, his body and his opinions on display, reported accounts of his sartorial tastes present a paradox. De Monvel admits that 'his attention to dress was a piece of extravagance, sufficiently striking', but goes on to claim that in his attitude toward clothing Brummell eschewed forcefully imposing his views on fashion, fearing accusations of effeminacy, presumptuousness or pedanticism. Apparently he preferred to confuse his followers with deliberately superficial and rather facetious announcements on such matters as the usefulness of champagne as a polish for boots.[17] As for his own wardrobe, Jesse notes that 'his morning dress was similar to that of every other gentleman - Hessians and pantaloons, or top-boots and buckskins, with a blue coat and a light or buff-coloured waistcoat... His dress of an evening was a blue coat and white waistcoat, black pantaloons which buttoned tight to the ankle, striped silk stockings, and opera hat.'[18] There was perhaps an element of perfection, an attention to detail and functional correctness in this get-up that marked it out from the habits of others. Certainly Brummell sought out tailors with the most impeccable connections and addresses.

**6** *Beau Brummell* by R.H. Cooke, *c.* 1835 (National Portrait Gallery)

Schweitzer and Davidson in Cork Street and Weston and Meyer in Conduit Street provided goods of particular distinction. The latter held the honour of dressing the Prince of Wales and the right to use Royal livery. It was the very elusiveness of this look, its elite connotations and resistance to wholesale emulation (its fabrics were of too high a quality, its quiet details too reliant on expensive craftsmanship and the social rules governing its wear too arcane for general copying) that both set Brummell apart and transformed him into the model for a new kind of urbane consumption, indelibly 'Londonate' in nature. Having emerged from relative social obscurity, Brummell was able to manipulate the opportunities which London's prime sites of pleasure and acquisition offered an ambitious social climber to subtly ambiguous ends. The result was a refinement of the ritualized lifestyle of the old aristocracy, transformed to serve the aspirations of a newly confident city and its affluent population. This process fixed a small network of London streets at the centre of such concerns for the next two centuries. As historian Peter Thorold remarks, for men such as Chateaubriand, who experienced the delights of London as French Ambassador in 1822, the social and sartorial performance of masculinity would never seem the same again :

One never stopped changing clothes… He was up at six am for a breakfast party in the country - and back in London for lunch. He then changed his clothes for a walk in Bond Street or Hyde Park. After that he changed for seven thirty dinner. Then came the opera and another set of clothes, followed - changing again - by the evening assembly known as a 'rout'. What a life, he thought; the galleys would be a hundred times preferable.[19]

# TRADING IN MASCULINE BEAUTY

The most tyrannical uniformity is exacted in London…wearing a hat an inch too wide in the brim, a waistcoat too short, or a coat too long, subjects the unfortunate and unconscious foreigner to a suspicion of vulgarity quite sufficient to banish him from the elegant circles of this gay metropolis. I have therefore begun my career by completely new modelling my costume, and for that purpose have put myself in the hands of the most celebrated professors. My hair has been cut by Blake, my waistcoat and pantaloons come from the hands of other artists of equal celebrity, each devoted to the particular line of his profession. Lock is my hatter and Hoby my shoemaker; and as I am assured… that : 'All is unprofitable, flat, And stale without a smart cravat, Muchined enough to hold its starch, The last key-stone of fashion's arch.' A kind English friend has taught me : 'By dint of hand and eye, How to obtain a perfect tie.' Indeed, I am so metamorphosed that you would scarcely recognise me. I can now pass unquizzed through a crowd of dandies; and I even had, a few days since, the glory of overhearing one of the most renowned of these heroes express his approbation of the brilliant polish which my boots displayed.[20]

Like Chateaubriand, who was suffering from the pressures exerted by London's fashionable obsessions at the same time, the Marquis de Vermont found his natural status as a Parisian nobleman of undisputed taste, challenged by the unwritten rules of

English society. In a bid to 'fit in', his search after the 'correct' London style clearly took him to those tradesmen clustered between Oxford Street to the north, the new Regent Street to the east, Park Lane to the west and Piccadilly to the south, whose reputations as purveyors of Brummell's philosophies-made-material gained them a special place on the itinerary of any aspiring dandy. As the architectural historian John Summerson proclaims in his magisterial study of Georgian London, this central section of the city witnessed the most profound physical transformation over the course of the eighteenth century. It grew haphazardly from a patchwork that in the late seventeenth century counted grand classical palaces along the north side of Piccadilly and measured trees and pathways to the south in what now constitutes Green and St James's Parks. To the north St James's Fields had already established itself as a square of decorous brick houses, but elsewhere ribbons of new housing edged across more dangerous footpad-ridden scrubland and small concentrations of rural industry. By the early eighteenth century the fields north and south of Oxford Street were criss-crossed by uniform squares of aristocratic town houses, punctuated by the white towers of a rash of new churches. As the decades passed older reminders of small-scale manufacturing and the shabby gabled remnants of village life gave way to rows of neat brick terraces, such as Brummell chose to inhabit, accented with mass-produced classical detail. And finally, when the next century opened, 'a ploughed line of demolition' snaked its way from the new Regent's Park down to St James's, imposing a stuccoed boundary between the genteel concentration of fashionable life to the west and the noisier domain of manufacture and trade to the east. Across the whole a network of shopping streets connected the desires and necessities of an affluent resident population to the new docks upriver, gateways for the products of an expanding empire and symbols of the new confidence. On top of this scene of organized chaos, Summerson positions a clear rationale :

London's growth has not been a matter of gradual and even incrementation, but of distinct waves of activity at intervals roughly of about fifty years... This interval corresponds with the cycle... in eighteenth-century trade... It bears an obvious relation to the alternation of periods of peace and war, and a less obvious relation to the increase of London's population. Each burst... had a character of its own - a different social character, representing a different stratum of the national wealth and bringing into prominence a different kind of taste.[21]

It is the nature of this development in taste that tracks most closely the rise of the West End as a centre for fashionable consumption, anticipating its reputation as the epicentre for early nineteenth-century dandyism. Its roots lay in the 'uncertain' and 'vernacular roughness' of the Restoration style, the tentative marking out of fresh boundaries which followed the movement of urban elites to new territories beyond Westminster and away from the City after the plagues and fire of the 1660s. From the early eighteenth century the desire of great country landowners to establish a permanent residence in the capital and maximize the rental income from their London estates resulted in the more directed development of a self-conscious architectural rhetoric (Palladianism) and a concentration of emulative style-seekers in the locales which such grandees decided to mark out as home. A period of 'refinement' and 'maturity' which saw increasing numbers of lesser country gentry and comfortable 'citizens' migrating to the West End preceded the 'Napoleonic building boom' when 'the rapidly increasing shopkeeper, artisan and labouring classes' joined the elite in a clamour for suitable accommodation. The social divide made more physical by the building of Regent Street was thus also represented in a division of taste which 'began to be eclectic on the one hand and strictly standardised on the other'.[22] In sartorial terms Brummell's persona pulled on the threads of such a history and situated its sphere of influence directly in the heart of this evolving townscape. In less abstract terms it also drew directly on the retail facilities set up to service a distinguished local population in pursuance of its finely modulated exterior surfaces.

Three streets in particular served Brummell's constituency, establishing themselves as magnets for those seeking items for the masculine wardrobe for decades to come. Architectural historian Jane Rendell states quite boldly that the point where all three broadly converged, the site of the Burlington Arcade, erected in 1818 for Lord George Cavendish, offered more than simple sartorial sustenance for men's bodies. While the streets in question (Savile Row with its tailors, Bond Street with its purveyors of hosiery, perfumes and fine accessories and St James's Street with its provision stores for connoisseur's wine and tobacco, its social clubs and its celebrated hatter) maintained at least a veneer of decorum, the Arcade symbolized a more complex understanding of masculine desire and the interweaving of sexual longing with all the other desiderata of a dandy lifestyle. Rendell clearly disapproves of the licentiousness that lay disguised beneath a matrix of 'respectable' trade, but also paints a vivid picture of the attractions that a 'ramble' in the West End could entail:

The area around the Burlington Arcade was a predominantly male zone. Bond Street was the site of dandyism and male fashion. Many bachelors lived in this area, in hotels and chambers, such as the Albany running parallel to the Arcade. They spent their leisure time engaged largely in drinking and gambling in the exclusively male clubs... Not surprisingly, the area was known for its high class brothels... The Burlington Arcade was closely associated with prostitution, especially the millinery shops... The glazed shop windows provided a perfect view of the shop girls and created a setting for images of 'professional beauties' concealed in tobacconist's snuff boxes and print shop displays.[23]

In terms of the dandy's inevitable focus on his own body rather than those belonging to others, the thesis that the West End maintained its magnetic pull largely on account of the existence of a sexual trade in courtesans and milliners does not tell the whole story. It is perhaps useful in pointing up the erotic context of commodity culture, but it underplays an integral part of the dandy's psychological make-up as it has been reconstructed by subsequent studies of masculine fashionability: that is, his apparent disdain for intimate relations with anyone but his own reflection and a concurrent maintenance of the highest degree of social discretion. The legends of Brummell and

**7** *Burlington Arcade* by H.S. Sargant, *c.* 1825 (Corporation of London)

D'Orsay trade on an assumption of sexual continence and a deliberate distancing of the dandified protagonists from the temptations that surround them, and this is a fastidiousness that extends to the etiquette of dressing and shopping.[24] It is this more homosocial rhetoric of self-love and its celebration of masculine taste and the idealized male body that runs most vigorously through the practices and spaces of London's male retail quarter from the eighteen-teens onward. This is not to discount the presence of heterosexual prostitution in the quarter, after all barely a corner of the capital escaped its shadow, but it is a plea for a more serious consideration of the dandy's overlooked significance as a consumer and promoter of a defining style whose meanings extended beyond the narrower concerns of sexual gratification. The Marquis de Vermont captured the purely commercial, as opposed to corporeal attractions of London's shopping streets when he appraised the spacious pavements, ceaseless traffic and brazen evidence of wealth which formed his first dramatic impressions of the city. It was their potential for fashionable consumption and display rather than for sexual adventuring that fired his imagination. The acquisition of luxury goods and clothing could be and often was an end in itself:

Evening was coming on at… my arrival, and a dense and yellow fog threw a gloom on all around. The convenience, however, of your trottoirs did not escape my notice. On these… crowds of well-dressed pedestrians of both sexes were hastening to their respective avocations, in spite of the unfavourable state of the atmosphere, and of the approaching night. Nor did I fail to remark the numberless elegant carriages and loaded carts which impeded our way… While the richness and variety of the shops, which were just lighted, dazzled my eyes and distracted my attention.[25]

Old Bond Street offered the most concentrated collection of the sort of shops which dazzled men like Vermont. Its origins lay in Sir Thomas Bond's speculations following the demolition of Clarendon House on Piccadilly in 1686. Pushing northwards through virgin fields as the next century progressed, it had been extended from Clifford Street by 1700 to form New Bond Street, reaching Oxford Street by 1721. Its elite and masculine associations were well established by the end of the 1830s when Old Bond Street numbered among its traders three businesses dealing in officers' uniforms, weaponry and the gold and silver lace which lent the requisite element of 'flash' to any self-respecting guardsman's outfit. Four civilian tailors supplied the basic elements of the dandy's wardrobe while a breeches-maker, a boot-maker, two hosiers, two perfumers and three hatters offered the necessary accessories. Other shops provided a wide range of those other commodities that aided the pursuit of the leisured life in London. Wine and coffee merchants, dairymen, a fishmonger, bakers and butchers stocked the larders of aristocratic town houses as carpet and china dealers, upholsterers, lamp-sellers and coach-builders ensured that their interiors and services were adequately modish. Beyond these necessaries, the street was also a focus for those seeking out the raw materials for the traditional gentleman's pursuit of collecting. Print-sellers, picture-dealers and several book-men occupied the premises not reserved for the fashioning of dressing, drawing and dining rooms. As Old Bond Street gave way to New, the specialization seemed to intensify with dressing-case makers, jewellers, gunsmiths, a saddler, a horse-hirer, an umbrella manufacturer, a watchmaker, a camp-equipment supplier, a curio-dealer, a cutler and a tobacconist competing for custom with further tailors, hatters and print- and book-dealers. One or two milliners were the only evidence of the feminine interests which would take possession of the street by the end of the nineteenth century, though it appears that the refined and exclusive reputation established since its seventeenth-century beginnings survived into the twentieth.[26] In a 1937 paean to the 'Dear Street', *Country Life* provided a faint echo of Vermont's earlier sentiments:

In this narrow, slightly curving street, with its continual procession of shining cars and interesting people, something of the spirit which makes trading an honourable occupation and not just a money-grabbing affair is preserved. You may see it by the shop windows, where perhaps only one thing is displayed, but that one a masterpiece... Bond Street is romantic because it suggests fine craftsmanship and connoisseur buying, because its goods are not all in the shop window.[27]

If Bond Street traded on the tastefulness of its polite facades (the bawdier displays of the print-dealers excepted) and its close association with an 'aristocratic' mode of consumption, the streets surrounding Savile Row to the immediate east were even more discreet in their devotion to the exclusive arts of dandyism. So much so that the uninformed Regency rambler might easily have remained unaware of their presence as he prowled the maze of pavements between Mayfair and the new Regent Street. This was partly due to the convention by which a tailor then visited the home of a client rather than vice versa, and also to the invisibility of the industrial processes of tailoring whereby cutters, pressers and stitchers were confined to basement and first-floor workrooms. This was a situation heightened by the social effects of Regent Street's geographical impact. As west and east became more clearly divided into zones of consumption and production the 'dirty' business of making-up on which tailors relied edged inevitably toward the cheap rents and labour of Soho and away from the refinements of Park Lane. Furthermore, the idea of a shop-front for elite tailors was at this time an irrelevance, indeed a vulgarity. Reputations were built by word of mouth within a close knit community of sartorial connoisseurs rather than on the back of a flashy window. In an era just before the publication of mass-circulation trade journals, the concept of promotion and display resided in the quality of the finished goods and their ostentatious flaunting on the back of some appropriately titled customer, which necessitated a close understanding of prevailing aristocratic tastes and intimate physical proximity with the social haunts and habits of the rich.[28] In this context the tight concentration of tailors within the confines of the old Burlington Estate with its liberal scattering of ennobled tenants was, then, unsurprising.

Within ten minutes' walk of their brass nameplates, Meyer of Conduit Street, Schweitzer and Davidson of Cork Street and Weston of Old Bond Street could descend on Brummell's house in Chesterfield Street for the customary fitting sessions and constant delivery of new items.[29] Further local clients famed for their free-spending habits and innovative tastes included the bawdy Lord Barrymore, a Byronic monster given to low-living and outrageous displays of horsemanship. Under his direction a small theatre was set up in Savile Row during the 1790s to house aristocratic amateur theatricals, attracting the attention of literary and dramatic bohemians such as Edmund Kean, the Kembles, Richard Sheridan and Byron himself. Lord Alvanley resided in nearby Park Street, following Brummell's lead in his choice of residence (around the corner from Chesterfield Street), and mode of entertaining. (Alvanley's elegant soirees were especially noted for the excellence of his apricot tart.) Brummell's direct successor, the Count D'Orsay also looked to this area of St James's to furnish his wardrobe. His tailor Creed traded from 33 Conduit Street and with George Stultz, who was established in Clifford Street from 1809, cemented the global reputation of the district as a Mecca for male exquisites.

This concentration of trend-setters was inevitably detrimental to more established locations for fashionable consumption and illustrates how perceptions of 'fashion' were at the same time mobile in terms of the ephemeral whims of the 'bon ton', and constrained by the more stately 'official' development of the metropolis. St James's Street, for example, with its ultra-respectable clubs and august provisioners of traditional masculine fare, became more closely associated with the old guard in both political and sartorial terms as the eighteenth century declined. As Charles Fox, the Prince Regent and Beau Brummell transferred their trade allegiances north of Piccadilly, St James's Street retailers like the hatter James Lock saw their order books filled by a more reactionary clientele; though ironically it was the seemingly conservative dress-rules imposed by Brummell that would ensure the longer survival of such firms.[30] Definitions of what was deemed to be fashionable were suspended in an uneasy tension between the parameters laid down by the traditional guardians of social and political power - the governing elite - and the proclamations of a newer urban breed, disdainful of authority and self-confident in their own interpretations of modishness. Whatever the sympathies of particular groups of consumers though, it is blindingly apparent that by 1821 journalist Pierce Egan's vivid characterization of fashionable society in the capital, *Life in London*, drew as much on the generous bounty of its retail sector, the varied fabric of its buildings, spaces and population and the increased fame of the West End for its sources as it did on the dictates of any singular autocrat of taste. Indeed Egan's iconic text, with its energetic heroes Jerry Hawthorn and Corinthian Tom, was a raucous celebration of London's new diversity. Combining aspects of the demotic and the refined it captured the popular imagination to such an extent that its episodes were adapted for the stage in four different versions, the most successful running at the Adelphi for more than 300 nights.[31] As such excitements suggested, the multiple trappings and desires of fashionable masculinity and the ever-lengthening streets of the capital had become entwined with each other in more general terms, driven perhaps by increasing competition for the ownership of a challenging new sense of London style:

Indeed, the metropolis is a complete CYCLOPAEDIA, wherein every man of the most religious or moral habits, attached to any sect, may find something to please his palate, regulate his taste, suit his pocket, enlarge his mind, and make himself happy and comfortable… In fact every SQUARE in the metropolis is a sort of map well worthy of exploring, if riches and titles operate as a source of curiosity to the visitor. There is not a street also in London but what may be compared to a large or small volume of intelligence, abounding with anecdote, incident or curiosities… and even the poorest cellar contains some trait or other, in unison with the manners and feelings of this great city, that may be put down in a note book and reviewed at an after period with much pleasure and satisfaction.[32]

# FASHIONING DANDY IDENTITIES

I feel induced now to describe, for the benefit of posterity, the pedigree of a Dandy in 1820. The DANDY was got by vanity out of Affectation - his dam, Petit-Maitre or Maccaroni , - his grand dam, Fribble - his great grand dam - Bronze - his great great grand dam, Coxcomb - and his earliest ancestor Fop. His uncle Impudence - his three brothers Trick, Humbug and Fudge ! and allied to the extensive family of the Shuffletons. Indeed this Bandbox sort of creature took so much the lead in the walks of fashion, that the BUCK was totally missing; the BLOOD vanished; the TIPPY not to be found, the GO out of date; the DASH not to be met with; and the BANG UP without a leader, at fault and in the background. It was only the CORINTHIAN that remained triumphant - his excellence was of such a genuine quality that all imitation was left at an immeasurable distance.[33]

The idea of the dandy has become something of a truism, an over-familiar player on the stage of early nineteenth-century culture and a generalized cipher for all manner of literary, artistic, philosophical and social developments. But it is worth taking a moment to reconsider the ways in which his self-indulged figure is also tied materially and specifically to the positioning of London as a centre for masculine sartorial interests. As Egan's description makes clear, his ubiquity in the nineteen-teens was bolstered by a longer genealogy of London types reaching back to those seventeenth-century Rakes and Fops who commandeered the coffee-houses and featured prominently in the cast lists of Restoration dramas. These were reprobate aristocrats whose identities pivoted around their sexual audaciousness, piercing wit and striking adoption of the more extreme features of the contemporary wardrobe; the tumbling perukes, extended lace cuffs, 'bizarrely' patterned waistcoats and vertiginous heels that symbolized irresponsibility and excess. More recently the Macaroni had used the potency of clothing to make a political and sexual statement that critiqued the status-quo during the 1770s. As Peter McNeil has shown, his zealous control over surface appearance utilized the effete and exquisite associations of continental tastes to signify a subversive attitude toward a variety of ingrained assumptions and prescriptions regarding various contentious social and economic concerns, from acceptable gender roles to the prerogatives of the crown.[34] His tight pastel-coloured suits, tiny hats and overblown maquillage drew controversy from the alien nature of their influences. This was a style of dressing and behaviour that, though based in London, seemed as if it hailed from another sphere. The spirits of these innovators, both real and represented, cluster around Egan's updated version, their more effeminate characteristics compromising the virility of later followers. The emerging ideal however, is placed head and shoulders above his predecessors, a clear example of the patriotic fervour that positioned the fashionable young West-Ender, with his discrete but perfected Mayfair wardrobe and his 'healthy' interest in the excitements of the ball-room, the boxing-ring and the horse-track, as the new Corinthian in a modern version of ancient Rome.

That the new Dandy was a concrete creation of London's commercial renaissance, and not simply an abstract figment of the satirist's pen, is made clear by the various commentaries which examine his physical trappings and the efforts taken to furnish his body with the requisite coverings and appropriate diversions.[35] The figures of the tailor and the hosier thus featured either as valuable guides to the new territory of the fashion city or avaricious lackeys in many descriptions of the lifestyles of modish male Londoners in the period, their own fortunes reliant on the extravagant spending of their clients. In the anonymous *Memoirs of a Rambler* of 1800, a Mr Dimity of Piccadilly is introduced as an astute interpreter of fashionability, a tradesman whose intimacy with the vagaries of dandyism was essential as a means of supporting a comfortable suburban household:

On my first coming to this dealer in white ties and white linen, he took me aside and with much earnestness observed : 'It has always been my ambition to employ sharp cunning fellows in my shop, I therefore trust that you will observe the established maxims so strictly adhered to by all snippers of muslin and clippers of cambric, which are : 'Take in everybody as you can, but suffer nobody to take you in. Deal pretty much in the marvellous, and always make two prices.' For if it were not for these things, how should my neighbour Froth, the haberdasher, keep his gig and country house at Newington Butts, or I my one horse chaise and villa at Hammersmith ?[36]

This notion, that standards of fashion were as much under the control of tradesmen as they were in the hands of elite consumers, was a concern that also surfaced in the pages of *The English Spy*, a competing account of the metropolis to that produced by Egan which appeared four years later in 1826. Writing under the pseudonym of Bernard Blackmantle, the author Westmacott used the same conceit of detailing the variety of London's pleasure haunts through a narrative revolving around the introduction of a provincial novice to the capital by a more experienced roue. The two accounts also shared the perceptive Robert Cruikshank as an illustrator. In tone, however, Blackmantle's text was less an extravagent celebration of high- and low-life than an expose of the amorality of a new leisure class, informed by the author's intimate connections with the rarefied salons and drawing rooms of the West End. The value of fashionable knowledge in this world held an elusive worth that was profoundly unsettling of the old social order. As one of Blackmantle's characters bemoaned:

It is now quite impossible to enjoy society and be comfortable in public without being associated with your tallow-chandler, or your butcher; or to take a pleasant drive out of town without meeting your linen draper or your tailor, better mounted or in a more fashionable equipage than yourself... It would be very hard indeed if those who enable others to cut a dash all the week could not make a splash themselves on a Sunday... It's a matter of business nowadays : Many of your kick-shaw tradesmen west of Temple Bar find it as necessary to consult appearances in the park and watch the new come-outs as I do to watch the stock-market : If they find their customers there in good feather and high repute, they venture to cover another leaf in their ledger; but if, on the contrary, they appear shy, only show of a Sunday, and are cut by the nobs, why then they understand it's high time to close the account.[37]

*Jerry in training for a 'Swell'*

**❽** The tailor Primefit attends to Jerry Hawthorne, from *Life in London* by Pierce Egan, illustrated by Robert Cruikshank, 1821 (Corporation of London)

Pierce Egan's sketch of the fictional Regent Street tailor Mr Richard Primefit betrayed a more relaxed and mutually profitable relationship between dandy and trade than the social frictions implied in Blackmantle's more conservative picture. Here the tailor is a modern champion, standing level with pugilists and gentlemen alike in a fresher reading of a reformed metropolis. Standing at the centre of a web of social connections, Primefit relied for trade on his own reputation as a 'genteel' craftsman and on word of mouth between the most fashionable men in London as to the superior nature of his skills and product; so much so that 'in London, no gentleman, who had been once in the books of Dickey would listen to the name of any other tailor, which rendered PRIMEFIT the 'go' for a tasty cut, best materials, and first rate workmanship'.[38] In return for the privilege of fitting out the famous and infamous, Primefit was accommodating with his credit terms and discrete in his guardianship of a profound professional knowledge regarding the secrets of dandyism. In other words the West End tailor enjoyed something approaching a cult following, Primefit's rise to fame echoing that of his real counterparts, Stultz and Meyer:

Things, at length, took the expected turn. Many long-outstanding bills came in. His capital accumulated. His business also increased in so extraordinary a manner that several clerks were necessary to keep it in order, and ensure punctuality… His character for fashion was so emphatic, that numbers of stylish tradesmen, who found it necessary to have a 'bettermost coat' by them for 'highdays and holidays' regardless of the charge, employed Mr Primefit… In short Mr Primefit had realised the climax of his exertions - he had measured his way into a carriage. DICKEY was principally distinguished for the cut of his coats. To CORINTHIAN Tom he was peculiarly indebted, as a leader of the fashion.[39]

Something of the metropolitan flavour embedded in the West End tailor's skills can be deduced from Egan's description of Primefit's methods in measuring up Jerry Hawthorne, Tom's country cousin, for a new set of clothing suitable for the bridle ways and promenades of Hyde Park rather than the village green. Much significance lay in the tailor's ability to play with contrasts of 'light and shade' in the displacement of items and the fall of the fabric, a very subtle moulding of the torso to reflect heightened taste and a certain delicacy of proportion (benefiting from recent reforms in tailoring methods that placed a mathematical understanding of anatomy at the centre of new cutting systems). The resulting transformation accentuated Jerry's broad rural frame, but also controlled it in such a manner that the sporting or military functions from which English tailoring took its primary references lost any practical associations, becoming instead a symbolic mode of urban display; the essence of a dandy sensibility set in direct opposition to the cruder connotations of a rude bucolic mode of masculinity. Town and Country had become discreet registers of fashion, embodied in the very design of dress :

During the time Mr Primefit was applying the measure to ascertain the frame of young Hawthorne, the Corinthian smiled to himself at the lusty, unsubdued back of his merry rustic coz., at the same time making comparisons, in his own mind, at the vast difference of the hinder parts of his dandy-like friends at the west-end of the town, when put into the scale against the country breed of Jerry. Tom, laughingly, told PRIMEFIT, that he had not been so well backed for a long time.[40]

That this articulation of an ultra-urban sartorial taste was also something more than the simple result of a concentration of tailoring expertise, or the desire of elite consumers to impose a localized hegemony of style as a badge of social inclusion and superiority, is suggested by historian Peter Mandler who tracks associations between lifestyle choices and political power-struggles on the national scene in the first half of the nineteenth century. Mandler illustrates how the effete self-presentation of late eighteenth-century aristocratic subcultures in London was deliberately modelled as the antithesis of the industrious and 'responsible' individualism peddled as a moral and religious position by the country gentry and the rising provincial middle classes. Thus the inheritors of Charles Fox's political philosophy with its 'preference for the metropolis over the country as the best and broadest microcosm of England', its insistence on 'an understanding that the aristocracy had a higher cultural mission than the self-interested pursuit of estate development, trade and banking' which typified the parochial concerns of the rural competition, and its perpetuation of a high-spending, high-living 'facade' behind which more serious responsibilities could continue unfettered, found a natural affiliation with the visual appeal of West End dandyism.[41] In this context the increased circulation of dandified styles of behaviour in the aristocratic quarters of London during the 1810s and 1820s makes perfect sense, with the consumption of clothing and other luxury items becoming an important badge of political affiliation for rich young men. Mandler details a variety of models from the 'roistering clubmen cluttering up the West End', their irresponsible actions cocking a symbolic snook to more 'worthy' estate and family pursuits, to the dual path offered to the young 'man of the world' whereby one followed a more overtly political route that espoused 'a kind of reactionary romanticism typified by 'Young England'', or 'a more radical romanticism which reflected army or navy experience'. At its most sartorial was another template, also a reaction against responsibility and the demands of the status quo. 'This was the ultra-fashionable, ultra aristocratic type, consciously opposing himself to the philistinism and rowdyism of the military world'.[42] Linking all four was the material context of London high society during the period, the adoption of a style that was whiggish and metropolitan in orientation - at odds with the rather puritanical culture approved of by the country at large. Its characteristics were 'a love of luxurious living, travel, sexual intrigue, conviviality, classical literature, oratory and the arts'.[43] What better engine for the promotion of dandyism as a serious London pursuit ?

The ultimate destination of such posing (and the point of its decline) is represented in Bulwer Lytton's 1828 novel *Pelham* where the eponymous hero adopts a persona closer to D'Orsay's outrageously styled posturings than to the more obviously controlled self-presentation of Brummell. As Alison Adburgham points out, by the late 1820s Brummell's enforced exile in Calais at the hands of his creditors had inevitably contributed to the slow decline of his control over sartorial matters in London. The tight, ingeniously tailored blue coat with silver buttons which had formed Brummell's rather militaristic trademark was replaced with an altogether more revealing, unpadded and svelte black alternative, more suited to the drawing room dramas and splenetic ennui that characterized the new-style dandy.[44] Pelham clearly relates how sexual, social and political progress was reliant on the adoption of just such a dandified identity:

I had resolved to set up a 'character' for I was always of an ambitious nature and desirous of being distinguished from the ordinary herd. After various cogitations as to the particular one I should assume, I thought nothing appeared more likely to be remarkable among men, and therefore pleasing to women, than an egregious coxcomb; accordingly I arranged my hair in ringlets, dressed myself with a singular plainness and simplicity (a low person, by the by, would have done just the contrary), and, putting on an air of exceeding langour, made my maiden appearance at Lord Bennington's.[45]

This contrived sense of 'dressing down' is contrasted with the more 'effeminate' affectations of Pelham's rival Russleton, a character clearly based on Brummell whose whole purpose in life is to present his body as an exquisite work of art. The old-school dandy proclaims that:

When I was six years old, I cut my jacket into a coat and turned my aunt's best petticoat into a waistcoat. I disdained at eight the language of the vulgar... At nine I was self-inoculated with the propriety of ideas. I rejected malt with the air of His Majesty and formed a violent affection for maraschino; though starving at school, I never took twice of a pudding and paid sixpence a week out of my shilling to have my shoes blacked... As I grew up... I employed three tradesmen to make my gloves - one for the hand, a second for the fingers, and a third for the thumb - for the great secrets of being courted are to shun others and seem delighted with yourself. [46]

That this rather frigid style, with its reliance on the skills of the tradesman and its promotion of a highly elaborated figure, was gradually giving way to a more relaxed and romanticized understanding of 'self' which drew on notions of an 'innate' aristocratic sense of taste, is shown by Pelham's rejection of the West End tailor as the sole arbiter of fashion. In a critique of the attitudes which had positioned Bond Street and Savile Row as the fount of sartorial knowledge thirty years previously, Bulwer Lytton anticipated the waning of a powerful metropolitan discourse which celebrated the talents of the gentleman's tailor and the elite provisions of its fashionable shopping streets. Control of the nature and direction of London fashion was, it seems, passing out of the dandy's hands, so much so that the fitting-up of the male body had become a discreet and personal rather than a public and self-promotional activity. Notably it is one of the most famous of those first-generation tailoring pioneers whom Pelham isolates for his attack:

Stultz aims at making gentlemen, not coats; there is a degree of aristocratic pretension in his stitches which is vulgar to an appalling degree. You can tell a Stultz coat anywhere, which is quite enough to damn it: the moment a man's known by an invariable cut, and that not original, it ought to be all over with him. Give me the man who makes the tailor, not the tailor who makes the man. [47]

Two further circumstances conspired against the continuing reign of West End dandyism as it had been conceived in the glory days of Brummell. The first was the opening up of Paris to British aristocrats after the abdication of Napoleon and the cessation of cross-Channel hostilities in 1814, and the second was the growing popularity of the dandy style among those who did not enjoy the 'natural' right to call themselves 'gentlemen'. In the first instance, it is significant that Pelham's self-fashioning is perfected like D'Orsay's in the Paris residence of an English Lord rather than on the streets of St James's. Where Anglophilia had generated a reverence for British sartorial taste in the 1790s and 1810s, by the 1820s and 1830s Paris was fully reinstated as an international centre for modish philosophies and luxurious living. The plush comforts of the Parisian hotel thus offered stiff competition to the more bracing conception of fashionable masculinity that resided across the Channel. This shift in the centre of sartorial gravity left those who still adhered to the London style looking rather anachronistic. Captain Gronow remembered that :

Thousands of oddly dressed English flocked to Paris immediately after the war… our countrymen and women having so long been excluded from French modes had adopted fashions of their own quite as remarkable and eccentric as those of the Parisians, and much less graceful… The characteristics of the dress of the gentleman was a coat of light blue, or snuff colour, with brass buttons, the tail reaching nearly to the heels, a gigantic bunch of seals dangled from his fob, whilst his pantaloons were short and tight at the knees; and a spacious waistcoat, with a voluminous muslin cravat and a frilled shirt, completed the toilette. The dress of the British military, in its stiff and formal ugliness, was equally cumbrous and ludicrous.[48]

Gronow's reminiscences are peppered with such caricatures and he takes great delight in detailing the dandified excesses of a series of London characters who illustrate a kind of decadence as far as the celebration of early nineteenth-century masculine fashion is concerned, providing fleshed-out versions of Cruikshank's grotesque visual satires. There was Lieutenant-Colonel Kelly 'haughty in the extreme, and very fond of dress' whose boots were renowned for their mirror-like shine, the secret blacking mixed by a valet whose widely envied services were auctioned off to the highest bidder when Kelly perished in a fire at the Custom House trying to rescue his precious footwear. Michel Angelo Taylor, a Member of Parliament was distinguished by his unusual appearance, glittering silver hair, a port-wine birthmark, leather breeches and 'an unstarched and exquisitely white neckcloth, the whole surmounted by a very broad-brimmed beaver'. Colonel Mackinnon, noted for his physique and agility, demonstrated the child-like and irresponsible characteristics associated with a West End lifestyle by 'creeping over the furniture of a room like a monkey' at modish parties; and Sir Lumley Skeffington, an old-fashioned macaroni 'used to paint his face so that he looked like a French toy; he dressed a la Robespierre and practised other follies… You always knew of his approach by an avant-courier of sweet smell; and when he advanced a little nearer you might suppose yourself in the atmosphere of a perfumer's shop'.[49]

All of these peacocks, collectively styled 'men about town' by Gronow, exposed the practice of dandyism to broader ridicule. There is a suggestion that their compulsion for exhibitionism placed them at the peripheries of genteel society, their clown-like activities the antithesis of the elegant code of behaviour set out by men like Brummell as the most appropriate for the habitation of London's new squares, parks and crescents (though by the 1820s such tight strictures had become more closely associated with the respectable, bourgeois and etiquette-book-buying inhabitants of Bloomsbury, utilized as a well-mannered rebuke to the excesses of the West End). More than this, Gronow hints at the shadowy social origins of these stars of the gossip columns and print shops, suggesting that fine clothes and extravagant attitudes had become a hollow signifier for aristocratic associations, sullied by rapid commercial expansion and the realization that a sense of fashionability could be bought as well as inherited. The ultimate proof of this state of affairs lies in the reams of popular ballads, caricatures and satires which instated the dandy as a general figure of fun, recognizable among all social classes and made ridiculous by his pretensions and base snobbery. Such representations must have littered the pavements of late-Hanoverian London. The following is typical of the oeuvre, sounding the death-knell for an elite fashionable identity which had brought London's shops, celebrities and fashion trades to the attention of the world. *Dandy Bewitched* is a facsimile of a letter from John Slink, a City clerk to his lover, a mantua-maker. It is a rather bathetic endnote to the social trend which Brummell and his like set in motion:

Dearest, the other day in St Mary's Wynd, as I passed through it, I purchased a pair of second hand Wellingtons that I got for five-and-sixpence, I had no money but the Broker seeing my genteel appearance, was kind enough to trust me. They are very high in the heel and I have been practising myself in the most fashionable way of walking on the heel, which in a great measure will hide the effect of my plain soles. I have got a pair of second-hand stays; and yesterday, I went to my tailor (who never refused to trust me) and ordered a suit of new clothes, and told him to put false braids in my trowsers, which he assured me that he would do in the neatest manner and to have them on Saturday night. So, that on Sunday you will much oblige your lover if you will be in readiness by eleven o'clock to ride out with me, not in one of those hackneys which I cannot endure, every person reading the owner's name under the window, but I shall look out for an exquisite Carricle, when as we ride we shall be taken for quality, which we really are, going to visit their property in the country:

*Of dandyship I sing, for you know it's just the thing,*
*Yes, you know it's just the thing to recommend you, O,*
*In the carricle we'll ride, and the sutty poor deride,*
*That we'll make support our pride to act the dandy, O.* [50]

## THE RAMBLER'S PLAYGROUND

While the image and identity of the London dandy gradually became accessible to a variety of social constituencies, moving so fluidly between them that the term eventually lost any direct association with a particular class of men, the haunts in which he was able to display his finely wrought exterior remained more firmly fixed by the opportunities and experiences which the capital had to offer. In this sense the development of masculine fashion in the period is anchored once again by the physical growth and material complexity of London's urban fabric. Having seen how the construction of the dandy-look originated from the tight concentration of aristocratic residences and elite tradesmen in the West End, it becomes necessary to consider the varied spaces and contexts in which such a sartorial philosophy was refined and put to work, for the relationship between the dandy and the pleasures of his home city was an intense and complex one. In many ways it reflected the hierarchical social networks which prevailed in aristocratic life generally, the dandy's activities mirroring the tightly policed round of levees, balls and assemblies which accompanied a season in town. But in others the practice of dandyism transgressed these formal boundaries, ensuring that that the categories of high- and low-life were not mutually opposed and introducing an element of social danger, of cultural miscegenation into the practice of fashion. This marked London out as an enduring focus for forms of fashionable stylization which owed as much to the energies of the street and the ferment of the crowd as they did to the deliberations of the salon. It might even be argued that it is precisely this dandified spirit of disrespect for the niceties of official society and an openness to the chaotic creativity of urban life which has positioned London as an alternative or competing locus for the production of fashion in a longer time-frame, setting the city in an on-going opposition to the more regulated fashion dictates of Paris since the late eighteenth-century.

As Rendell and others have demonstrated, the idea and practice of 'rambling', allowed the dandy free movement across the pleasure zones of the metropolis, offering up a near pornographic fantasy of London as a cornucopia of corporeal delights for the discerning gentleman. Preceding its mid-twentieth-century incarnation as a weekend hobby for the suburban lower-middle classes which provided the opportunity to hike across the greenbelt and indulge in healthful exercise, the early nineteenth-century version was an altogether more urbane and dissolute practice. *The Rambler's Magazine*, published in London during the 1820s, was clear in its definition of the typical reader's interests, styling itself as the 'annals of gallantry, glee, pleasure and bon-ton. A delicious bouquet of amorous, bacchanalian, whimsical, humorous, theatrical and literary entertainment. Our motto is be gay and free! Make love and joy your choicest treasure; look on our book with eyes of glee, And ramble over scenes of pleasure'. A collection of erotic prose, lascivious engravings of classical and orientalist couplings and scurrilous gossip concerning the intrigues of high society, the journal provided a template for the practice of dandyism which linked the Mayfair balls attended by infamous courtesans such as Harriette Wilson, the fashionable Sunday parades in Hyde Park which punctuated the Season and the coarser celebration of male bonding represented by the drinking and gambling dens and the pugilistic competitions of the proletarian East End. Playing these scenarios off against each other while remaining unflustered at the centre of each was the figure of the 'clothes-wearing man', his unobtrusive tailoring providing the requisite armour for a world which was morally dubious and often physically dangerous. In this context the maxims of authors such as Bulwer Lytton regarding the importance of dress and self-image take on the ring of truth. Far from simply dressing to fulfil the demands of an overweening narcissism, the man about town found it necessary to adopt a costume and attitude that set him at an advantage in a savage and competitive social scenario. The dandy was quite literally equipping himself to engage in a form of sexual and social warfare. Pelham's instructions for the aspirant London dandy were entirely apposite:

- Always remember that you dress to fascinate others, not yourself.
- Keep your mind free from all violent affections at the hour of the toilet. A philosophical severity is perfectly necessary to success.
- Remember that none but those whose courage is unquestionable can venture to be effeminate.
- The handsome may be showy in dress, the plain should study to be unexceptionable; just as in great men we look for something to admire - in ordinary men we ask for nothing to forgive.
- A man must be a profound calculator to be a consummate dresser… there is no diplomacy more subtle than dress.
- There may be more pathos in the fall of a collar, or the curl of a lock, than the shallow think for. Should we be so apt now to companionate the misfortunes of Charles I if his pictures had portrayed him in a bob-wig and a pig-tail? Vandyke was a greater sophist than Hume.
- The most graceful principle of dress is neatness - the most vulgar is preciseness.
- Dress contains the two codes of morality - private and public. Attention is the duty we owe to others - cleanliness that which we owe to ourselves.
- Dress so that it may never be said of you 'what a well-dressed man' but, 'what a gentlemanlike man!'
- Avoid many colours and seek by one prevalent and quiet tint to sober down the others. Apelles used only four colours, and always subdued those which were florid by a darkening varnish.
- Nothing is superficial to a deep observer! It is in trifles that the mind betrays itself.
- There is an indifference to please in a stocking down at heel - but there is malevolence in a diamond ring.
- Inventions in dressing should resemble Addison's definition of fine writing, and consist of 'refinements which are natural, without being obvious.'
- He who esteems trifles for themselves is a trifler - he who esteems them for the conclusions to be drawn from them, or the advantage to which they can be put, is a philosopher. [51]

It comes as no surprise, following such a list, that the image of the London dandy most often recorded by the caricaturists was that of the young man in his dressing room, being prepared as if for a command performance by an army of tailors, hairdressers, corsetiers, shoemakers and valets. In an inversion of Hogarth's *The Countess's Levee* from his *Marriage A La Mode*, the artist Heath depicted his heroes Lubin and Dashall from the satirical 1822 series *Fashion and Folly* being attended to by the cream of Mayfair tradesmen. Lubin sits manfully astride a chair in the centre of his dressing room while a barber, various combs balanced in his own coiffure, attends to his locks. To his right a tailor adjusts the waistline of his coat in front of a full-length mirror, his valet presents his riding boots from behind, while a draper proffers textile samples from the left. His friend Dashall, resplendent in striped Cossack trousers and matching waistcoat reads a newspaper for knowledge of the latest scandals, lifting his patterned dressing gown so as better to warm his rear in front of the fire. In the following plate the two descend the steps of their Mayfair residence, expensive toilettes complete and horsewhips in hand,

9 'La toilette : Lubin fitting out' from *Fashion & Folly* by W. Heath, c.1822 (Corporation of London)

en route to Tattersall's, the fashionable horse auctioneers at Hyde Park Corner. Such is the glory of their attire that a passing baker inadvertently thrusts his wares into the face of a maid, transfixed by this fleeting vision of extreme fashionability.[52] Further down the social scale, the transformative potential of fashionable dressing and the necessity of ensuring that its details lived up to the splendour of the occasion was underscored in publications such as *The Dandies Ball or High Life in the City*, a crudely engraved and coloured illustrated ballad of 1819 which represented the attempts of city clerks to emulate the grand extravagance of those aristocratic masquerades and dances held at West End locations such as Almack's or the Argyll Rooms, but in the humbler domestic drawing rooms of Bloomsbury or Clerkenwell:

Mr Pillblister, and Betsy his sister, determined on giving a treat;
Gay dandies they call, to supper and ball, at their home in Great Camomile Street.
Mr Padum delighted, for he was invited, began to consider his dress.
His shirt was not clean, nor fit to be seen, so he washed it, he could not do less.
Here's the stays from the tailor, for Mr MacNailor, 'Oh Jeffery ! lace it quite tight !'
'I'll hold by the post, that no time may be lost, at the ball I'll outshine all tonight.'
'I'll dance with my charmer', said Mr Bob Palmer, 'I'm determin'd tonight at the ball.'
'I've dined on the fishes, and washed up the dishes, and wait for the barber to call.'[53]

Beyond the obvious uses of a dandified style of dressing that through lacing, padding or expert cutting could be requisitioned as an aid to the sexual adventuring which the freer mixing of the sexes sanctioned at such venues allowed ( in the early decades of the nineteenth century physical proximity between men and women was intensified by the popularity of new more intimate dances - and the tendency of contemporary dress for both genders was to accentuate the erotic potential of secondary sexual characteristics), the adornment of the masculine body could also be associated with urban pastimes exclusively devoted to the company of men. Tattersall's, alluded to in Heath's caricature, played a central role in bringing together male bon-viveurs from across the capital's social and cultural divides. Pierce Egan described it as 'the most complete place in the metropolis' and recommended that 'if you have any desire to witness 'real life' - to observe character - and to view the favourite hobbies of mankind' a visit was compulsory. 'It is the resort of the pinks of the swells - the tulips of the goes, - the dashing heroes of the military - the fox-hunting clericals, - the sprigs of nobility, - stylish coachmen, - smart guards, - saucy butchers, - natty grooms, - tidy helpers, - knowing horse dealers, - betting politicians, - neat jockeys, - sporting men of all descriptions, - and the picture is finished by numbers of real gentlemen. It is the tip-top sporting feature of London.' [54] Furthermore, in the image of Lubin at his toilette it is no coincidence that Heath chose to depict a print of two boxers as a fitting decoration for the walls of the dandy's boudoir. In the spectacular half-naked figure of the pugilist many of the contradictions of the dandy could be reconciled.

Alongside compulsory attendance at the Hyde Park 'church parades' on Sunday afternoons where the bloodstock purchased at Tattersall's made a fitting mount for the wardrobe purchased in Bond Street, the dandy might seek out a wide variety of contexts for displaying his body and his tastes. Besides the Wednesday evening balls at Almack's and the frequent appearances in St James's Street gentlemen's clubs, the more dangerous streets east of Temple Bar offered an alternative arena for the distillation of an emergent London style. Pierce Egan again provided a chronicle of fashionable pursuits beyond the golden enclosure of the West End in his *Boxiana or Sketches of Ancient and Modern Pugilism*, rejoicing in the individual characters of celebrated boxing champions and relishing the raucous escapades of the 'fancy' - fight-followers whose passion for the clear romanticism of the sport crossed class boundaries. An interest in the manly arts of boxing excused the dandy from accusations of effeminacy while intensifying his celebration of the perfected masculine figure. In reference to the most popular association for aristocratic patrons of the ring, Egan stated that 'it was... for purposes of the truest patriotism and national benefit that the Pugilistic Society was formed... The great object of it is to keep alive the principles of courage and hardihood which have distinguished the British character, and to check the progress of that effeminacy which wealth is apt to produce.'[55] Members could even distinguish themselves by the purchase of a special uniform including the blue coat and yellow kerseymere waistcoat made more famous by Brummell, the letters 'P.C.' engraved on their buttons. Hard by the West End itself, in St Martin's Street close to Leicester Fields, the Fives Court attracted 'the most respectable audiences' and provided the space in which 'amateurs of scientific pugilism' could develop their skills.

Further east the Castle Tavern in Holborn was opened as a haunt for 'sporting bucks' from the West End by retired fighter Bob Gregson in 1810. Egan noted that his six-foot, fifteen-stone frame was the focus for much admiration. 'A finer or better proportioned athletic man could not be met with... He was considered by the celebrated professor of anatomy at the Royal Academy a most excellent subject to descant upon...

He was likewise selected by the late Sir Thomas Lawrence as a fine subject...his general deportment was above all absurd affectation; nothing supercilious was to be found in his manner... [he] was always well, nay fashionably dressed'.[56] Succeeded by the equally 'swell' Tom Belcher as landlord in 1814, this paragon of a classless London fashionability presided over a business whose ambience competed strongly with more central and select venues for fashionable resort. 'Patrons came out in mobs to give it support, necessary to make it a striking feature with the bloods, the bucks, the men of ton, and the etcetera, which make up the sporting circles.' Its success was repeated in countless other sporting houses, many of them run by prize-fighters from Smithfield, to Moorgate to the Old Kent Road. That similar retreats could be found in Fitzroy and Grosvenor Squares, in Bond and Jermyn Streets attests more strongly still to the manner in which the dandy-style gripped the character of the capital, drawing on and contributing to what Peter Thorold has called 'the fascination of London in 1800... its vitality, its enormous size, the choice of things to do, the ease of living, the clamour, the sheer metropolitan sensation.'[57] This is why the style of the early nineteenth-century dandy, which linked the naked body of the working-class fighter to the tailored figure of the aristocratic rambler in an egalitarian celebration of masculine heroism, can rightly be termed the first and perhaps the most important of a succession of fashionable identities intimately bound up with the development of the city itself. His shadow falls across the next two centuries as a template for dressing according to the opportunities which a particular urban context demands, fading a little as divisions between East and West Ends became more entrenched in the following decades and the nature of producing and wearing clothing in London grew to reflect more clearly the chasms between sections of the population and the competing cultures of particular districts, in a monstrous Victorian metropolis that was more often described in dystopic terms. By the standards of an optimistic World City in the 1820s though, dandyism lent an agreeably fair and self-assured face to a thriving urban society:

In cockneyland, the seventh day
Is famous for a grand display
Of modes, of finery and dress
Of Cit, West-Ender and Noblesse,
Who in Hyde Park crowd like a fair
To stare, and lounge and take the air,
Or ride or drive, or walk and chat
On fashions, scandal and all that.[58]

# The Immigrant:

## EAST END, WEST END 1840-1914

In the seventy-four years between 1840 and 1914 which marked London's heyday as a World City, the metropolis was frequently conceived of by commentators as a series of spatial relationships, from east to west and centre to suburb. Like the ancient Rome of legend its highways traced a network of broader global connections that fed out from the city's core. Cultural, financial, social and martial links all joined together at this celebrated hub of Empire, replicating the sensations and concerns of the far flung colonies at their administrative and ceremonial centre. Thus in a passage from his impressionistic text *The Soul of London* of 1905 Ford Madox Ford elegantly described the varying perspectives involved in an imagining of the capital's topography. In a city of diverse contrasts, of striking poverty and ostentatious wealth, of crowded slums and palatial villas, of opulent shops and mean factories, the whole could make sense only by a description of the linked variety of its parts. For Ford, as for many men of his class and profession, the contrasting architectural styles and confusing geographical configurations of London carried with them all the exciting trappings of the explorer's descriptive repertoire, but transplanted from the veldt and the jungle to the asphalt and brick of an urban milieu. Furthermore in travelling across and between the districts of the city, the nineteenth-century journalist engaged almost in the manner of a fashionable consumer with a shifting social and aesthetic scene whose potential for aiding a process of self-characterization through clothing was limitless. In imperial terms the role of shopper, dresser and colonialist overlapped:

Speaking broadly, the man who expresses himself with a pen on paper sees his London from the west. At worst he hopes to end with that view. His London of breathing space, his West End, extends from say Chiswick to say Portland Place. His dense London is the city as far as Fenchurch Street, his East End ends with what he calls Whitechapel. The other sees his London of elbow room extend from say Purfleet to say Blackwall. He is conscious of having, as it were at his back, the very green and very black

**❶❿** *A bird's eye view of London from Lambeth by T. Sulman, c. 1859 (Corporation of London)*

stretches of the Essex Marshes dotted with large solitary factories and small solitary farms. His dense London, his city, lies along the line from Blackwall to Fenchurch Street. Beyond that the City proper, the City of the Bank and the Mansion House, is already a place rather of dilettante trifling. Its streets are tidied up, its buildings ornamented and spacious. The end of the West End is for him Piccadilly Fountain, and this latter quarter of large, almost clean, stone buildings, broad swept streets, and a comparative glare of light, is already a foreign land, slightly painful because it is so strange.[1]

In its architectural variety the built environment of Imperial London offered a stage for self-performance and sartorial exploration as evocative as anything which might have lain at the end of a lengthy sea passage to Canada, India, Southern Africa, Australia or the far east, though as Ford suggests, its inhabitants cleaved to the familiarity which local vistas and landmarks encouraged. Within the seeming permanence of its streets and squares, its courts and closes, however, the inexorable movement of peoples and a multiplicity of racial 'types' further endorsed the idea of a globally connected city whose social boundaries and human geographies were in a constant state of flux, tied as they were to the rhythms and economics of the colonizing process. Edwin Pugh writing in *The City of The World: A Book about London and the Londoner* of 1908 described how:

Foreign quarters abound, and living specimens of almost every race under the sun are to be met with in the streets in their native garb. There are Russians and Poles in their raw state in Church Lane off the Commercial Road; Orientals of every shade of complexion, from lemon yellow to black, Turks, Moors, Kabiles, Armenians, Syrians, Persians, Hindus, Chinese, Japanese, Siamese, Malaysians, Polynesians and Negroes in Limehouse and Poplar; Italians at their Romish observances in Back Hill, Clerkenwell; Germans in Lehman Street and Fitzroy Square, a whole cosmopolitan colony in Soho, and Colonials and Yankees everywhere.[2]

# THE URBAN EXOTIC

The hold of literary constructions such as these on the popular imagination of the Victorian and Edwardian public was a powerful one, and it is to the descriptive talents of such authors as Ford, Pugh and others who aimed their words at a middle-brow audience that I wish to turn in the course of this chapter. Written for provincial and colonial visitors to London and for a growing local constituency of middle- and lower-middle-class readers whose knowledge of the city related to their own broadened experience of it as commuters, consumers or employees of an expanding service and administrative sector, these texts were both explanatory and imaginative, aiming to make sense of a bewildering diversity through the employment of a literary register which we might define as that of the 'urban exotic'. Here was a strategy for dealing with cultural difference by turning the threatening aspects of urban life and the project of Empire into spectacle, and it was descriptions of the dressed (and sometimes naked) bodies of city dwellers, of London style and its constantly mutating colonial context which proved to be one of the most effective mediums by which the city's complex status as an Imperial and national capital could be communicated. As London 'stood in' symbolically for the Empire as a whole, so the physical appearance and dress of its inhabitants was used by writers, artists and ethnographers as a productive code for interpreting the various relationships between place, identity and power that marked its social landscape. These were represented in such a way that no singular, unchanging sartorial type could be associated with its fragmented terrain. Even the famous cockney was a literary creature contained within tightly defined boundaries, at home only within the sound of Bow bells, and both the recently arrived alien and the complacent suburban were similarly characterized as contingent bit-players in a grand narrative of carefully monitored and nuanced movement through and across colonized space. Journalist Thomas Burke suggested as much when he claimed in his autobiography *Nights in Town* of 1915 that

London is not one place, but many places; she has not one soul, but many souls. The people of Brondesbury are of markedly different character and clime from those of Hammersmith… The smell, the sound and the dress of Finsbury Park are as different from the smell, the sound and the dress of Wandsworth Common as though one were England and the other Nicaragua.[3]

As literary historian P.J. Keating has explained, nineteenth-century commentators on the urban scene were attracted to this 'exploratory' writing style largely because of its magical ability to 'evoke a variety of simultaneous and often ambiguous connotations' that matched the multi-layered experience of the city itself. On another level its themes 'encouraged a literal… interpretation' of social and racial difference that fed the more conservative instincts of a middle-class marketplace. 'For author and reader alike, it was dangerous to allow either the working or the immigrant classes to gather in dark… little known areas… there was something tribal, primitive and unchristian about them'.[4] Texts which aimed to uncover and illuminate their habits effected a semblance of control and compassion, extending the reforming zeal of the missionary to those threatening territories closer to home. 'It is not always possible, or sensible to distinguish in this peculiar literature of urban life between fiction and non-fiction', but the best of these writers who included Mayhew and Dickens, James Greenwood, John Hollingshead, Charles Manby Smith and George R. Sims shared a sympathy for the subjects who inspired their work, anger at the social and economic conditions which caused their distress and a direct and lucid prose style. They also adopted a common approach to the field that was qualitative rather than quantitative: a willingness to argue their point of view by means of dramatically presented case-studies and highly emotive language. This may lessen the value of their work to those historians of a more scrupulously empirical bent, but their romantic interpretations do offer rare insights regarding both attitudes toward, and the visceral experience of, urban lifestyles that were ephemeral and otherwise unrecorded. Most importantly, such writing attempted to open the eyes of the reader to what was near at hand and possibly over-familiar… 'to the great variety of London life and its perplexing social stratification', rather than to the simple capital-labour conflict that dominated so much of Victorian political economy and moral philosophy.[5] Furthermore the voyage of exploration necessary to comprehend this state of affairs need only consist of a ten-minute walk from St James's to St Giles, for along its route in microcosm lay examples of all the problems and inequalities of the modern globe.

So, the sartorial imagery employed by such explorers was calculated to appeal partly to the reader's social conscience and partly to his or her class fears. Possible retribution for neglect was constantly threatened, but because the crucial urban relationship highlighted in the literature was between rich and poor, rather than capital and labour, retribution was conceived of in terms of contamination rather than physical violence or industrial unrest, and it was here that the spectre of the poor alien immigrant, floating across districts and between boundaries, carried most weight. His shadowy, ragged presence is particularly marked in Gustave Dore and Blanchard Jerrold's iconic *London: A Pilgrimage* published in 1872. Art historian Ira Nadel suggests that the power of Dore's images lay not in their realism (which to the dress historian is deeply compromised by the engraver's debt to traditional academic strategies of composition and his romantic generalization of the details of bodies and clothing) but in their symbolism, which taught the viewer a grammar for perceiving the city and its importance for the age. Dore and Jerrold posed as 'pilgrims, wanderers, gypsy loiterers' set on exploring the highs and lows of the London experience, always seeking 'the imaginative side of the great city's life and movement'. The major theme of their work centred on the idealized social and economic unity of a metropolis connected physically and symbolically along the length of the River Thames, which itself flowed out through the docks toward the ports of the Empire. This notion of a physical unity was itself slightly anachronistic by the early 1870s in a London which was experiencing a rapid division by occupation, living conditions, transportation systems and the lack of any central governing authority. Consequently the idea of separate East and West Ends with their own distinctive populations was by now an unavoidable geographical reality, though one whose psychic boundaries were frequently breached. In imaginative terms the illustrator and the journalist succeeded in breaking through those distinctions so that the 'unutterable external hideousness' that Matthew Arnold saw in London in *Culture and Anarchy* became for Dore and Jerrold a phantasmagorical and organic unity that linked the fairytale scenario of Holland House and the Ladies' Mile to the sublime mysteries of the Limehouse Opium Den or the Seven Dials Rookery. As Nadel states,

The reality of the city for Doré is dualistic - at once detailed and imagined, identifiable and illusory. Doré revealed the urban world of Victorian London as one of depth and multiplicity, and the success of *London: A Pilgrimage* resides in its ability to take the city and its inhabitants and transform them into the surface and symbol of Victorian life.[6]

'A City Thoroughfare' from *London : A Pilgrimage* ❶❶ *(right)*
by Gustave Dore, 1872 (Museum of London)

Beyond the importance of travel and migration as themes which aided the projection of nineteenth-century London through literature and print culture, the movement of workers and economic refugees across and between cities and nations was also a material fact of nineteenth-century life, at least until the 1880s when the growth of more regular employment for the unskilled, the mechanization of much piece work, the demise of wakes, feasts and fairs and the triumph of shop over packman ensured a greater degree of urban stability and the walling in of those whose lives had previously been organized according to the seasons and a negotiation of the highways. Historian Raphael Samuel referred to this itinerant population as the 'comers and goers', an important but fugitive constituency whose culture and appearance profoundly affected the atmosphere of the city at particular times of the year: 'Wayfaring life had a definite place in the moral topography of the nineteenth-century town. Railway stations always attracted a floating population to the vicinity; so did the wholesale markets... Brickfields, on the outskirts of town were regular dossing places, along with gasworks, railway bridges and viaducts'. Weirdly invisible, it was almost as if the browns and greys of the indigents' rags blended into both the local architecture and the local economy. 'There were Irish quarters in every centre of industry and trade, 'Little Irelands' whose inhabitants remained notoriously migratory in their habits... Waterfront districts too, always bore a peculiarly migratory character'[7]... though here the alien qualities of life were less hidden, more

distinctive : 'The quarters of every town that lie near the wharves and banks always seem to deteriorate', wrote Lady Bell in her philanthropic book *At the Works* of 1907. 'There is something in the intercourse of sailors... who come and go, nomadic, unvouched for, who appear and disappear, with no responsibility for their words or deeds, that seems to bring to the whole world a kinship of lawlessness and disorder.'[8]

❶❷

'London Nomads' from
*Street Life in London*
by John Thomson, 1877
(Museum of London)

# THE EAST [END]

It comes as no surprise then that when the exploratory writers of Victorian London chose to identify the 'urban exotic' in its most concentrated and spectacular form, they looked to the Port of London and the docks downriver as its most natural location. For Charles Knight in his extensive *Encyclopaedia of London* published in the early 1870s, the streets of Wapping signified a miniature fashion-system all of its own, set up purely to service the sartorial and material desires of the nautical wayfarer:

Whatever Wapping may appear to the eyes of landsmen, to the British sailor it is without doubt, a region of romance... We go through its long and narrow streets... turning up our noses at its dirt and age and squalor. But... from the moment we pass Tower Hill, and those immense warehouses to the right - rising storey upon storey, and large enough apparently, to be the storehouses of an empire rather than of a single metropolitan dock - every other shop is in some way or other devoted to his wants, his instructions, his recreations... Here we have the wholesale slop seller occasionally condescending to throw a half unpacked bundle of jackets or shirts into his window, and who can at the briefest notice rig out a ship's crew: there the retail dealer who is not too proud to exhibit nearly his whole substance to the light of common day, and covers his entire front, from the pavement to the first floor with snow white ducks and rough pilot coats, oil skin overalls and every variety of hat, from the small jaunty round to the coal heaver fashioned... The aristocratical shop-keeper of Wapping we take to be the mathematical instrument maker whose windows, so full of neatly finished and highly polished brass articles, in so many varieties of form, might even cut a figure in Bond Street.[9]

Knight's conception of the local economy is an ordered one which utilizes the rhetoric of Empire to suggest lines of travel and communication (both real and symbolic) which reach out from Wapping to the West End and beyond to the dominions. The chaos of the dockside has been sublimated in a picturesque reading which prioritizes the abundant but wholesome exotica of window displays and warehouse catalogues, drawing pointed comparisons with the opulence of Bond Street. Other interpretations were not so accommodating, isolating the riverside as a contaminated no man's land in which theft and immorality arose as a natural consequence of the locale's unboundaried perimeters, open to the free movement not just of goods and people but of vice. Clothing, its decency or otherwise, made a potent symbol in this context, and as the East London QC Montague Williams recalled in his autobiography 'Round London' of 1896 :

It would have been madness for any respectable woman, or for that matter any well-dressed man, to proceed thither alone. The police themselves seldom ventured there save in twos and threes. The inhabitants of Ratcliffe Highway lived upon the sailors. There were a great many lodging houses there, still more clothiers and outfitters, and any number of public houses and beershops, nearly every one of which had a dancing saloon at the back of the bar... No sooner did a vessel reach her moorings than she was swarming with boarding touts, crimps, outfitters, runners and other rapacious beasts of prey... Sailors of every nationality were to be met there, including a great many Portuguese, Spaniards, Italians, Greeks, Norwegians and Scandinavians. The Highway was indeed a veritable modern Babel. Among the disreputable characters to be met there were men dressed as sailors who sold parrots and parakeets.[10]

The drawing of a link between a perceived foreign, and generally oriental, duplicity and the selling of fashionable accoutrements was a strong theme in the literature. It was endorsed in 1906 by Count E. Armfeldt when he described the 'Oriental' population for George Sims's majesterial three volume project *Living London* :

There is the Turk from Constantinople who has no shop, no warehouse, and sometimes no address, and yet carries on a lucrative trade in old point lace; there is the Syrian who sells beautiful dolls dressed in their native costumes, and there is the insinuating carpet hawker from Jerusalem. All these have their clients who never forsake them. There is too the kohl vendor from Egypt, who goes to the houses of the Jews and who will pencil the eyebrows and the eyelids so as to give intense lustre to the eyes. There is the Japanese tattooer who earns his twenty guineas in two or three sittings... each of them can be seen in the streets of Oriental London.[11]

Beyond their role as pedlars of the exotic, however, Armfeldt found a greater fascination in the bodies and dress of visitors from beyond Europe, objectifying their difference in a fetishistic prose style that constructed a sublime version of the East in the midst of London, which betokened the unequal relationship of colonizer to colonized. As he states,

Visions of palm trees and mango groves, of mosques and pagodas, rise in the imagination as one beholds the swarthy sons of the Orient, whose quaint costumes bring colour to the London Streets, whose presence is emblematic of England's far-reaching commerce and power. The Maharaja who wears a diamond star... the Japanese who dress in solemn black, the Persian philosopher and the Parsee student one meets in the West End are all interesting figures... But to understand what Oriental London means from the point of view of character, costume and life scenes, one must travel from the fashionable west to the humble east, for it embraces all the various scenes of society high and low... It is in the crowded thoroughfares leading to the docks... That one meets the most singular and most picturesque types of Eastern humanity.... The pale yellowish Chinaman from Peking who almost trails his pigtail, and whose loose flowing robes are caught by the breeze, and whose soft thick felt shoes glide silently through the streets, and his brother from Canton or Hong Kong who wears sailor's clothes, and whose hair is neatly plaited round his head and covered with a large golf cap; the red turbaned Lascars whose toes are as nimble as a monkey's hands, and whose sea chests contain treasures of odds and ends of cast-off European clothing mixed with bits of oderous Bombay ducks; the alert up-to-date Japanese, whose pilot jacket has capacious pockets bulging with weird looking little idols... and the Cingalese, whose figures are hid in long overcoats, and who shiver with cold in the sun of an English summer, can all be observed on the quays of the docks, and in the favourite haunts of asiatics.[12]

# THE FOREIGNER ABROAD

LEAVING THE CHINESE LEGATION.

**1 3**

'Leaving the Chinese Legation' from *Living London*,
Volume I by George Sims, 1906 (Corporation of London)

This sense of alien splendour, of the colourful immigrant's costume symbolizing the global prowess of London's trading and governmental activities, was not simply reserved for descriptions of the dress of 'Asiatics'. The pages of *Living London* are littered with accounts of the city's foreign enclaves and their status as transplanted fiefdoms, emblematic of a spectacular 'otherness' and subject to the tourist gaze, but equally closely knitted in to the cultural and economic rhythms of the Imperial capital. Besides the seafaring peoples of the docks, Armfeldt also described the Italian community of Clerkenwell whose members were generally employed in serving the streets of the city with mechanical music or fast-food items. Dressed for the feast of Our Lady of Mount Carmel in mid July, 'the young Neapolitan dandy wears for the first time his brand-new broad-collared jacket, his rich looking figured waistcoat cut to exhibit an immensely white shirt-front and set off by a green or red necktie, and his flaming silk handkerchief from Sorrento'.[13] In Soho Armfeldt lauded the atmosphere of cosmopolitanism, refined over the years as 'the cherished home of foreign artists, dancers, musicians, singers and... performers, and the sanctuary of political refugees, conspirators, deserters and defaulters of all nations'.[14] Here in a district associated more with the imaginative and creative potential of emigration in a psychic and intellectual rather than a physical sense, sartorial identities appeared more fluid and open to self-determination. Transplanted from the dockside and freed from his status as just another exotic commodity, the wily foreigner dissolved into the productive confusion of the city, taking full advantage of its transformative potential. As Armfeldt stated,

To the uninitiated Soho is a land of romance - a Bohemia and an Alsatia. But to the British country cousin it is mainly a conglomeration of odd characters. He may imagine himself in the Latin Quarter, or within the boundaries of a far-off ghetto; he finds himself in a crowd of... alien types - hatchet-faced Greeks, strong featured Jews, sallow Frenchmen, yellow-skinned Levantines... and ebony sons of Africa. To behold these people on their arrival in the little hotels of Soho is both interesting and instructive. Many of them have undergone sea voyages as the labels of their luggage denote; and they reveal themselves in the curious garb of their native countries. In a day or two they will, with few exceptions, be all dressed in the clothes of modern civilization. The red and white turbans... of the Turks, the yellow koofieh of the Persians, the toques of the Montenegrans, the fur caps of the Russians and the Poles will disappear, and so will the stately kaftans, the picturesque baggy trousers, the embroidered vests... and the greasy sheepskins. They will all be relegated to the bottom of old-fashioned hair-covered trunks.[15]

By the first decade of the twentieth-century several authors of 'urban exotic' prose felt that this process of fitting in, of cultural homogenisation, the blurring of ethnic boundaries and of personal and local differences was becoming more pronounced. Armfeldt conceded that 'Soho always will have its romance and its mysteries. [Yet] its most glaring pictures of cosmopolitan life are being rapidly obliterated; but though it is no longer Babylon, it will ever remain Babel'.[16] Similarly, back in Wapping, Thomas Burke bemoaned that 'There was a time, years ago when the East End was the East End - a land apart... But the omnibus has changed all that... it has so linked things and

**❶❹**   *Piccadilly*
by Thomas Shotter Boys, 1842 (Corporation of London)

places that all individual character has been swamped in a universal chaos, and there is now neither East nor West... boundaries are things which exist today only in the mind of the borough councillor... and the London Docks are a region whose chief feature are cockney warehouse clerks'.[17] In some ways the picturesque immigrant now existed only as part of the romantic repertoire of popular writers, keen to promote the increasingly troubled cause of Empire. Historian Jonathon Schneer, in his recent book on London in 1900, suggests that genres like 'the Sherlock Holmes stories, like Music Hall entertainment, West End theatre, the spectacles at Earls Court, the London Zoo... preached a rather simple message. Brave and wise Englishmen had established a great empire over vast reaches of the world inhabited by uncivilized, dark-skinned people. This was good for those who had been colonized and for the colonizers. Meanwhile foggy, prosaic London accepted as was her due the fruits of Empire. Often the fruits of Empire were "dividends at 4½ %". But when they were dart blowing pygmies... or puff adders from India, white men such as the brilliant Holmes and trusty Dr Watson would deal with them as they dealt with Italians and Jews. The price of Empire was an eternal vigilance, but it was a price well worth paying.'[18]

In a sense, then, the vivid descriptions of immigrant communities and their dress, which featured so heavily in mid- to late nineteenth-century literary and journalistic works on London, can be viewed as a rather paranoid means of containment. But they also invite less negative interpretations as they trace the open networks and opportunities for change and disguise offered by the overlapping and multi-layered geographies of the Imperial city. We shouldn't forget either that these are descriptions which defined the immigrant primarily through his or her appearance and attire, or that the commodity of clothing itself can stand as a symbol of travel and escape. The London retail industry clearly recognized this and clothing emporia from Liberty's Department Store to Steven's Auction Rooms to Petticoat Lane traded on the global and romantic connections of their wares. As the final section of this chapter will suggest, the real clothing practices of immigrants (as producers and consumers of dress) were perhaps more humdrum. Economic and social necessities frequently demanded that the vulnerable foreigner adapt to local circumstances, and historians of immigration have shown how incoming communities gradually adopted practices of public assimilation in order to 'fit' while reserving the memories and customs of the old country for the private world of the home.[19] Arguably it is only in the torrid writing of novelists such as Thomas Burke that the alien achieved a compromised glamour:

Black man - white man - brown man - yellow man -
Pennyfields and Poplar and China town for me !
Stately moving cut-throats and many coloured mysteries
Never were such lusty things for London lads to see

Three miles straight lies lily-clad Belgravia
Thin lipped ladies and padded men and pale
But here are turbanned princes - and velvet-glancing gentlemen
Tom-tom and sharp knife and salt-caked sail.

*Then get you down to Limehouse, by rigging, wharf and smoke stack*
*Glamour, dirt and perfume, and dusky men and gold.*
*For down in hulking Limehouse there's the blue moon of the Orient*
*Lamps for young Aladdins, and bounties for the bold![20]*

## OXFORD CIRCUS, TRENTINO AND NOTTING HILL: LONDON STYLE

It is perhaps a facile comparison, but the confusion of moods, divergent experiences and tense connections between opposing parts which made up the unknowable and mysterious whole that was the London of writers like Burke is not so far removed from the complexity of textiles and accessories which described the wardrobe of the late nineteenth-century fashionable Londoner herself. This is evident in the sublime confection of a Princess Line dress owned by the Museum of London and made by the milliners C. Applin of Cork Street, sometime between 1878 and 1882.[21] So majestic (and not a little outre) is its combination of passmenterie trimmings, rust and gold embroidery, modern machine-made lace, ruched and boned black silk and satin weave silk ribbon that, according to family lore, the husband of the owner commissioned a special walnut wardrobe in which to house it. Inspired by a Parisian model, it has been constructed in the West End of London and utilizes a blowsy visual and social language native to its metropolitan context. As a product its physical characteristics are at one with the rapacious new retail culture which spawned its forms.

By the early 1860s the trade of the court dressmakers and milliners whose premises crowded the streets between Piccadilly and Oxford Street were visibly altering the tenor of the neighbourhood. The troubled Pantheon, for example, stood as a symbol of transition from the formal values and urbane language of aristocratic display, formerly associated with neighbouring Regent Street, to that debased focus on the pleasures of fashionable consumption which increasingly marked characterizations of the West End. George Sala, a pioneer of lifestyle journalism and chronicler of West End mores, appreciated the shift:

**❶❺**    Princess Line Dress by C. Applin of Cork Street, *c.*1878-1882 (Museum of London)

So into the Pantheon, turning and turning about in that Hampton Court-like maze of stalls, laden with pretty gimcracks, toys and papier mâché trifles for the table, dolls and children's dresses, wax flowers and Berlin Crochet work, prints and polkas and women's ware of all sorts… the world is as yet a delightful Pantheon, full of flowers - real, wax and artificial, and all pleasant - sandalwood fans, petticoats with worked edges, silk stockings, satin shoes, white kid gloves.. pet dogs, vanilla ices… and scented pink invitation notes. [22]

In this inventory of profuse gewgaws, Sala captured the exotic pleasures that the West End had to offer, mirroring the less-refined, more 'dangerous' exoticism of the East End. The sugary confections of goods whose only purpose appeared to be decorative found further echoes in the new structures and businesses that were increasingly closing in on John Nash's stuccoed Regent Street facades. Across the road from the Pantheon, the London Crystal Palace competed for the custom of young women in particular. Designed by Owen Jones in 1858, its coloured glass roof supported by painted iron columns sheltered a crowded souk-like space. 'From the galleries', noted the topographer Charles Knight, 'we look down upon the ground floor and find it arranged with counters in a very systematical order, loaded with uncountable trinkets… articles of millinery… lace… gloves… jewellery… children's dresses… porcelain ornaments… cut glass… alabaster figures… and a host of other things, principally of a light and ornamental character.' [23]

Oxford Circus itself was originally occupied by dignified family businesses. The presence of W.C.Jay, Mourning Warehouseman imbued the ornate, corinthian facades with a solemnity that sat strangely with the celebration of sensuality that surrounded it. In the manner of a 'memento mori', Henry Mayhew recalled how the interiors of the shop froze the desire to consume: 'with its tall gothic windows; it was softly carpeted, so that you scarcely heard your own footsteps as you trod along.. we noted the quietness, the harmonious hush of the whole place, and were impressed with the total 'un-shop-like' character of the establishment'. [24]

By the turn of the century, Jays still maintained its silence, but around it compulsory stock sales, railway-company hoardings, tabloid-newspaper announcements and American iced drinks jostled with the remains of a nineteenth-century carriage trade. The incursions of a noisy mass-culture were clearly undermining the elite and hushed integrity of the site. To think in terms of noise is perhaps an apt metaphor in trying to come to terms with this shift. Oxford Circus, then as now, sucks in and amplifies sound, both visual and aural, and this is a function that Peter Bailey has helpfully located within a discourse of urban modernity. 'It can be argued', he says, 'that physical and psychic survival in the city demanded a more finely tuned and active alertness to its many layers of sound… Thus we may understand modern street noise as a montage.. with shock-like juxtapositions… mastered by a newly developed sonic subconscious… Noise is a common compound signifier, most often of excess or vulgarity… The social translation is plainest in charges of vulgarity in dress.. as with the Edwardian music hall performer Kate Carney of whom it was reported "she wears such loud dresses you can't hear the buses go by".' [25]

**1 6** *Regent Street Quadrant*
by the London Stereoscopic Photographic Company, *c.*1886 (Museum of London)

So in some ways, Nash's stucco, now dirtied and peeling, failed in its primary and original function as a barrier for the undesirable sounds and sensations that clamoured against its surfaces. The tram and the underground train brought the restive suburban masses through its portals, while the sweated trades, the dirty clothes and the compromised immigrant bodies that were formerly annexed from view and hearing by the processes of mapping and planning, increasingly seemed to make their presence felt at the centre. Cheapness, vulgarity and life 'Up West' had clearly become interchangeable terms, now clearly audible or visible rather than carefully controlled. Local traders had long encouraged their elite male browsers in the consumption of goods that ranged from the sartorial to the sexual, but without seriously compromising the reputation of their streets as anything but the focus for elegant and genteel perambulation. Sala for example could recall his youthful fascination with the shop-windows of Regent Street with seeming innocence, though the nature of his desire is clear:

the larger half of my affections were secured by the waxen effigy of a lovely young lady, highly rouged, with the most ravishing blue glass eyes imaginable and very long silky lashes, whose hair was arranged... something like uncooked pork sausages which had been artfully convoluted... To me this mute beauty in ringlets presented additional fascinations of an almost ecstatic kind. First, by means of clockwork concealed in the pedestal... she was continually, slowly and gracefully revolving... And, again her snowy white arms were bare.. and she wore a ravishing corset of emerald green satin, sprigged with pink flowers and richly adorned with black lace. Whether she was the pride and ornament of a hairdresser's or a staymaker's shop, I can scarcely recall to mind. [26]

Its posé plastique attractions safely muffled behind glass, Sala's mannequin merely reflected the warmer bodies available for purchase only several minutes' walk away. As Gordon Mackenzie let slip in his rather prurient history of Marylebone, the district immediately to the north-east of Oxford Circus provided a morbid mirror image for the sugar-spun offerings of Regent Street: 'The Oxford Street area has a hinterland which at different times has been noted as a haunt of highly commercialised prostitution... The Victorians in particular contrived to make of this a sordid district of mean streets and shady businesses.. eighteenth century street names such as Night Pit Lane or Hartshorn's Rents proclaimed its sleazy character.' [27] Coloured by Michael Sadleir's melodramatic novels *Fanny by Gaslight* of 1940 and *Forlorn Sunset* of 1947 which were set in the locale, Mackenzie's appraisal carries with it the whisper of erotic wish-fulfilment, but that doesn't invalidate the importance of such accounts in the moulding of a potent myth, a sort of anti-romance of Oxford Street which has continued to bolster its reputation right up to the present. Social degradation was indeed never far from the barricades formed by the shop fronts to the south, though it was the seasonal and unreliable needle-trades necessary for the fashioning of their goods (and staffed largely by a local population of Russian Jews) that were responsible for the grinding poverty; prostitution was merely viewed as its ugly symptom. Charles Booth captured the arising contrasts:

Neither Shaftesbury Avenue, nor Charing Cross Road, nor Cambridge Circus belong in sentiment to the locality, any more than Regent Street, Oxford Street or the Strand... In spite of the great gashes so near its heart, the separate life of the district still survives. Leave any of the great streets I have mentioned, step but fifteen paces and you find yourself in another world, with another people... First comes darkness and a sense of stillness and peace after the rattle and blaze of the great streets, and then suddenly at the turn of another corner you are at once plunged into the spirit of the district itself... The air is bright with flaring lights and resonant with voices. [28]

For Booth, the world of fashionable goods infected the honesty and humanity of those whose lot it was to service its demands. The West End as he saw it was a mirage of a way of living, detached 'from the sense of responsibility which arises naturally from living in the reflected light of our past actions and pursued by their consequences'. The very modernity of its landscape uprooted both consumer, retail worker and dressmaker through the chimeric promise its goods held out of an escape into a more glamorous future. 'The result', he bemoaned, 'is a strange world; at best

**❶ ❼**  'The Old Clothes of St. Giles' from *Street Life in London* by John Thomson, 1877 (Museum of London)

not altogether wholesome; at worst inexpressibly vicious... Partly perhaps, as a result of this influence, the population of the district differs much in character from that of east or south London... its people are more 'conscious'. If they are bad they know it; if they are poor they feel it more.'[29]

By way of conclusion, the piquant story of a black silk dress, comprising bodice, skirt and underskirt, dating from the turn of the century and donated to the Museum of London by the maker's granddaughter, pays witness to Booth's prejudices and is aptly suggestive of the alienating realities which attended the life-stories and sartorial choices of the workers whose labour contributed directly to the appearance of fashionable Londoners and whose physical presence emphasized the moral and haptic character of the World City.[30] It was made and owned by Irma Cocco, born Irma Cescotti in Isera, Trentino, Italy in 1876[31]. Irma was trained as a court dressmaker, but moved to London in about 1900 as a result of an illegitimate pregnancy, apparently conceived with an English lover. She went into service and in 1905 married Pietro Cocco, an Italian boot-maker and -repairer of the Portobello Road. Trading on her skills she continued to produce clothing for herself, for her growing family and possibly for private clients, but her life remained dogged by ill fortune. Denied a pension due to her Italian citizenship yet bound to support many dependents, Irma died in poverty in the 1960s.

She left several children and grandchildren, one of whom offered the Museum Irma's clothes. The biographical details which lent them meaning were as threadbare as the fraying items which remained her only legacy; for her family they had come to represent the shame of their mother's past, and offered a tangible reminder of personal and dynastic ruin. A series of photographs also demonstrate the passage which Irma travelled from a carefree prosperity to the burdens of a forced emigration, placing the Museum of London dress in the midst of a sartorial and a personal journey. Three images from the early 1890s capture her youth in Italy. In the first she stands in profile, gazing up from underneath a parasol. Her long dark hair is tied loosely back in a chignon and her pale lace-trimmed blouse and full dark skirt further bespeak a stylish simplicity which emphasizes her fragile beauty. In the second image the pensive atmosphere is dispelled by a coquettish playfulness. Irma, laughing, has assumed a more worldly posture. Pulling aside a heavy curtain as if emerging onto the stage, her dark dress is chic in

❶ ❽ Black silk dress made by Irma Cocco (Cescotti), c.1900 (Museum of London)

its severity, set off at the collar by a choker in a similar material. Her hair, still pulled back into a knot, is now provocatively ruffled, its fringe frizzed according to contemporary fashion. And on her hand which pulls her skirts up to her hip, there is the unmistakeable glint of jewellery. The final Italian image, taken by a Milanese photographer, shows Irma with two friends, dressed more elaborately in 'dressy' outfits suitable for the passaggiato. Her costume, with its puffed sleeves, ruched collar and fanciful embroidered panels makes romantic reference to the sixteenth century while complementing the modish shawl collars, leg-of-mutton shoulders and straw hats of her companions.

Once arrived in London, Irma's demeanour takes on a more circumspect air, her expression frozen into a mask of resigned disappointment. Her choice of clothing, however, always displays elements which recall the desirable status of her Italian youth. In a photograph from around the turn of the century, though her face has filled out and her hair is set into the rigid rolls of the matron, her neatly striped, pin-tucked blouse, plain skirt and the elegant swathe of black silk at her neck both echo the earlier development of her

❶❾ Irma Cocco (Cescotti),
c.1890-1922 (Museum of London)

personal style and pay appropriate attention to the strict codes of hygiene and sartorial etiquette expected of a woman recently entered into the rank of governess or lady's maid. It is in this context that one might read the Museum of London dress with its respectful palette, skilful handiwork and gesturing toward the 'frou-frou' fashionability which was beginning to inform popular style in the city by the first decade of the twentieth century. In a sense it is a polyglot costume, reflecting those influences which commentators identified as a key component of modern metropolitan life. In 1902 Mrs E.T. Cook practically described Irma when, in her account of the *Highways and Byways of London* she noted that

the Italian women who, with their 'men' and their babies, accompany the street organs, are generally trim and smiling, and, so far as foot-gear and general neatness of appearance is concerned - are immeasurably the superiors of their English slum-sisters. The Italian woman seems, - indeed in London, at any rate, - always vastly superior to the Italian man…. She is cleaner, smarter, pleasanter…. In the early morning hours, her 'court' is a perfect babel of chatter and noise… Not only Neapolitans, but Sicilians, Tuscans, Venetians, are represented; indeed the dialects and slang used are so unlike, that the different circles of this Italian colony often themselves fail to understand each other. In the evenings, and generally on their doorsteps, the men… gamble; while the women… patch clothes, chatter and gesticulate in true native fashion… It is a strange life, and stranger still is the manner in which various types and nationalities have thus for generations "squatted down" in special districts of the metropolis, and filled them with their traditions, their atmosphere, their personality. [32]

Following her marriage, Irma is shown in subsequent photographs valiantly attempting to retain the reputation for stylishness that must have accompanied her early years and presumably identified the Italian woman in London; but she was clearly struggling with the demands and responsibilities of a growing family in an alien environment. Her pairing of choker and blouse, for example, survives in images of 1905 and 1915, but this signifier of continental sophistication suggests a kind of tired hopelessness and by 1922 all pretensions to a leisured existence have been eradicated, replaced by the home-spun printed-cotton overall that had become the generic uniform for the inter-war working-class 'cockney' matriarch.

Such are the tales told by old clothes. Whether in the hedonistic and labour-intensive embellishment of a Cork Street gown or the quieter, almost desperate stitching of an immigrant dressmaker's wardrobe, it is evidently possible, just, to locate a sense of the Victorian city as the fractured mirror for a teeming population of ethnic, economic and social migrants whose very appearance lent London its hybridized personality and unfathomable soul. As Mrs Cook concluded: 'The cosmopolitanism of London tends to draw to it the sweepings, as well as the choice spirits, - the worst, as well as the best, - of all other nations and climes. "Hell is a city much like London," said the poet… and he spoke truth. Views, religious and otherwise, differ largely as to what Hell may be; one opinion, however, may be safely hazarded; that it will at any rate be cosmopolitan.'[33]

# *The* H*ctress:*

## COVENT GARDEN AND THE STRAND
## 1880-1914

The Strand has long been a site of flux in the history of London's spatial relationships - a point of transit between places, roles and attitudes. Before the Great Fire, when the Cities of London and Westminster were separate conurbations, it was the primary conduit for land passage from one to the other. Its length echoed the parallel flow of the Thames and channelled commuters between the centres of commerce and government. Indeed at one time the Strand formed the river's northern bank. During the sixteenth and seventeenth centuries the southern perimeter of the street was flanked by the well-appointed houses and gardens of those wealthy and titled Londoners who felt it necessary to maintain a median position between affairs of trade and the politicking of the court. To the north and south-east of the Strand, Lincoln's Inn, Chancery Lane and the Temple also afforded easy access to the services of the law, while from the turn of the eighteenth century the coffee houses, taverns, bordellos and print and book dealers who resided in the narrow medieval streets and courts that led up toward Covent Garden and Drury Lane provided for the intellectual and corporeal needs of a growing and increasingly sophisticated local population.

By the mid-nineteenth century the residential aspect of the street had been superseded by these more professional and touristic concerns, yet besides its serious role as a carrier of goods and information from the seat of commerce to the throne of government, the Strand also continued to fulfil a more ambiguous function as a focus for the pursuit of pleasure. It was this aspect, manifested through the theatres, restaurants and popular-magazine headquarters which crowded in on the vicinity, which singled out the area for notoriety from the 1860s to the early 1900s.[1] Such a conflation of wealth, business and entertainment positioned the Strand as London's premier leisure zone at a time when the fashion industry itself was also coming to embrace those concepts of accessibility, rapid change and popular topicality which were now built into the street's own fabric and history. The intertwining of these modern forces in the popular figure of the turn-of-the-century actress forms the focus of this chapter, for although the Strand and its inhabitants sit less obviously in a history of fashion production, retailing or consumption in London than say Spitalfields or Bond Street, their contribution toward the forging of a new cosmopolitan definition of fashion premised on the themes of publicity and celebrity was highly significant for the further development of a London style.

# METROPOLITAN DEVELOPMENTS

In 1908 the Edwardian journalist Edwin Pugh clearly recognized the productive contingency of the Strand's very particular but rapidly changing environment of play and display when he noted its ' tall pinched... and squat dumpy buildings, brick and red and grey granite and stucco', a stone 'coping adorned with a fresco of classical figures in bas relief, advertising some up-to-date brand of physical culture - plate glass windows, expansive and boldly glittering, and windows such as one associates with small insolvent chandler's shops in squalid suburbs; hotels that are towns in themselves, mighty caravanserai... Here are such contrasted edifices as a transmogrified Exeter Hall, once the scene of religious congresses, now an ornate restaurant, palatial but popular and cheap'.[2] In 1892 the unveiling of the Strand improvement scheme, which proposed the widening of the narrow thoroughfare as it bottle-necked at Temple Bar, and the opening up of a new direct route to Holborn via Aldwych and the Kingsway, marked the beginning of a rationalization of vistas and traffic circulation in the vicinity which spelt the slow demise of such electrifying and edgy eclecticism. Discussions regarding the scheme can be traced back to the 1860s and the desire of the Metropolitan Board of Works and its successor the London County Council to cleanse the district of its more unruly connotations. These were symbolized most potently in the subsiding wreck of the seventeenth-century triumphal arch at Temple Bar which was removed from its original location at the border between the two cities in 1878 to rest, most appropriately, in the estate of a brewing millionaire in Cheshunt. Its squat form had featured as a backdrop in several satires of fashionable folly. In one of 1770, an exquisite beau meets social disaster in its shadow, suspended by his breeches from a butcher's hook while a dissolute crowd applauds his discomfort.

By 1899 an Act of Parliament announced the first demolitions of obstructing streets and buildings, and such squalid scenes of debauchery as those recorded by earlier caricaturists were smashed into oblivion by the wrecker's ball. In an apt sign of the times, any remaining spectres from the Strand's past were almost literally fenced in by the ultra-modern firm Partingtons, 'an enterprising advertising contractor [who] erected a huge hoarding in front of the doomed houses - the largest hoarding ever seen in London, and covered it with advertisement posters which were remarkably well chosen for equality of size and for their artistic merits'.[3] A contemporary photograph shows regularly spaced promotions for such democratic masculine luxuries as Capstan Cigarettes and Allsop's Pale Ale, quotidian household commodities including Bird's Custard and Cerebros Salt, and aids to fitness like Sandow's Embrocation, and Bovril which promised to 'repel influenza'. In recognition of the Strand's continuing role as a provider of entertainment, bills for the Criterion and Adelphi Theatres partnered vividly illustrated flyers for such spectaculars as *Faust* at the Lyceum and *Ben Hur* at Drury

Lane. When the hoardings finally came down the emergent sweep of the Aldwych promised a sanitized notion of pleasure which bore more in common with the slick imagery of Partington's advertisements and the homogenized tastes of a new mass audience than with the carnivalesque 'topsy-turvydom' and piquant diversions associated with the old Strand. This shift from exclusivity to accessibility was nowhere more evident than in the rebuilding of the infamous Gaiety Theatre. As the *Globe* newspaper reported on 12 August 1903:

The Gaiety Theatre entered into its final stage of existence yesterday afternoon when Messrs Home & Co. submitted for auction the stage on which so many histrionic triumphs have been achieved, the gilt erections of the prosceniums, the floors, panelled doors, partitioning, tons of lead and even the bricks. Only a week ago dresses and other effects used by members of the Gaiety companies were sold under similar conditions, and attracted the attention and the bids of a large number of costumiers and others.[4]

Located on an island between the Strand and Catherine Street, the old Gaiety Theatre had been managed by John Hollingshead since 1868. It provided lightly erotic burlesques to a predominantly male market and shared in the homosocial buzz of neighbouring businesses. Hollingshead recalled that 'old taverns and 'a la mode' Beef shops abounded' during its earliest incarnation, serving chops and porter to passing trade. He characterized the resulting atmosphere as 'festive', further hinting at the presence of 'flash night-houses' such as Jessop's, and the proximity of pornography dealers in nearby Holywell Street. But these more disreputable businesses were themselves coming under pressure from the massive expansion of popular journalism in the area during the final quarter of the nineteenth century. As it moved toward Fleet Street the Strand was forced to accommodate the editorial offices and printing rooms of a rapacious yellow press. Thus a former brothel came to house the premises of the *Echo* newspaper, and under the editorship of George Newnes the eponymous *Strand Magazine* established itself, alongside its resolutely popularist stable-mate *Tit-Bits*, in palatial style close by in Southampton Street.[5] The traffic of progress was not all one-way, and Hollingshead lamented the demise of an older, more literary mode of gentlemanly journalism typified by Charles Dickens's *Household Words*, the defunct premises of which were (rather ironically) converted into the dressing rooms and offices of the Gaiety.[6] The expansionist activities of Hollingshead's theatre were themselves a factor in the very developments which he affected to regret.

The Gaiety brand of innovation had also been marked by the appointment of George Edwardes on Hollingshead's retirement as manager in 1886. Edwardes's most significant contribution to the business was his reorganization of the plots and pace of the old burlesques. These were transformed into the hybrid genre of musical comedy which, while retaining the erotic undertones of burlesque in its celebration of the physical attractions of young actresses, rejected the pantomimic conventions of the 1870s and 1880s in favour of topical, indeed fashionable settings that drew on the modernity of the contemporary high life. Such a shift also attracted a slightly more mixed audience which now included female parties, suburban couples and tourists. This new constituency was enticed by the consumerist fantasies of the lavish productions and the attention Edwardes paid to the comfort and interests of his clients. When the Gaiety reopened in October 1903, in new premises designed by Ernest Runtz on the junction of the Aldwych and the Strand, its unrestrained fittings proclaimed an unashamed populism. Finished in grey Portland stone with strips of green marble, its cupola supported a golden female figure blowing on the trumpet of Variety. She was a version of the famous siren who had always adorned the interior act drop of the theatre, described lovingly by McQueen Pope in her 'diaphanous clothing or drapery, with a girdle round her waist, in the buckle of which shone a real jewel, and in her hand above her head she held a lamp which actually... burned, for there was an electric light behind it'.[7]

The symbolic figure of Variety epitomized the drive toward a self-conscious modernity which vindicated Hollingshead's 'view of the need to construct on a thoroughfare in the full tide of progress'.[8] Yet regardless of the dubious triumphalism of the fourth estate, or the parallel rationalization of the entertainment sector, the tenor of the vicinity continued to draw its distinctive atmosphere from the anti-authoritarian conviviality and rather puerile concerns of an all-male coterie of writers, actors and bon-viveurs, who insisted on the pursual of sybaritic goals which the planners and new entrepreneurs thought they had all but repressed. Such men still formed the core audience for Hollingshead's and then Edwardes's risqué bills of fare and found their cultish interests extending out into the life of the surrounding streets. W. McQueen Pope, the theatrical memoirist, counted himself among this exclusive elect and fondly remembered that

The Strand was essentially a man's street... it was no shopping centre, and such ladies as you might meet there were either escorted by their men folk from lunch at Gatti's, staying at the Hotel Cecil or the Savoy, or taking their children to buy toys at the Lowther Arcade... Or if the ladies did not fall into any of these categories, then they were shop assistants out on business, possibly some of the rapidly growing army of typists, or most likely of all actresses or music hall performers.[9]

Women were evidently present on the Strand, but as McQueen Pope suggests, their compromised presence purveyed a highly theatricalized version of femininity to their observers, premised around problematic notions of display and commodification whose disruptive connotations were not dispelled or diluted by the respectable cover of genteel fashion retailing which prevailed further west in the domesticated department stores of Regent and Oxford Streets. Here in London's untamed pleasure zone the erotic content and glamorous visual registers of a more robust sense of female fashion were starkly revealed for a predominantly male audience with unsettling effect. Lesbian journalist and raconteur Naomi Jacob was also receptive to this dissonance, recalling the provocative mix of products available for sale in the Strand's eclectic and rather seedy selection of shops, noting that 'there was and still is a very famous gun-smith's in the Strand - Vaughan's, who were also pawn-brokers, and did a considerable number of

**2 0** The Strand, *c.*1900 (Museum of London)

deals in highly expensive jewellery. Most elaborate precautions were observed for the protection of the stock, the guns, the furs which many wealthy women pawned during the summer, because by law a pawn-broker must keep any goods accepted by him in perfect order'.[10] Even more evocative of a forbidden and titillating sensuality was the presence of Rimmel's, 'The Scenter of the Strand', whose exotic wares included 'Etoile du Nord, Romanoff, Ihlang Ihlang, Vanda, Henna, Cuir de Russe for 2s 6d per bottle. Or Toilet Vinegar, said to be 'highly refreshing and salubrious' for 1s. Lime juice and glycerine for the hair was 1s 6d, whilst Velvetine, 'a refined, imperceptible toilet powder' was 1s... When they advertised in theatre programmes, which they often did, they supplied a scent which was applied in some way to the paper and retained its pungency for many years'.[11]

Perfume and fur, the stock in trade of the Strand, clearly suggested the tactile presence of the actress and a close interweaving of her professional identity and the identity of the street. Like the scent in a theatre programme, her spectacular image seemed to hang in the air - pungent with sexual possibilities. The touristic observations of Justin McCarthy MP, who in 1893 noted that 'the longer one lives in London, the more the Strand comes to be a phantom haunted thoroughfare', alluded to the manner in which the area's thespian and pornographic associations conjured up barely disguised sexual fantasies for its liberated male and female ramblers:

Can one wonder that the cavalryman is such a hero and idol to the servant girl? Look at him with his scarlet coat, his jingling spurs, his sabre, his moustache, his gold lace, his shiny buttons, his smart jacket, his tall well-knit figure, and put yourself… in poor Mary Jane's place, and think what a god of her idolatry he well may be!… Is there any corresponding womanly splendour which could equally dazzle the butcher's boy? A ballet girl perhaps, with her gauzy petticoats, and her pink legs, and her powdered and rouged face, and her smiles and her suppleness and her general splendour of attire? Well no doubt she must seem to him like some creature from another sphere. And then the circus-riding woman in the velvet bodice and the short skirts and the pretty buskins, who stands upright on the horse's back and leaps through all the crashing hoops… with pretty pantings of fatigue and bewitching little shudders of exhaustion; surely she must seem a vision of youth, beauty and spangles - a plump phantom if ever there could be such a thing of delight.[12]

The chimerical soldiers and show girls of the Strand may well have figured large in the private imaginations of turn-of-the-century Londoners, but the flesh and blood figures of the living actors and actresses from whom such fantasies drew their co-ordinates, played an equally active role in establishing a modern iconography of fashionable celebrity which set up alternative models for stylish contemporary living to those previously promoted by the dictates of the aristocratic Season or the West End and the Parisian dressmaker. When McCarthy claimed that there 'was not a spot along the whole length of the Strand but I associate it with some name and face of a passing celebrity'[13] he was also bearing witness to the rising prominence of a newly minted and rather daring conception of the fashion leader that drew on the heritage of its environment. As this chapter will go on to demonstrate, it was the industrial, aesthetic and administrative structures of popular musical theatre, the mainstay of the Strand, which provided the impetus for this important development in London's sartorial manners.

## KITTY LORD AND HER SPANGLED COSTUMES

The Museum of London owns a selection of stage costumes dating from about 1900 which were worn by the variety actress Kitty Lord, whose career on the stage spanned the years 1894-1915. Little is known about Miss Lord, other than that she played at the

Kitty Lord, *c.*1900 (Museum of London)

major London music halls (The Tivoli, The Oxford, The Paragon and The Hippodrome) and that she worked with professionals of the calibre of Fred Carno, Ida Barr, Maurice Chevalier and Gladys Cooper.[14] Surviving theatre bills from the first decade of the twentieth century also record her working in Paris and Naples, where she is described variously as an American Star, an 'Eccentric' Englishwoman and an International 'Eccentric' Star. (Eccentric here might refer to the spectacular extravagance of the act and seems to have been a generic term for solo dancers and singers.) At the Ambassadeurs Theatre in Paris, her act falls as scene fourteen of twenty-four in a pageant oriented toward feminine concerns, but with clear concessions made to the scopophilic demands of those men in the audience. Tableaux of fashionable life set in flowered courtyards, the post office, the dressmaker's and the palm house are interspersed with appearances by the dance troupe 'les flip flap girls' and what appear to be posé plastique versions of historical and artistic scenes. The programme itself carries advertisements for hatmakers, perfumiers, shoes and women's underwear.[15] Though her name did not survive her, it would seem that Miss Lord shared some common ground with those fashionable celebrities whose connection with the Strand was turning the street into a modern synonym for the high life.

The rare survival of three distinct sets of costume belonging to Kitty Lord suggests that she was versatile enough to work across the staple character parts associated with the popular stage. Two roughly cut dresses in brightly coloured light silk and silk chiffon fabrics suggest the 'motley' or approximation of tattered rags necessary to clothe the principle roles of pantomime prior to their robing in more extravagant garb during the ubiquitous transformation scenes. Both incorporate the fringed shawls of stereotyped poverty which hang limply around the shoulders. The first, a short tunic reaching down to the knee, is medieval in conception, perhaps suitable for the role of Dick Whittington. Made by Edouard Souplet of 18 Rue de Douai, Paris, it utilizes contrasting quarters of crimson, aquamarine and yellow in the manner of fourteenth-century mi-parti.

❷❷ 'Motley' costume belonging to Kitty Lord, c.1900 (Museum of London)

Heraldic motifs, swirling scrolls and exaggerated stitches have also been roughly painted onto the surface of the textile in a dark red pigment for graphic effect.[16] The second ensemble in the motley style takes its references from the eighteenth century. It boasts a long V-shaped bodice and fuller skirts, parted in the middle to reveal layers of deliberately tattered underskirts in the same material. The whole has been patchily dyed in murky tones of pink, brown, yellow and aquamarine, stencilled over with deep red and brown roses and hatched representations of rents and worn patches, then liberally covered in pink and blue sequins. The faded grandeur of the costume is perhaps suggestive of the role of Cinderella.[17]

Two further sets of costume fall more directly into the idiom of burlesque, though the first could well have been worn in an orientalist extravaganza such as Aladdin or Ali Baba and the Forty Thieves. A yellow-silk thigh-length tabard woven with geometrical Chinese designs, finished with borders of pink and grey silk and with short sleeves knotted from pink silk and yellow velvet ribbon, is encrusted with applied floral motifs of generalized Indian or Persian provenance, constructed from violet, silver and green sequins.[18]

❷❸ 'Aladdin' costume belonging to Kitty Lord, c.1900 (Museum of London)

This is accompanied by a decorative belt and purse in a golden-yellow velvet, made to be worn around the waist and covered with pearl buttons, sequins and glass gemstones.[19] A floor-sweeping cape in canary-yellow brushed cotton is bordered with machine lace, turquoise sequins and pearl buttons, its corners embellished with stars of seed and drop pearls and ruby and emerald sequins.[20]

❷❹ 'Burlesque' costume belonging to Kitty Lord, c.1900 (Museum of London)

The second set is perhaps the most stylistically coherent of all three ensembles, and most closely relates to the visual idiom of contemporary high fashion, especially those items of clothing associated with the boudoir. A more contoured short tunic in a shell-pink silk has its cream floral pattern picked out in swirling designs of ruby and emerald sequins and clear-glass gemstones. Its sleeves are woven from dark-red velvet ribbons and its black and red velvet borders decorated with a scallop-shell design picked out in glass bugle beads over black net.[21] This is partnered by a long cape of the same pink silk, bordered by deep-red velvet and a line of emerald sequins. The interior of the cape opens to reveal large appliquéd bows of the same deep red material.[22] A pair of pink-satin eighteen-hole boots, made by H & M. Rayne of London and embroidered with a design of silver braid and ruby sequins, were clearly intended to be worn with this set of items.[23] Integral to these last two sets and the focus of much contemporary debate concerning the morality of popular theatre, particularly the performance of burlesque, are a pair of ribbed woollen tights, cut and padded to the required shape and coloured to suggest bare flesh.[24]

Photographic studio portraits of about 1900 show Kitty Lord wearing similar, though not identical, costumes to the ones described above. In these provocative promotional images her spangled tunics fit tightly and are worn over a corset which thrusts her heavy figure into the desired 's'-shaped curve. They ride high and close over the tops of her smoothly stockinged thighs, and simple satin dance slippers replace the boots. The open sleeves of her garments draw attention to the exposed flesh of her upper arms and a low sweeping neckline supports a flowing cape which in one image is edged in ermine. In several portraits Miss Lord sports a wide-brimmed and ostrich-feathered 'Merry Widow' hat over loosely dressed hair. Her neck and fingers display conspicuous jewellery and she supports herself regally with a tall cane. The overall effect is an opulent one, combining the poise of the acrobat with the over-emphatic posturing of the principal boy. These are clearly outfits designed to dazzle and excite the audience. They hint at a spectacular excess and transgress contemporary ideas of decency.

In common with many expensive bespoke dresses of the period, Kitty Lord's costumes (with the exception of her exquisitely finished boots) are surprisingly rough in terms of their hidden construction. Most of the effort of manufacture was directed toward surface effect, and for these skills the actors and impresarios of the Strand could rely on a network of local provision. Until fairly recently actors had been expected to furnish their own wardrobes, often utilizing contemporary dress unless the production was set in a specific historical period.[25] But for the strata of performance in which Miss Lord was involved, more specialized expertise was called for. Mrs May of Bow Street was a recognized costumier for burlesque and the pantomime. An article in *The Stage* of October 1883 described her work for the famous Alhambra productions, noting her studio's completion of a harlequin's dress which weighing 'as much as an ordinary suit of clothes' was constructed of hundreds of pieces of cloth of various colours...each had from fifty to a hundred spangles attached to it'.[26] Across the road from Mrs May, the establishment of Mr Strinchcombe also produced items for popular theatre, as well as for commercial fancy-dress balls, and among these the stage reporter 'found a very useful commodity in the shape of 'rags', this latter being most difficult for the actor to obtain without the destruction of some useful garment'.[27] Kitty Lord's motley costumes were presumably sourced from similar stock.

The sequins and paste which lent lustre to Miss Lord's glittering stage persona would have been provided by even more specialized retailers, several of them relying on sweated labour in the East End. In the 1880s a Mr Hales of Wellington Street devoted his business 'to the manufacture of dress ornaments' supplying metallic motifs to both Masonic and friendly societies and to theatrical companies. His 'silver plate' and 'water fringe' were woven on a loom by a Mr Tutton of Bethnal Green and though 'it was not difficult to mentally transplant the shining texture to its destination and see pit, gallery and boxes gazing with admiration on its glittering effect, yet neither the hard-working weaver nor his wife had seen a pantomime for the past quarter of a century'.[28] For foil paper Mr Bousquet of the Barbican offered the only London-made alternative to German imports and similarly bullion fringe was exclusive to traders in Paris and Lyon. Its adaptability for theatrical and liturgical uses was noted by the reporter who suggested that 'the next... time the reader sees a graceful female prince figuring merrily in burlesque with bullion fringe adding charms to her flexible limbs, he can comfort himself with the reflection that his spiritual adviser is equally dependent on the silver plate artificer for effect'.[29] Cut-glass jewels backed with coloured foil were 'obtained from Bohemia and finished in Paris by such houses as that of Touchard's for whom Mr Hales [was] the sole agent in London'. And spangles fashioned from a flattened ring of copper wire, or pearls derived from small glass globules dipped in a solution of iridescent fish scales and wax were available from a Mr White, also of Bow Street.[30]

Similar boots to those which must have attracted a great deal of attention for Kitty Lord formed the staple product of W.H. Davies of Bow Street. The reporter for *The Stage* was entranced on entering this business with 'several rows of blue, pink, buff and other coloured shoes... of silk and satin' being prepared for the 300-strong corps de ballet attached to a production of *Cinderella* at Drury Lane. Also lovingly described were 'an Eastern shoe of sea green satin… for Madame Lockhart in her performance with Jock and Jenny, the wonderfully well-trained elephants', with its 'Louis XV heels three inches and a half high', and 'a pair of cardinal satin embroidered turret boots with no less than 22 buttons… with a long gold lace… for Miss Julia Warden in pantomime'.[31] But if the production of theatrical footwear was guaranteed to set male writers off on lavish declamations of unrequited passion, then the provision of hosiery pushed journalistic hyperbole to even greater heights:

…the adolescent individual who is smitten with flaxen curls and hectic flush, little knows the number of industries called upon to contribute to such result. Take, for instance, the hosiery display in a burlesque, extravaganza, or pantomime. How difficult it is to realise that the major portions of the costumes there exhibited have been manufactured perhaps in some little out of the way country village, or have endured the chimney atmosphere of a smoky provincial town. The whole thing seems too ethereal ever to have emanated from the brawny hands of the British Workman.[32]

As *The Stage* suggested, theatrical dressers depended largely on the stocking industry of the Midlands for their supply, though some establishments such as Mr Reid of Longacre and Burnet's of Covent Garden machined a small quantity of hosiery on their premises for rushed and special orders. It was naturally the display of the product in the shop which garnered most attention, and a breathless description of the actress 'Miss Delavere of The Frivolity' (a rather transparent disguise for the rising fame of various Gaiety Girls during this period) selecting her requirements conveys the frisson which this garment engendered. 'Some of the tights, which were exhibited in both cotton, wool, and silk were really marvels of artistic work. The silks for the 'front row' could be looked at and admired even without the footlights' glare. The flowered silk opera hose… would melt the heart of the sourest cynic… All the colours of the rainbow were there in abundance. Silk stockings, bought by weight and sold by weight; gloves almost long enough for an enterprising telegraph pole… combined to form a dazzling display of stage dressing.'[33]

From motley to hosiery the theatrical clothing trades which abutted the Strand clearly dealt in a currency which was larger than life, and shameless in its promotion of effects that were blatantly artificial and erotic.[34] These were the necessary qualities demanded by enterprising performers such as Kitty Lord and her audience. As the high-living newspaperman James Douglas avowed in 1909, this deft playing with arousing degrees of artificiality had become a defining skill among those who considered themselves to be metropolitan moderns both on and off the stage. It was an early twentieth-century inverted version of the eighteenth-century craze for sensibilité, here practised as provocative burlesque in The Alhambra Theatre of Leicester Square :

We go.. into the promenade. It is a seraglio where man is a sultan and woman a houri. It is aglow with dim lamps, soft with the susurrus of silks, languorous with subtle perfumes.

Miles away below us the ballet languishes in its golden frame…The dancers are syllables in a visible song… They are the gestures of an artificial femininity. The civilised woman is always artificial, but here her artificiality is multiplied. A woman is natural only when she is alone. She wears the armour of artifice in public, and the aim of the ballet is to generalise her artificiality. It submerges her in a long undulation of fluid femininity…. The rouged lips, the painted cheeks, the pencilled eye brows, the bistred eyes, the blackened eyelashes, the pearl powder, the gaudy skirts, the stretched texture of tights, the threads of hose… the jumble of mimic and real life - all this upsets your centre of levity and plunges you into a brief insanity…. You lose sense of your values. You are in topsy-turvyland… Here beauty is business and business is beauty. And the oddest thing is your own incongruity. You are ashamed of your dress clothes. These dancers in short skirts are absolutely unconscious… They are at ease in their convention. Probably they blush when they don the garb of the outer world.[35]

## STYLES OF FASHIONABLE THEATRE: FROM BURLESQUE TO MUSICAL COMEDY

The extraordinary diversity of theatrical costume manufactured in late nineteenth-century London owed much of its splendour to trade demands related to the rapid development of various genres of performance, each finely-tuned to keep pace with public tastes and obsessions, and associated with particular styles of stage presentation. The effects of this were not limited to the sphere of show business alone. Between c.1865 and 1914 the Strand-focused entertainment industry, dominated by Hollingshead and Edwardes at The Gaiety, refined several forms of address which resonated with the energies of a fashionable life existing beyond the world of the theatre, while also inspiring the continuing vitality and importance of those energies in the day-to-day life of the capital. The twin strategies of vestimentary design and embodied display engineered in the spaces of the costumier's and the dressing room, and in the broader context of the pursuits of a rejuvenated leisure class, thus generated a unique synergy in their common definitions of modishness. In this evolution toward a London-centric prescription for modern fashionable dressing, Kitty Lord's costume appears to represent a design cul-de-sac, its risqué brevity and gaudy drama suitable only for the narrower and rather clichéd concerns of Variety, Pantomime and Music Hall performance. Furthermore, at a superficial level its flouting of acceptable codes of decency obviously rendered its eye-catching properties inappropriate for the salons of the supposedly respectable. However, many of the subversive values which its pattern incorporated, not least its play with ideas of self-promotion, masquerade and artificiality, took a pivotal role in supporting the emergence of the more sophisticated, directional and adaptable dress styles which prevailed in the fashionable culture of the city by the eve of the First World War.

Miss Lord's stage apparel owed its essence to the loose rules laid down for the performance of burlesque from the 1860s onward. As a literary form burlesques had enjoyed great popularity during the middle years of the nineteenth century, and the premise upon which they were built - to appropriate and lampoon the plot and language of a familiar text for topical and satirical ends - formed the basis of many humorous publications, especially in *Punch* magazine. In the theatre the premise remained the same, with abbreviated and adapted versions of the classical dramas, Shakespeare, modern opera and theatre forming the staple fare of an evening's entertainment, often interspersed with visual interpretations of famous paintings and sculptures or events from history (what became known as posés plastiques). On stage, however, the erudite knowledge which informed the burlesques of the popular press was lacking, and the dramatic form became associated with a bawdier form of comedy and increased opportunities for the revelation of the female body. William Davenport Adams in a review of the development of burlesque across its several media was thus equivocal in his description of its extension to the stage:

I have not thought it necessary... to offer any apology for stage burlesque. One must regret that it sometimes lacks refinement in word and action, and that in the manner of costume it is not invariably decorous; but that we shall always have it with us in some form or other, may be accepted as incontrovertible. So long as there is anything extravagant in literature or manners.... So long will travestie find both food and scope. That is the raison d'être of theatrical burlesque - that it shall satirise the exaggerated and the extreme. It does not wage war against the judicious and moderate.[36]

Robert Allen's excellent study of the rise of the burlesque performance in the United States suggests that its increasing popularity went hand in hand with the growing sophistication of equestrian drama and ballet. All three genres relied on a notion of 'feminized spectacle' in order to produce that sense of pleasure essential for commercial success, while 'containing the moral and social transgressiveness that pleasure necessarily entailed'.[37] Their costumes shared common features, including the stockinged legs, emphasized bust and liberal use of spangles evident in Kitty Lord's apparel. In this manner, Allen argues, the heroine of burlesque stood in opposition to, indeed lampooned the characteristics of the well-established melodramatic heroine, whose stereotypical qualities 'pervaded sentimental novels and sermons alike, and whose image was reproduced in paintings, prints and magazines' from the 1840s onward.[38] This sentimental figure, with her constraining and compliant dress and attitudes, symbolized the truthfulness and innocence of the idealized 'angel in the home' whose example was so influential in the education of young middle-class women during the period, especially in the ultra-religious atmosphere of the New World. Burlesque impertinently shattered the coherence of this construct through the purposeful challenge set by its sartorial and sexual effrontery.

It is not just coincidental, then, that the actresses and models of performance associated with burlesque in American theatres of the 1860s and 1870s originated in Britain, and specifically in the urbane environment of London; for such visual and moral effrontery drew its knowing co-ordinates from the rapaciously commercial and closely analysed styles of female presentation long pioneered in the capital's West End streets, stores, brothels and theatres. To take just one example, the famous journalistic portrait of that compromised young follower of London's West End fashions known as 'the Girl of the Period', who was familiar to readers of Eliza Linton's furious and reactionary columns in the *Saturday Review* during the late 1860s, had helped explode the veracity of the 'angel in the home' stereotype and provided a template for continuing satirical and sartorial experimentation. With her devotion to fast dress, cosmetics, smoking, self-indulgent shopping, low theatre and trashy literature, the 'Girl' had become an anti-heroic icon of the times. .

The first imported British star of American burlesque was Lydia Thompson, who in 1868 toured the United States with her troupe Ixion, parodying the stories of the classical legends, but also affording opportunities to ridicule the hypocrisy of celebrated Society sex scandals, to ape the current fashion for the Grecian bend (a favourite target of Lynton's) and to promote contemporary popular songs and minstrel dances. Her personal style, while couched in the vaguely neo-classical language of high theatrical tragedy for the comical purposes of the burlesque idiom, was also inflected by non-theatrical sartorial and social codes which would have been very familiar back home in the Strand and in other fashionable West End locales. She was clearly a Girl of the Period. Inspired by her visit, a letter to the *New York Times* of May 1869 summarized the requirements for an aspirant burlesque actress. The writer provided a check-list which no doubt resonated for readers in the green rooms, millinery shops and boudoirs of London. But its content offered a shockingly alien picture to American subscribers. The letter asked 'Is your hair dyed yellow? Are your legs, arms and bosom symmetrically formed, and are you willing to expose them? Can you sing brassy songs and dance the can-can and wink at men...? Are you willing to appear tonight, and every night amid the glare of gas-lights, and before the gaze of thousands of men, in this pair of satin breeches ten inches long, without a vestige of drapery on your person?'[39] And if such exhibitionism wasn't upsetting enough, a roughly contemporaneous correspondent in the *New York Clipper* was even more explicit about the debt this outrageous style owed to degenerate London precedents:

They do say that nearly all our native American actresses are about to leave for England in order to go through the necessary training to fit them for an appearance before an American public. They have a manufactory over there where novices are taken in and put through a regular course of sprouts for the New York market. Legs are repaired and made to conform to the American standard; bosoms are filled out and developed more in accordance with existing notions; the blackest hair is transformed into the purest blond; while modesty, delicacy and innocence are at once made to give place to impudence, profligacy and immorality, as better suited to the American market.[40]

It is perhaps ironic that the theatrical genre of burlesque which came to be so closely associated with American personal freedoms and commercial innovation should have drawn its influences from the established popular and illicit sexual cultures of London.

Thirty years later, having been modified by forward-looking entrepreneurs to suit the outlook of conservative mid-westerners, it would be sold back to the British theatre-going public in the mass-manufactured form of Vaudeville and via such snappy icons of progressive modernity as the Gibson Girl. But in the 1860s and 1870s its power to shock resided firmly in a conception of fashionability and display that was recognized as being strictly retrograde and un-American, though quite commonplace in the morally dubious and historically loaded milieu of the Strand (as well as in Piccadilly, The Haymarket and Tyburnia). Lecturing at a meeting of the London-based Church and Stage Guild in October 1870 to the proposal 'Is Burlesque Art ?' the speaker Blanche Reiver did not have to look too far for his scandalous examples: 'Everywhere do our eyes rest on burlesques on that which has been called the divine form of woman... Whenever I see a very limited waist attached to an almost unlimited bust, I immediately suspect either tight lacing in the one direction or padding in the other... I cannot imagine that anyone can believe the unnatural to be beautiful, for proportion is the only true beauty. What is out of proportion is an exaggeration, an extravagance, a burlesque.' This deliberate flouting of the natural which Reiver perceived in the fashionable dress of ordinary London women was in his mind not so far removed from the perverted inversions of the popular stage, for 'there is a still more hideous burlesque in existence... I allude to those shameless women, who never having spoken a line on the stage in their lives, arrogate to themselves the title 'actress'. They do not go on the boards to act, but merely to exhibit themselves! and for these creatures to be called 'actresses' is simply to burlesque in a ghastly, gloomy, ugly way, that honourable calling.'[41]

Reiver predicted the future for burlesque in his invocation of a theatre devoted primarily to fashionable exhibitionism. A bias toward sartorial display had always been central to the genre and was an unsettling quality frequently picked up by theatrical journalists, who in their attempts to categorize its strangeness come close to providing a reading of the complex aesthetic system of late nineteenth-century fashionable women's dress by default. Allen cites the writer Richard Grant White, who in 1869 called attention to the manner in which burlesque 'forces the conventional and the natural together just at the points where they are most remote... The result is absurdity, monstrosity. Its system is a defiance of system. It is out of all keeping'.[42] William Dean Howells, writing in the same year, is more explicit in his references to the charge of deliberate perversity frequently levelled at contemporary standards of beauty, stating of burlesque performers that 'it was certainly a shocking thing to look at them with their horrible prettiness, their archness in which was no charm, their grace which put to shame'.[43]

For Allen the proper interpretation of such commentaries demands a recourse to literary historians Stallybrass and White's much cited conception of the 'low other', which provides a means of unpacking burlesque's transgressive capabilities.[44] This grotesque component of the carnivalesque is thereby revealed as a formation commonly 'despised and denied at the level of political organisation and social being whilst it is instrumentally constitutive of the shared imaginary repertoires of the dominant culture'.[45] Such a reading would certainly help to explain the gradual incorporation of burlesque into the theatrical mainstream by the 1880s, when, according to Allen, its descendants retained the inversive and parodic qualities of burlesque humour, but based their appeal on a more feminized and accessible variant of the visual spectacle of the extravaganza, especially the pantomime. It would also support a decoding of the opposite flow, whereby the very looseness and 'irrationality' of the burlesque spectacle's dramatic construction 'allowed it to scatter its wit across a wide field of contemporary fashions and foibles' informing the appearance and mores of its newly expanded audience.[46]

Pantomime provided the perfect medium for extending the attractions of burlesque. In the London theatre world of the 1880s and 1890s it pulled the biggest, most socially mixed crowds. Like the writers of burlesque, its producers, composers and directors drew on traditional stories (European fairy tales rather than Greek legends), 'gave them a modern or topical twist, larded the dialogue with puns and verbal wit and spiced it with songs adapted to familiar music gathered from opera, ballads and the music halls'.[47] This new hybrid form had also evolved beyond recognition from its eighteenth-century roots in the simple Commedia del'Arte. The ambitious scale of its performances and its fantastical sets and costumes set it well apart from its demotic antecedents. By way of reviewing the spectacular production of *The Forty Thieves* staged at Drury Lane in the winter of 1886-1887, the correspondent of the *Illustrated Sporting and Dramatic News* chose to offer his critique in verse. The resulting poem offers a sense of the manner in which some of the visual elements of burlesque now fed into the huge military organisation that had become late nineteenth-century pantomime:

*By living rainbows now the stage is spanned,*
*As in succession file on band by band*
*The Amazons in astral arms arrayed,*
*Shimm'ring in satin, blooming in brocade.*
*The dazzling eyeballs grow with gazing dim*
*As now before them in confusion swim*
*The sheen of silver and the glow of gold,*
*The rich-toned velvet draped in mossy fold,*
*The floating wealth of silk of every tint,*
*The buckle's glitter and the lance's glint,*
*The spangled kirtles and the gleaming vests,*
*The nodding plumage and the radiant crests,*
*The jewelled weapons and the cuirassed breasts.*
*Whilst ladies who with awe this sight regard,*
*Whisper, I'm sure it cost four pounds a yard.*[48]

The final couplet of that review infers that the refashioning of pantomime, despite its debt to the fantastical rhetoric of burlesque, looked firmly to engage the consumerist interests of the women in the audience. It did this by virtue of its playing on the superior technological support provided by larger theatres such as Drury Lane and the Lyceum, whereby stronger and more directed lighting, together with greater floor space for the

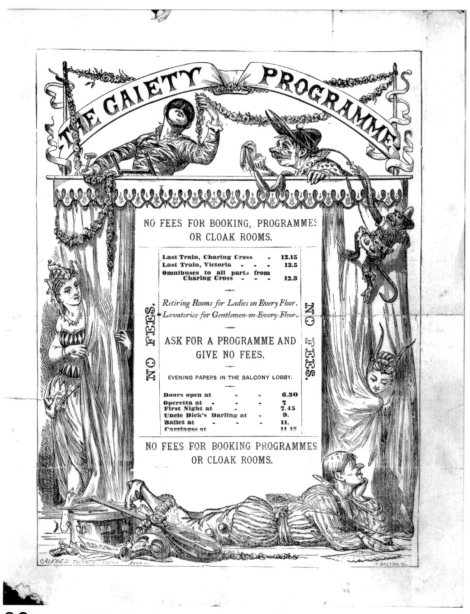

The following text appears within the image:

THE GAIETY PROGRAMME

NO FEES FOR BOOKING, PROGRAMMES
OR CLOAK ROOMS.

| Last Train, Charing Cross | - | 12.15 |
| Last Train, Victoria | - - - | 12.5 |
| Omnibuses to all parts from Charing Cross | - - - | 12.3 |

*Retiring Rooms for Ladies on Every Floor.*
*Lavatories for Gentlemen on Every Floor.*

ASK FOR A PROGRAMME AND
GIVE NO FEES.

EVENING PAPERS IN THE BALCONY LOBBY.

| Doors open at | - - | 6.30 |
| Operetta at | - - | 7 |
| First Night at | - | 7.45 |
| Uncle Dick's Darling at | - | 9. |
| Ballet at | - - | 11. |
| Carriages at | - - | 11.15 |

NO FEES FOR BOOKING PROGRAMMES
OR CLOAK ROOMS.

NO FEES  NO FEES.

**2 5** Programme for the Gaiety Theatre, 1870 (Museum of London)

complex composition of massed ensemble scenes, echoed the sophisticated marketing and display strategies of the new department stores. In scenarios such as this, the refracting gilt spangles and glass gems of the adapted burlesque costume, with its colour-saturated and richly textured surfaces, became an apt receptacle for feminine aspirations and expressions of wonder. Unlike burlesque with its more exclusive appeal to a minority (male) audience, pantomime satisfied the urge to consume on a grand and unprejudiced scale through its profligate visual codes and temporal approximation of popular fashions. The sexual content of the performance did not disappear entirely in this shift of emphasis, but was arguably displaced into a specific form of commodity fetishism. Producers of modern pantomime such as Augustus Harris also imported ostentatious Music Hall stars onto the stage of theatres like Drury Lane for the purposes of injecting a contemporary frisson into the proceedings. And Harris was well aware of the sensual appeal still made to male members of the audience by his massed ranks of chorus girls and dancers, kitted out in provocative style as amazons or fairies. In his review of a production of *Cinderella* staged at the Lyceum in December 1893, William Archer recognized the dual attractions - both covetous and corporeal - of such excessive displays:

One pleasure succeeds another without intermission... Miss Minnie Terry is charming as the sylph Coquette, who presides over the jewels and scents, the handkerchiefs, gloves, fans and powder puffs of the Fairy Boudoir... Chorus and ballet are most carefully selected, and present an uncommonly high average of beauty; the dresses (by Wilhelm) are admirably tasteful and fanciful.[49]

Historian of nineteenth-century theatre Michael Booth suggests that pantomime shared the characteristics of contemporary melodrama in its concern with the narrative potential of stage spectacle and its incorporation as an integral part of the dramatic structure of its form. He draws a distinction however, between the tendency of melodrama to 'imitate social and urban life on a... scale appropriate to the magnitude of human emotion... express[ing] in striking visual terms the sensationalism inherent in its nature' and pantomime's more singular bias toward the creation of a pure and other-worldly fantasy.[50] This assumption that verisimilitude was not of primary importance to the producers of *Cinderella* or *Babes in the Wood* is true only to the extent that such productions were necessarily located in the non-realist realm of imaginary kingdoms by dint of their traditional storylines. What it overlooks is the strong correlation that existed between the stage concept of fairyland and a contemporary understanding of London's commercial and popular cultures as parallel sites of fantastical effects and desires. As the reviewer of a 1900 production of *The Sleeping Beauty and the Beast* proposed,

The Drury Lane pantomime, that national institution, is a symbol of our Empire. It is the biggest thing of the kind in the world. It is prodigal of money, of invention, of splendour, of men and women; but it is without that sense of beauty or the restraining influence of taste. It is impossible to sit in the theatre for five hours without being filled with weary admiration... The monstrous glittering thing of pomp and humour is without order or design; it is a hotch potch of everything that has been seen on any stage... We have Yvette Guilbert's gloves and Marianne's hair, we have the motor car, the two-penny tube and the flying machine, we have a transformation and a Harlequinade, we have a coon-dance, music hall songs, ballets, processions, sentimental songs and occasionally even a good joke... always with fresh foolery and fresh glitter, in a real crescendo of effects.[51]

Musical comedy emerged in the 1890s as the genre which made explicit the escapist potential of London's fashionable scene as a fitting and coherent subject for spectacular theatre. It ironed out the internal contradictions of burlesque and pantomime, drawing on the promotional strengths of both to create a new kind of performance premised on the idea of glamour and stardom. And it made its home at the Gaiety. Besides its contemporary settings, its highly controlled delivery, and its tone of light frivolity borrowed from French revues, the most dramatic departure in Musical Comedy was in its attitude toward costume. As one subsequent memoirist put it, 'Tights were banned and Bruton Street frocks and Savile Row coats... were substituted for the costumes which the wardrobe mistresses or Covent Garden costumiers had run up for earlier Vaudeville players.'[52] George Edwardes staged an early example of the type at the Prince of Wales theatre in October 1892. *In Town* was set in theatre land and its reviewer in *The Players* devoted a great deal of print to the description of the wardrobe :

Some very, very smart frocks are worn by the 'chorus ladies of the Ambiguity Theatre' in the first act, Miss Maud Hobson being well to the fore in the way of style and presence. Her dress... is quite of the smartest I have seen for some time. The skirt, which is made in a demi-train, lined underneath (and seen only when the wearer moved) with pale pink silk, was composed of a beautiful shade of dove coloured silk - over this was worn a bodice of the richest purple velvet, designed in a new and very quaint manner, the fronts being cut very long so as to form kind of tabs... Miss Hobson wears with this dress a large spoon shaped bonnet with a black velvet bow... The eyes of many of the female portion of the audience grew large with envy as they watched this creation and its tall and graceful wearer move about the stage.[53]

The reviewer did not stop at a description of stage dress, but went on to note the mantle of a member of the audience 'made of turquoise poult de soie, and lined all through with the same material in a most delicate peach colour'. Such synergy was clearly novel, underlining the claim of another reviewer that the play 'embodies the very essence of the times in which we live'.[54] A concern with the faddishness and ephemerality of contemporary fashion arguably left the new comedies vulnerable to accusations of superficiality, but this was perhaps preferable to the older charges of vulgarity which had been levied at burlesque. Indeed, in many ways the frothy subject-matter of the plays helped to bracket them with other highly innovative departures in illustration, commercial advertising and journalism, where a gossipy tone and a wry understanding of contemporary 'trends' signified a sophisticated 'continental' sensibility. The reviewer of *The Gaiety Girl*, which succeeded *In Town* at the Prince of Wales in 1894 before transferring to Daley's, grudgingly acknowledged the import of these shared influences:

This type of musical farce is not an elevating or intellectual art form, but it is at least an improvement on the solemn and stodgy Gaiety burlesque of the old school which it seems to be supplanting. In selecting Mr Dudley Hardy to design the handsome memento which was distributed in the theatre, the management showed a nice sense of appropriateness. Along with French methods of draughtsmanship, the tone of the French

comic papers is gradually permeating a large section of English journalism; and A
Gaiety Girl is, on the stage, an unmistakable symptom of the same tendency. 'Spiciness'
is the distinguishing trait of this class of work.[55]

That such 'spiciness' might now be evoked through the directed use of contemporary
rather than burlesque costume was both a reflection of the growing acceptance of the
outré lifestyles increasingly displayed for their own sake in the public spaces of the
promenades and restaurants that punctuated the neighbourhood of the Strand, and
evidence that the well-oiled machinery of a professionalized and commercially astute
entertainment industry could translate such manners onto the stage with easy
confidence. When The Gaiety Theatre produced its first musical comedy The Shop
Girl in 1894, the critical reaction focused particularly on its well-regulated glossiness,
its manufactured sense of modernity. Commenting on the character of the leading
actress, The Theatre stated that 'one is tempted to forget she is anything more than a lay
figure, intended for the exhibition of magnificent costumes. In this respect, however,
she merely fulfils the law of her being'.[56] An extended description of the production in
The Sketch further revealed the promotional mechanisms which lay behind the froth:

The first sensation connected with the performance was one of surprise at the costume.
Nineteenth-century dress had succeeded for once the absence of dress peculiar to the
century of Gaiety burlesques. On the prompt side the 'stage beauties' were collecting for
their entry in such costume as they might wear in the street. What would an old time
Gaiety Girl think of such a condition of things, I wonder? With the termination of the
first act, the old Gaiety traditions asserted themselves... Soon shapely women, in the
traditional Gaiety attire, which was probably originated for summer wear only, came
from their dressing rooms... There was a combined sparkle of eyes and diamonds, a
frou-frou of scant but delicate drapery, as someone came off singing or went on smiling...
From the front, several of the dresses, or suggestions of dresses, looked somewhat daring,
but on the stage they appeared quiet enough. There was such a business-like air about
the proceedings... that a Sunday School meeting... could not have been more free from
offence.[57]

Historian Peter Bailey locates the musical comedy within those broader regimes of late
Victorian modernity which included the routines of the office and the factory
production-line, the military drills of imperialism and the speculative systems of the
financial markets.[58] And while it is certainly possible to read the fashionable stage
confection as another regulatory device, controlling unruly desires and encouraging
unthinking consumption among the broadest possible audience, it is necessary to
recognize the psychological compensations which the form offered. As Bailey suggests,
'within a generation.. London women came to use the greater range of cheap consumer
goods in ways that not only followed the promptings of popular fashion and femininity
but realised a more independent sense of self. Although a blithely manipulative mode,
musical comedy may have stimulated such new imaginative gains for women in a more
overtly sexualised identity that was no longer merely hostage to the designs of men'.[59]

The trajectory of sexualized stage presentation that ran from burlesque to *The Shop Girl* lay behind such stimulation and is framed by those changes which saw the Strand mutate from a shady refuge of pornographers, hacks and stage-door johnnies to a brightly shimmering thoroughfare of hotel lobbies, catering companies, theatrical extravaganzas and advertising hoardings. Entirely symbolic of this shift was the figure of the actress herself, about whose body consumers could now weave all manner of aspirational dreams without fear of moral censure.

# THE ACTRESS AND HER STYLE

The cult of the actor and the actress is a new development - of the nature of Carlyle's 'hero-worship'. The actor looms large in the public eye; London lies at his feet. His portrait is everywhere - at the photographer's, the bookseller's, on posters, picture postcards, and even on table services and other articles of china.[60]

The Italian journalist Mario Borsa was an astute observer of the London theatrical scene as it evolved in the first decade of the twentieth century. He recognized that the prosperity of the stage, evidenced through a 44 per cent increase in audience figures, an 18 per cent rise in the total number of theatres, and a 45 per cent expansion in the music-hall sector over the previous ten years, was testament to a public insatiability for an easily accessible glamour which was peculiarly English in nature. As he stated 'the British public goes to the theatre in search, not of intellectual enjoyment, but of a placid and comprehensive gratification of all the senses. On the stage it expects to behold palatial edifices, gorgeous dresses, spectacular effects; in the auditorium propriety, elegance and comfort. The characteristic English taste for a judicious combination of utility and beauty nowhere reveals itself to greater advantage than at the theatre'.[61] The turn-of-the-century actress perfectly incorporated these properties by virtue of such factors as an emergent star system, which regulated her public image according to prevalent desires; a concurrent cult of the celebrity, which placed her at the centre of popular interest; and the existence of a well-networked fashion culture, which bracketed the thespian identity to a sartorial renaissance. In the concluding section of this chapter, a study of three very different actresses, all associated with the Edwardian theatres of the Strand, demonstrates the powerful influence these factors wielded in progressing a style that was closely identified with the culture of London's West End.

The chorus of one of the hit songs of George Edwardes' production of *In Town* illustrated well the manner by which this new generation of actresses were fitted up to represent an approximation of popular aspirations for the high life, proclaiming:

*We are the fair Ambiguity Girls*
*Worshipped by bankers and brokers and earls*
*Gorgeous in genuine diamonds and pearls*
*Daintiest mantle and hat!*
*Though we are terribly modest and coy*

*Nice little lunches we rather enjoy*
*Chicken and quails with a glass of 'the Boy'*
*Surely there's nothing in that!*
*We are so beautiful dancing in tights,*
*Mashers adore us for hundreds of nights*
*Sending us bracelets and little invites*
*Waiting outside on the mat!*[62]

Constance Collier, who graduated from the chorus of the Gaiety Theatre to the heights of classical theatre, was acutely aware both of the ambiguous status enjoyed by the actress promoted solely as an icon of fashionability, and of the highly constructed and transient nature of her image. Her career had been launched on the basis of little else. In her autobiography she constantly returned to the idea of the theatre as a chimerical space of transformation in which spectacular scenes of excess could be conjured out of nothing and might also rapidly disappear at the whim of the management. Significantly, her memoirs open with a description of a pantomime transformation scene witnessed during her Bradford childhood: 'it was a blaze of glittering glory. The background went up revealing a gigantic silver oyster shell, out of which stepped the fairy queen... Lovely girls in tights the colour of pickled cabbage posed on water lilies, or moved across the stage; magnificent flowers... blossomed everywhere; gauzes went up and down and everything moved like a kaleidoscope. Suddenly there he was - My Harlequin! Tip, tap - the oyster shell became a tree... A whirl, a twist - down came the sausage shop, sausages and all, and the clown with a poker. The transformation scene was ended in all its glory'.[63]

The fragile contingency of thespian glamour implied by the scene above haunted Collier, whose continuing prosperity was guaranteed by her beauty rather than any contrived pretentions toward serious acting. At the Gaiety between 1893 and 1895 she enjoyed all of the trappings of celebrity which Edwardes engineered to keep his charges in the public eye. Her wardrobe was provided gratis by 'two famous dressmakers, one in London and one in Paris'. For special occasions Reville lent mantles and hats, and her throat was dressed by 'a famous jeweller'. All such finery was recorded three times a week by the society photographer Downey, and Collier's image was subsequently used to advertise 'all sorts of ware, and face creams and soaps'.[64] The flimsy foundations of such magnificence were, however, everywhere in evidence and Collier made sympathetic reference to the 'lovely photographs of bygone stars' which decorated her agent's office 'with [their] enormous hips, in tights and swans-down-trimmed boots. Very faded, fly-blown pictures they were'.[65] The faded actress was also a permanent feature of the day-to-day life of the fin-de-siecle theatre and Collier remarked how:

It is amazing how short is the successful life of the girl who goes just for the glamour and excitement of the stage; how soon for her the outer darkness - the most ghastly life in the world... Gradually her few trumpery possessions go - no more flowers, no more champagne, no more parties... I knew some of those girls who, when their beauty began to fade hid their shabbiness beneath fur coats and jewels; they put all their wealth in the shop window of life and , behind their seeming prosperity, were often very hungry… I knew one of them very well in the old days. I met her once in the Strand. It was summer, and she was wearing a beautiful fur coat which was fastened up rather tight… I asked her if she wasn't very hot… Tears came into her eyes. She opened the coat and showed me a very thin, threadbare little dress.[66]

While blatant melodrama clearly played well to Collier's voyeuristic fans, the precarious realities of a profession which had always shared some common ground with the world of prostitution lent a chilling veracity to such morality tales. Collier herself was able to fall back on a repertoire of skills which protected her from sexual compromise or destitution. Though even these hinted at a too-close engagement with the corrupting world of the demi-monde and an abandonment to Sevengali-like manipulation, both signs of the tendency to compromise which adhered to the figure of the actress in the popular imagination. In her 'resting' periods she modelled for artists including Solomon J. Solomon, Byam Shaw and Charles Conder, and Edwardes had trained her in 'dancing, singing, elocution and fencing, as he did to all his girls who showed promise'.[67] Such accomplishments undoubtedly served Collier well in her transition from popular pin-up to celebrated player of the famous tragic roles. Yet her reminiscences betray a continuing faith in the greater currency of the former mode of presentation, which in Collier's day still defined a calling premised on a passive abandonment to regimented display rather than on individual interpretation or notions of personal empowerment:

Oh how I suffered from the admiration of my friends! I was taken up by all sorts of people, treated as if I were an authority on the difficulties of speech, told that my poses were purely Greek, asked all sorts of questions as to whether I had taken them from Flaxman or the Tanagras; if I had studied in South Kensington or the [British] Museum… I didn't dare say I hadn't the remotest idea… All that I had managed to achieve came naturally.[68]

While Collier's self-conscious naivety was a little disingenuous (for this was the period during which dancers such as Isadora Duncan and Loie Fuller were also trading precisely on the idea of a practice of performance that was 'primitive' and intuitive), her attitude is strongly suggestive of prevailing expectations that the actress's public persona was necessarily manufactured and inauthentic. In its very artificiality lay its eroticized fascination and its safely contained sense of spectacular otherness. Against this ideal of mass-produced glamour, and as powerful in its projection of a distinctive mode of theatrical fashionability, was positioned the cultish and perhaps more self-determined figure of the character actress. The pointed lyrics of The Shop Girl trumpeted her rising popularity in forthright terms:

I'm a lady not unknown to fame
Critics call me by my Christian name
And you see my photograph on show

*Just wherever you may care to go!*
*I've been taken in my dinner gown*
*Looking modestly and shyly down*
*Or kicking high with petticoats that fly*
*The smartest girl in town.*[69]

Smartness was certainly an apt description for Marie Tempest, who from 1895 had performed the lead roles in Edwardes's comic operas at Daly's Theatre. Lauded in 1914 as 'one of the best dressed women in London', she had a fashionable image which was also located around the concept of artificiality, but in Tempest's case this was not in any way imposed by a patriarchal management. An expert in the art of self-promotion, she drew inspiration from the urbane environment in which she worked, and she laboured hard to project a coherent representation of her tastes and prejudices to an appreciative audience. According to one critic 'this of course means that she thoroughly understands her own personality, a highly important thing for an actress'.[70] In the case of her stage costumes, this attitude meant that she eschewed the services of a theatrical costumier, preferring to commission fashionable dressmakers such as Jay's in London and Doucet, Worth and Felix in Paris.[71] The resulting garments, whether made for stage or civilian life, were always distinctive. The satin cloak made by Hiley which she wore for the final act of her performance in *The Artist's Model* (1895) received press comments for its ingenious pattern of inter-locking storks. And Tempest recounted several instances when her everyday clothing drew unwelcome attention from passers-by. Her biographer recorded two anecdotes centred on altercations in Regent Street. The first in which 'she was wearing a green velvet dress covered with black lace' illustrated her celebrity status and her ready wit. 'The skirt hung over a water-fall, a bird cage contraption then worn, fixed to the bodice. Marie Tempest suddenly felt discomforted and turned to find herself confronted by a man, holding her water-fall in his hand. 'I think that this is yours Miss Tempest' he said. 'Not at all, you have made a mistake', she answered, and walked on'.[72] On the second occasion a prostitute accosted her while she was window shopping and ordered her off her 'beat' on pain of a thrashing with her umbrella. Such stories pitted 'her own fierce individualism... with her inherent respectability' and revealed the tensions which lay at the heart of the actress's social predicament. In Tempest's case these were resolved through her skilful understanding of the transgressive power of masquerade and its usefulness as an active career stratagem.

Individualism in dress coupled with a regard for propriety was thus a promotional idea pioneered by Tempest. As she recalled 'fashion in clothes changed and within the Morris rooms of the day languid ladies reclined, draped in Liberty's robes. They wore slabs of uncut stone in their brooches and their wrists were noisy with slave bangles. I did not wear them'.[73] Rather than follow the trend for aesthetic or bohemian dressing that was taken up by so many others in the theatrical community, she favoured a sharper sophistication engineered to play well with her suburban and provincial followers, dressing 'with precision rather than artistic abandon'. The underlying premise of her personal style segued with the sentimental morality, reactionary political outlook

❷❻ *Marie Tempest* by Bassano, 1887 (National Portrait Gallery)

and belief in 'keeping up appearances' beloved of her rising lower-middle-class audience, anticipating the concept of conservative modernity that would go on to define popular taste after the First World War. Her biographer noted that 'her feelings about clothes are deep and serious. Self respect, courage, duty to others: these are the terms she will use in explaining why she cares so seriously about what she wears'.[74] These were qualities she was able to explore more fully in the designing or acquiring of her stage costumes after her resignation from Edwardes's company to star as Nell Gwynn in *English Nell* which played at the Prince of Wales Theatre in 1900. Nell had become a popular icon of English femininity in the jingoistic years around the turn of the century and Tempest's 'celebrated cart wheel hat of white chiffon, lined with yellow and trimmed with large black and orange plumes' which she wore in the final act, cemented her own place in the nation's affections.

Tempest's independence as an actress was underlined by her insistence on the personal control of her wardrobe. The early fashion and lifestyle journalist Mrs Aria interviewed her for a 1906 book on the history of costume and uncovered forthright opinions regarding appropriate design: 'To the designer, it seems to me, the actress is merely a note of colour in his general scheme. Only that, and nothing more ! I would urge that exactly the same kind of costume cannot possibly be becoming alike to tall majestic women and a little insignificant nay retroussé person like me!... I always think that a woman ought to have a large share in the designing and arranging of stage dresses, for she can understand what is becoming far better than a man.'[75] Her own efforts in this direction clearly made the desired impact, for James Douglas writing three years later in 1909 described an electrifying stage presence as visually and sartorially compelling as any later celluloid version of stardom produced in the golden age of Hollywood:

Marie Tempest is the last cry in the comedy of feminine artifice. Eve would stare and gasp at her frocks... Marie Tempest is ineffably artificial and divinely meretricious, from the jaunty hat on her saucy head to the red gold wavelets of her hair; from the naughty ruff round her naughty ears to the tempestuous hang of her tempestuous skirt. She belongs to her clothes... [Marie Tempest] adds a new terror to simplicity... Her polished brightness is inhuman for she has improved nature out of existence... She is an absolute amalgamation of the body and the soul, a miraculous union of all the senses, everything in working order, from the first hair to the last eyelash, a continual effervescing triumph of calculated harmony and sharp design and flawless symmetry. Marie Tempest is a blend of Longchamp and the Rue de la Paix, of Trouville and Monte Carlo, of Dieppe and Dinard.[76]

The Marie Tempest 'look' evidently set a challenge to the insipid prettiness associated with the Gaiety and its protégés, not least in its consumerist echoes and commercial possibilities. Critics agreed that 'her influence on fashion was astonishing... Her pannier dress, which startled the first night audience of 'At the Barn' (1912) appeared a few weeks after in the enclosure at Ascot... She made yellow fashionable... When she wore fur, London wore fur. She was a prophetess in dress and it was a role that pleased her greatly.'[77] However, though 'the shrine of her devotion [had] always been the shopping street', Tempest's interests stopped short at engaging directly with the marketing of fashionable products for profitable ends. Material links with London's fashion and retail sector were initiated instead by her competitor Mary Moore (another protégé of Hollingshead and Edwardes), whose association with various couturiers capitalized more fully on the potential for publicity inherent in popular theatre and high fashion.

Her productions of the late 1890s brought to fruition the expectations which had been raised in the opening chorus of *The Gaiety Girl*, first produced in 1893 :

*Here come the ladies who dazzle Society*
*Leaders of etiquette, pinks of propriety,*
*Creme de la creme of the latest variety*
*End of the Century girls!*
*Strictest observers of social formalities*
*Wearers of modern modistes specialities*
*Only residing in tip top localities*
*Flocking where fashion unfurls*[78]

Moore's elegant 'drawing room' plays were perhaps easier settings for sartorial experimentation and dissemination, providing a discrete space for display that would have been more difficult to achieve within the operatic scale of the productions associated with Marie Tempest. Her audiences at Wyndham's Theatre which she managed with her husband Sir Charles were also typically more 'refined' than those who flocked to Daly's or the Gaiety, offering a realistic and remunerative target to those collaborators who wished to market their product via the stage. Moore's costumes therefore aimed at a level of magnificence and sophistication appropriate to Society as opposed to suburban events. She remembered that 'one of my first succesful gowns - which was hugely copied - was a black watered silk with sequinned bodice, and soft billowy sleeves of white chiffon and lace. Large sleeves were then all the fashion. I wore this in 'The Case of Rebellious Susan' [1894] and it was so becoming I had the gown copied for private wear. One Sunday, when spending an evening at the Metropole Hotel, Brighton, I donned this dress for the first time, only to discover on entering the dining room that there were three other facsimiles of it there already.'[79]

Moore paid close attention to the dressing of all the productions she was involved with, developing sound business partnerships with various couture houses who shared her belief that the stage provided 'the finest medium for dressmakers to advertise their wares'.[80] Parisian designers including Beer, Deuillet and Lacroix contributed to plays including *The Liars* (1898), *Lady Epping's Lawsuit* (1907), and *The Mollusc* (1908). In the case of the last-named production she even went to the lengths of reupholstering the interior of the Criterion Theatre to match the Nattier-blue chiffon-velvet of her gown.[81] Besides providing stage costumes, French companies would also discount items that Moore promised to wear at prestigious events such as appearances at Ascot. The actress recalled that 'for these occasions I generally had two or three dresses sent over from Worth's Paris house, which - as they had my pattern over there - arrived ready to put on, without all the trouble of fitting. How delightful it was to receive such lovely gowns at a special prix d'artiste. In those days one could afford to dress well!'[82]

Moore generally deferred to Paris as the home of sartorial innovation, but she also famously turned to the risqué London couturier Lucile for the dressing of *The Physician* in 1897. Moore recounted a particular coat 'of black charmeuse, covered with sequins and lined with ermine which showed when she moved' adding that 'I used to go and look at it growing under Madame Lucile's direction, and my only criticism each time was 'more sequins', as I wanted the material completely covered, as I had seen it on the French stage'.[83] The relationship between patron and client was clearly not easy, as in her own reminiscences Lucile complained:

I had made Mary Moore a dress of coffee coloured lace, embroidered with sequins. It seemed to me to suit her perfectly, but it had long sleeves, which I had not known she particularly disliked. She refused to wear it, said that I was trying to make her look old... Fortunately for me Sir Charles Wyndham took my side... and she wore it for the first night. She had one of the greatest triumphs of her career, and generously wrote and told me so, completely taking back her previous objections.[84]

Despite such setbacks, Lucile continued to provide dresses for Moore and for other celebrity actresses such as Lily Elsie, Gertie Millar and Irene Vanbrugh.[85] Her signature style with its fluid line and floating textures successfully blurred the boundaries between stage and civilian dress, embracing that sense of theatricality which inflected the cultural life of the capital between the turn of the century and 1914. In her own modest words Lucile 'had a message for the women I dressed. I was the first dressmaker to bring joy and romance into clothes, I was a pioneer. I loosed upon a startled London, a London of flannel underclothes... a cascade of chiffons, of draperies as lovely as those of Ancient Greece'.[86]

This chapter, though supporting Lucile's assessment of London's renewed propensity to accept permissive and pleasurable entertainment as a central component of the city's appeal and cultural clout, locates the underlying causes of that shift in a wider network of influences than the self-promotional efforts of one woman. It was a change which emanated from the 'residual zone' of the Strand - a site, as Tracy Davis reminds us, carrying long associations with 'the greater informality of the evening', an informality which 'deliberately confused the mixture of official and unofficial public spaces and behaviours'.[87] Such creative confusion as that promoted by the turn-of-the-century theatre offered real imaginative compensations to its audience, especially its female audience. Borsa correctly identified the hunger of this crowd for novelty and freedom of expression : 'the shopgirls, milliners, dressmakers, typists, stenographers, cashiers... telegraph and telephone girls... who avail themselves of the liberty allowed them by custom, and the coldness of the English masculine temperament, to wander alone at night from one end of London to the other, spending all their money in gadding about, on sixpenny novels, on magazines, and above all on the theatre'.[88] For them the sequins which adorned both Kitty Lord's costume and Lucile's gowns glittered more brightly than anything produced by Worth in Paris, illuminating the question raised by the chorus of The New Aladdin staged at The Gaiety in 1906 and lighting the way for the emergence of a modern metropolitan style:

*What's the matter with London?*
*That's what we want to know:*
*It once was a city you'd hardly call pretty,*
*Not very long ago.*
*What's the matter with London?*
*Everyone's making a fuss,*
*For we have just realised*
*London's idealised,*
*London and all of us.*[89]

❷❼ Oxford Street shopping scene *c.*1920 (City of Westminster Local Archives Centre)

# *The* **H**ostess and the **H**ousewife:

## FROM MAYFAIR TO EDGWARE
## 1918~1939

During the decades separating the world wars two fictional women set out on errands in the West End of London. Superficially similar in terms of their middle-age, their conservative outlook and a shared propensity to expand on their interior lives while undertaking the familiar activities of shopping, entertaining and supporting the needs of their families, these genteel icons of inter-war Englishness revealed, through their actions and opinions, the preoccupations that defined prevalent versions of fashionable femininity during these transitional years in the history of the capital's leisure culture. The first character to imprint her personality on the imaginations of an early twentieth-century readership was Mrs Dalloway, eponymous heroine of Virginia Woolf's novel. In terms of her canonical status and class background Mrs Dalloway enjoyed precedence over Jan Struther's Mrs Miniver, the other symbolic character in this comparison. The work in which she featured would come to be considered a key example of modernist and feminist literature, while the protagonist herself, as the wife of a Tory Member of Parliament, resident in a grand Westminster house, represented the upper echelons of British society. In this respect her actions on the bright June morning in 1923 in which the novel opens trace the rhythms of an elegantly glamorous lifestyle. Stepping out to select flowers in preparation for a grand party that evening, Mrs Dalloway's experience of London is, on one level, emblematic of a privileged understanding of the West End, and of Mayfair in particular, as the picturesque and long-standing haunt of the fashionable elite:

It was June. The King and Queen were at the Palace. And everywhere, though it was still so early, there was a beating, a stirring of galloping ponies, tapping of cricket bats; Lords, Ascot, Ranelagh and all the rest of it; wrapped in the soft mesh of the grey blue morning air, which, as the day wore on, would unwind them, and set down on their lawns and pitches the bouncing ponies, whose forefeet just struck the ground and up they sprung, the whirling young men, and laughing girls in their transparent muslins who, even now, after dancing all night, were taking their absurd woolly dogs for a run; and even now, at this hour, discreet old dowagers were shooting out in their motor cars on errands of mystery; and the shopkeepers were fidgeting in their windows with their paste and diamonds, their lovely old sea-green brooches in eighteenth-century settings to tempt Americans... and she, too, loving it as she did with an absurd and faithful passion, being part of it, since her people were courtiers once in the time of the Georges, she, too, was going that very night to kindle and illuminate; to give her party.[1]

Walking through Green Park, out along Piccadilly, and stopping to peruse the window display of Hatchard's bookshop before crossing up into Bond Street with 'its flags flying; its shops; no splash; no glitter; one roll of tweed in the shop where her father had bought his suit for fifty years; a few pearls; salmon on an iceblock',[2] Mrs Dalloway uses the route of her stroll to reflect on her past relationships. Fashionable London, with its hierarchical trappings of Empire and ancient family traders, is a mnemonic, heavy with associative values. For Woolf, as well 'London was a centre for emotions and memories, a site of social satire, and a celebration of life itself'.[3] And in Mrs Dalloway's musings, the fractured experience of modernity and gender which so troubled the author hangs on an understanding of the city imprinted with the marks of privilege. This element of snobbery is evident in the heroine's observations on those fellow shoppers whose social origins were lowlier than her own: 'The British middle classes sitting sideways on the tops of omnibuses with parcels and umbrellas, yes, even furs on a day like this, were, she thought, more ridiculous, more unlike anything there has ever been than one could conceive.'[4]

It was in the purview of those 'ridiculous' British middle classes that Jan Struther set the concerns of Mrs Miniver when she penned her occasional columns for inclusion on the Court pages of *The Times* between 1937 and 1939. Introduced to reflect the rising 'importance that the domestic and private life had come to assume in national life', the success of Struther's sketches of the daily round and its minor vicissitudes was testament to the central role played by the contented wife and mother in the psyche of 'respectable' middle England by the end of the 1930s. Indeed, so valued were these qualities by war-time propagandists in America that they were later immortalized by Greer Garson in the 1942 MGM film loosely based on the patriotic themes of the column. In her original incarnation Mrs Miniver 'leads the comfortable life of the professional middle class... she has a house in a Chelsea Square, and a second home - 'Starlings' - in Kent, a professional husband, Clem, (a domestic architect with an office in Westminster) and three children'.[5] Occupying a social niche some way below the exalted position of the

Dalloways, the Minivers nevertheless enjoy a comfortable style of life, orchestrated around the simple pleasures of a quiet bourgeois existence. In this respect Mrs Miniver's uses of the city differ from those of Mrs Dalloway, whose attachment to the West End has stronger ancestral and emotional ties that manifest themselves through an aestheticizing attitude which keeps her at a remove from the lives of her fellow citizens. In one episode Mrs Miniver braves the Christmas crowds at a West End department store (the kind of establishment that Mrs Dalloway would have shunned):

One of the minor arts of life, thought Mrs Miniver at the end of a long day's Christmas shopping, was the conservation of energy in the matter of swing doors. With patience and skilful timing it was very seldom necessary to use your strength on them. You could nearly always follow close behind some masterful person who had already done the pushing... This seemed obvious enough; but there was an astounding number of people who seemed to glory in taking the line of most resistance, hurling themselves against an approaching door and reversing its direction by brute force, as though there were virtue in the act. They must lead, she reflected, very uncomfortable lives.

Placing herself neatly in the wake of a bull-necked woman in tweeds, she slipped out of the shop. There was a raw wind; sleety rain was beginning to fall, blurring the lamplight; the pavements were seal-sleek; it was settling down into one of those nasty evenings which the exiled Londoner longs for with a quite unbearable nostalgia.[6]

Admittedly the deft Mrs Miniver similarly distances herself from the hordes of bovine suburban bargain hunters, assuming the effete delicacy which also characterized Mrs Dalloway's perambulations, but in all other respects this *mise en scene* constructs a version of feminine fashionability that could not be more different from the exquisite expense of Mayfair. Yet in these two opposing descriptions we find evidence of the defining characteristics that governed the production and circulation of an identifiable London style in the 1920s and 1930s. In Mrs Dalloway's 'glittering and tinselly' affectations resided the glamorous registers of taste associated with the contemporary idea of London as a decadent social whirlpool, while Mrs Miniver's neat and tweedy practicality bespeaks the homeliness of a new mid-twentieth-century consensus.[7] Both constructions reflect a contemporary dialectic: between distinction and homogenization, escapism and common sense, tradition and modernity. They also inform the focus of this chapter on the concurrent sartorial provision made by manufacturers and retailers for the real-life counterparts of Mrs Dalloway and Mrs Miniver between 1918 and 1939.

# THE MODERNITY OF LONDON

This is the England of arterial and by-pass roads, of filling stations and factories that look like exhibition buildings, of giant cinemas and dance halls and cafes, bungalows with tiny garages, cocktail bars, Woolworth's, motor coaches, wireless, hiking, factory girls looking like actresses, greyhound racing and dirt tracks, swimming pools, and everything given away for cigarette coupons. If the fog had lifted I knew that I should have seen this England all around me at that northern entrance to London, where the smooth wide road passes between miles of semi-detached bungalows, all with their little garages, their wireless sets, their periodicals about film stars, their swimming costumes and tennis rackets and dancing shoes. The fog did not lift for an instant... we crawled... and I had ample time to consider carefully this newest England... It is of course, essentially democratic... You need money in this England, but you do not need much... It is a large scale mass-production job, with cut prices. You could almost accept Woolworth's as its symbol.[8]

In 1934 the playwright and novelist J.B. Priestley drew attention to the processes of suburbanization and Americanization which he felt had transformed the physical and psychological landscape of England after the First World War. In a well-known passage describing the return by car to London after a tour of the country, he vividly captures both the material tenor of that change, with all of its gimmicky, commercialized sheen, and the patronizing distaste displayed toward its manifestations by the political, literary and class elite (of which he himself was a part). Perhaps most threatening, to those who masked their fear of modernity beneath a voluble critique of its mass-manufactured surfaces, was the accessibility of these new products and lifestyles to a growing constituency of youthful, working- and lower-middle-class, often female subjects, who held no truck with the stratified access to pleasure and luxury that had supposedly prevailed at the close of the previous century. As Priestley went on to state: 'The young people of this new England... do not live vicariously... by telling one another... how beautiful Lady Mary looked in her Court dress; they get on with their own lives. If they must have heroes and heroines, they choose themselves, from the ranks of film stars and sportsmen and the like.'[9]

Increased access to new goods was particularly marked in London and its growing suburbs. Arguably this had been the case for centuries. The close association with fashionable novelty was related to London's long-standing status as a capital city, the centre of political, social and economic life in the country at large, and an imperial nexus with connections via trade and governance to the rest of the world. But, by the end of the 1920s the idea of mobility underlying all of this had become a central tenet of the city's continuing pre-eminence and rapid expansion. Priestley's re-entry into its ever widening boundaries was tellingly made on an 'arterial' route, providing proof for the claims of social scientists that

No change in the last generation has had more far reaching effects upon the life of the whole community in London than the improvement of transport facilities. It has influenced almost every Londoner, both in his work and in his play. It has extended the urbanised area, increased the mobility of labour, offered a partial solution to the problems of housing and overcrowding, assisted in standardising wages and prices, and increased opportunities for culture, recreation and amusement.[10]

❷ ❽ *Victoria Bus Station* by Wolfgang Suschitzky, 1939 (Museum of London)

New kinds of transport, in the form of automobile, motor bus and underground train, held the key to London's modernity. The familiarity of these cleaner and more reliable networks encouraged those social revolutions which furthered a partial erosion of the old segregation of communities along class and ethnic lines and heralded the greater freedoms of some women to work in clerical and industrial occupations outside of the home and participate in a wider range of leisure activities. It also invited expanding numbers to extend their shopping expeditions beyond the horizons of the local market or high-street retailer. As *The New Survey of London* (an updated version of Charles Booth's social and economic study of the late nineteenth-century city, revised to take account of change since the war) remarked, 'large numbers of suburban dwellers converge on various centres for their shopping by means of the cheap fare facilities offered, with results which may be seen in the general prosperity of the great multiple stores, not only in the West End, but also in such places as Peckham and Brixton'.[11]

Of the more contentious effects observed to arise from this general process of connection and 'opening out' was an increase in standardization of services, prices and quality. While this was cause for some celebration, and a clear indicator of progress, the consequences for the quirkier aspects of London's geography and character were viewed in a more equivocal light. Abandoning the objectivity demanded of a reporter for the *New Survey*, one observer bemoaned that 'perhaps a word of regret may be allowed to escape for the passing of something original and colourful in the drab monotony of a great city'. Nowhere was this more evident than in the changing appearance of working-class Londoners:

The visible signs of class distinction are disappearing. Chokers, Derby coats and ostrich feathers are rarely to be seen. The dress of the younger generation of working men and women, so far from having any distinctive note of its own, tends merely to copy, sometimes to exaggerate, any particular fashion current in the West End. In the same way paint and powder, once regarded in this class as the marks of the prostitute, are freely used by respectable working girls. With men the pipe has given way to the cigarette, and where it persists it is no longer a clay but a briar.[12]

Higher up the social scale, commentators such as the Hon. Mrs C.W. Forester, fashion columnist for the *Daily Telegraph*, also noticed a 'flattening out' of differences between the dress codes of the various classes in London. 'In our present day life dress is the great leveller', she claimed. 'There may be the distinction between rich and poor, but not between class and class. The dress creators make for all who can command their services.'[13] In Forester's case an increased engagement with fashion across social groups was, however, welcomed. It supported the livelihoods of a sizeable percentage of London's population, encouraged a healthy degree of creative aspirational effort and deflected attention from 'less desirable and possibly dangerous' pursuits (presumably of a sexual or narcotic nature, though these are not specified). In the newly-minted advertising language of the period, fashion provided a tonic, a psychological shield against the buffeting forces of contemporary urban life and a refreshing complement to the energizing experience of the stream-lined twentieth-century cityscape. As Forester asserted: 'The modern Harley Street specialist who recommends an orgy of shopping as a cure for nerves is as wise as another fashionable physician who affirms that a new hat is generally a better tonic than most of his prescriptions.'[14] And within the uniform features of modern dress was encoded a celebratory motto of emancipation: In simple conformity lay strength of purpose and the will to succeed:

Women of business! Take the chances that clothes provide; seize on a special cut and colour, and make it your own… It strikes a note of individuality that has merit; further, it simplifies the extras and accessories… Brown or beige shades, for example, are generally becoming, useful and easy of successful attainment. Any workaday woman of almost any age looks ever so nice in a coat frock of a medium tabac or dark brown shade… A brown felt close-fitting hat, with shoes, hosiery and gloves in the tan shade, completes a satisfactory scheme.[15]

# THE MODERNITY OF MANUFACTURE

The means of production by which the modern London look was manufactured was an inheritance of the late nineteenth century, informed by the social, distributive and technological advances ushered in since the First World War. A bewildering range of specialized crafts and industries still existed to service discreet markets, but the prevailing drift toward standardization experienced in the social sphere also affected the making of fashionable dress in the metropolitan area. The Trade Board Acts of 1909 and 1918 regulated the iniquitous conditions of the many out workers or 'sweaters' who had grafted for the ready-made sector since the 1840s, but this also had the effect of squeezing the profits of many of the small independent clothing companies and dressmakers who had relied on that supply of flexible labour. The beneficiaries of such legislation were the larger factories, often owned by the new multiples and chain stores, whose enlightened employment policies and investment in technology offered attractive inducements and stability to those who would formerly have depended on piece work at home. Post-war restrictions on immigration similarly worked in favour of standardization, cutting off the supply of skilled Jewish workers and rendering fine hand-making an increasingly rare commodity, especially when the sons and daughters of established fashion or tailoring firms were turning away from the rag trade for steady jobs in more remunerative or reliable industries.[16]

Nevertheless, in terms of product, personnel and location, the London fashion trade was still marked by its diversity. 'Thus', as S. Dobbs, writer of an authoritative 1928 treatise on the conditions of Britain's clothing workers recorded,

In the "sittings" of Soho we shall find skilled tailors, discontented with their lot, but still maintaining the traditions of their craft, and, on the other side of Oxford Street, countless busy Jews and Jewesses, in subcontractors' workshops, working steadily on less artistic but more up-to-date lines, and though engaged on a lower class of trade, earning more money than the handicraftsmen who despise them… We shall find also the fashionably attired 'flappers' in the millinery and dressmaking workshops of famous London houses, and contrast them with the struggling middle-aged dressmaker in Cornwall [or]…. The efficient, well-paid operatives in the mammoth factories of Leeds.[17]

Though dispersed and marked by their variety, the clothing workers of 1920s London accounted for a sizeable proportion of the city's 4.5 million population. Dobbs computed that around 160,000 workers earned their living from the production of clothing in the capital, with another 20,000 spread out across the adjoining counties. Of these, nearly 80,000 were attached to the tailoring trades, 55,000 to women's wear, 16,000 to hosiery (shirts and underclothes), 2,000 to corsetry, and 6,000 to millinery. The majority of men (40,000) worked in tailoring, while women dominated all of the other sectors bar millinery, where the gendered split (as in tailoring) was about even.[18] It should be noted that these figures included personnel whose labour was variously employed in ancillary services, management and sales; the sort of distributive and desk jobs which were synonymous with modernization.[19] But these bald statistics also disguise the ineffable mystery which, despite rationalization, still attached itself to the world of the London 'snip':

The task of the investigator in London is perhaps more arduous than it is in other parts of the country… The average factory is small; the average employer is a Nobody, in a city where even Somebodies count but little. The worker's organisation is weak…. There is no obliging Chamber of Commerce anxious to display its wares; no convenient local records exist. Moreover, the area to be covered is almost too large for a single individual to cope with; lost in a forest of which he can only see the trees... Jew and Gentile, skilled and unskilled, factory operative and home-worker, tailor and seamstress and milliner, here they all are, and yet in their endless variety they constitute but a single element in the many sided life of the city, and but a fraction of its teeming millions.[20]

In contrast to tailoring, the London dressmaking sector witnessed the most profound reorganisation during the period, having 'been almost entirely transformed by factory methods'.[21] Embracing all non-tailored outer garments, undergarments and baby linen, the trade benefited from the greater simplicity and standardizing influences in women's fashionable dress. Divided broadly into a wholesale manufacturing and a retail bespoke branch, the industry ran the gamut of production methods from 'a free use of power machinery and extreme sub-division of labour' to intensive and highly skilled handwork. The manufacturing departments of large West End drapery stores incorporated both systems, but generally production-line work was restricted to the wholesalers who supplied export orders for the colonial markets and standardized goods such as overalls, aprons and wraps to the chain stores. This left hand-making to the small court dressmakers and independent retail outlets, with some finishing processes such as braiding, embroidery and smocking sent out to a dwindling number of home-workers.

The dressmaking trades were scattered across the metropolis. Small costume, mantle and blouse firms joined the established tailoring subcontractors north and east of Oxford Circus in the 1930s, laying the foundations for the rag-trade district that still exists there in the fashion-company headquarters and wholesale outlets of the twenty-first century. Further east, wholesale factories shadowed the pre-existence of sweat-shops. 'In Poplar and Limehouse,' as Dobbs observed, ' we pass every now and then a clothing factory of some description... Docklands... boasts a number... mainly engaged in the production of low grade garments. It is on the earnings of the women here employed that many a dock labourers' family depends for its regular means of subsistence'.[22] Elsewhere factories clustered in Clerkenwell, Hackney and Walthamstow (the latter renowned for its shirt, pyjama and light-clothing manufactories), and in the south and west the districts of New Cross, Woolwich, Willesden and Shepherd's Bush supported similar outlets.

The retail bespoke dressmakers situated themselves closer to their private customers, following a more refined pattern of distribution that took in Westminster, Marylebone and Kensington. From here the creative lines of influence stretched back to Paris, or originated from within the London industry itself. The New Survey commented that 'in the highest class of businesses models are either designed by the firm... or bought from outside... Since the imposition of the import duty on silk it has become not uncommon for copies of French models to be made up for importation in woollens or canvas with a view to avoiding the payment of duty'.[23] Further out in the suburbs, independent dressmakers relied on the more mature client, whose specific and old-fashioned requirements were not met by the standardized goods available in the chain stores.

This was augmented with steady alteration and repair work. When called, occasionally, to complete an order for a special occasion (such as the christenings, weddings, bar mitzvahs and company functions whose importance demanded professional attention) suburban dressmakers worked largely from fashion plates and generally utilized fabric supplied by the customer.

Distinct from dressmaking, but central to the construction of the modern London look, was the production of ladies' tailored costumes, incorporating coats and separates (jackets and skirts). This 'wholesale mantle' trade was closely allied to the Jewish-dominated tailoring sector, following the older division of function between entrepreneurs who provided the capital, the designs and the cloth, and skilled master-tailors who took on the responsibility of making-up. Less affected by the economies of scale prevailing in the factory-system, the arising small units of manufacture (constituting a tailor, a machine presser, feller and finisher) were often situated in the domestic context of a living room or the back-yard or basement of a large house in the inner suburbs of north and east London. Their size made such units supremely adaptable to the shifting demands of fashion and season which dominated the output of this sector. In times of increased activity master-tailors called on the support of family and community, leading the *New Survey* to repeat the claim that 'at the height of the season men normally occupied as stall holders in Petticoat Lane may be found as pressers in the workshops of relatives who are ladies' tailors'.[24]

The cut-throat competitiveness and sharp sensitivity to change which characterized the wholesale mantle trade lent a vibrancy which was reflected in the noise, heat and chaos of its working spaces. 'Speed, that is what strikes you directly you enter a workshop,' noted one contemporary reporter, 'everybody is working at top speed - machining, pressing and talking all at one time. The dumb workers talk with their fingers. The Jewish people talk in their language, with here and there a smattering of French and German.'[25] It is important to remember that it was this robust but anonymous cosmopolitan culture which shadowed the sleek modernity of London's more famous fashion protagonists who emerged in the 1930s to meet the desires of patrons like Mrs Miniver. In 1937 the journalist Alison Settle posited a series of names whose fame would go on to recast the reputation of the city as an elite centre for bespoke clothing, serving women as much as men. But their fortune coincided with the development of a wider infrastructure of manufacture and distribution that informed the character of London as a fashion city to an equal extent:

Who are they, the leading British designers? There is Victor Stiebel, a young South African, of whom his French rivals speak with the greatest respect for the purity of his design; a simple, unassuming young man with none of the temperamental ways which one has learnt to expect from the dress world. Cleanness of colour, fabric, line are a passion with him. Norman Hartnell was the name first spoken of among women as the fashion leader who re-focused the eyes of the foreign dress-buying world on this country... To say 'Hartnell' is to conjure up a picture of full-skirted pailetted frocks, of fox collared, smooth-clothed coats, of dresses which were born to attend parties. Digby Morton was the third name among the young men entering the ranks of designers. A brilliant handling of colour marked him out and he was the first to receive the recognition of foreign buyers, because he created only that which they look for in these islands, country clothes, sports clothes, morning clothes.... The same was true of Winifred Mawdsley, a house to which the American buyer has always turned with confidence because Winifred Mawdsley herself was the originator of the sports-clothes department. She it was who built the early reputation of Fortnum and Mason, creating their sweater and cardigan, tweed skirt and pullover branch.[26]

**29** Wedding Dress for Mrs Carl Bendix, designed by Norman Hartnell, 1928 (Museum of London)

# THE GLAMOUR OF MODERNITY

To 'conjure up a picture of full skirted pailetted frocks, of fox collared, smooth-clothed coats, of dresses which were born to attend parties', is also to evoke those glamorous, 'Dallowayesque' aspects of inter-war London life that stood in opposition to the 'sweater and cardigan, tweed skirt and pullover' practicality of Mrs Miniver, or the monochrome shades of factory, showroom, sweatshop and warehouse which characterized London's demotic garment trades. Hartnell's 'gowns' were produced for wearing in a largely nocturnal London landscape which offered a fantastical impression of modernity, suffused with nostalgia and shimmering in negative against the rational, egalitarian concerns of the daytime.[27] As Stephen Graham noted in his 1925 account of London's nightlife:

Our days are democratic; our nights are feudal. For if there is a seeming equality by day, there is an evident disparity by night. Though dukes and tramps may walk Piccadilly in the sunlit hours there is no such companionship in the night. Then doss house and mansion are like serf's hut and baronial castle. Thus the past has a stronger hold on the night than it has on the day... Night sends each to his home, to his own place.[28]

Though it still resonated with the hierarchical division of venues and pastimes which had delineated the pleasure-haunts of London's rich and poor in the nineteenth century, the capital's entertainment economy enjoyed a period of unprecedented expansion, relative safety and carefree hedonism during the inter-war years. The new electric lighting of the West End illuminated a space in which women especially could relax, reasonably free from the fears of attack or censure which had attended the gas-lit maze of the nineteenth-century 'city of dreadful night'. In the popular imagination, London after dark in the 1920s and 1930s was a place of high spirits, extreme decadence and smart clothing; the natural habitat of those 'bright young things' who populate the novels of Evelyn Waugh and the plays of Noel Coward. It was also a venue newly opened up to the suburban middle and lower-middle classes, as a focus for reputable recreation in the dance halls and cinemas which provided a version of glamorous spectacle tailored to supposedly less sophisticated palates. Little wonder that only during these years (according to one influential author) 'does there appear a literature in which the London night is celebrated'.[29] Stephen Graham certainly captured its chimerical attractions with gusto :

The West End has its attractions... Electric light wastes there like life itself. It glows, it dazzles, it flares to heaven. All the moths of London come and stare at it; the lights of pleasure and the lights of vice. Something not to be missed by the visitor to London is to drive in an open car up Piccadilly at night to the Circus. All the sedate clubs are like lodges. All the lamp posts, now painted to look like aluminium, have a processional aspect, as if they indicated the way to court, to the great gates... Effulgence rolls to you along the magnificent avenue... Silk hats take colour reflections. Light holds everyone in movement. It is grand.[30]

Piccadilly Circus, with its new electrically lit advertising hoardings, symbolized the slick modernity of the city and offered one of the few nodal points (Leicester Square was another) in which the night-time crowds achieved a democratic unity. Against 'the red crystal bottle which pours port into a waiting glass... the gyrating coloured pin heads of new pin soap... the baby with the illuminated forelock sucking a bottle of Nestle's milk... the gilded letters of the Chinese restaurant' and 'the bright white light of the Monaco', revellers of every class and creed found their aspirations reflected through the lambent wonder of modern commercial art. Besides the constantly transforming imagery of mass-consumption, the crowds who crushed into the Circus also offered up a vision of contemporary femininity which was strangely disorientating, for 'there you may see the three little girls in blue, the summer girl with slashed skirt, the public house hussy with the bunch of bobbed and hennaed hair, girls chaperoned and unchaperoned, regulars, pirates, the cerised lips, the pencilled brows, starers, loiterers, hurriers...'[31] To an extent Graham's description simply re-enforced the old Victorian expectation that 'women in the night landscape were either whores or angels'; and while an opening-up of the nocturnal city in the 1920s had, as Joachim Schlor points out, rendered such reductive categorizations partially defunct, female pleasure-seekers were still 'often only present' in popular representations of London's nightlife 'as window dressing, as decorative elements'. Thus those actresses, singers or prostitutes of the type who might sport 'the cerised lips, the pencilled brows' were reduced to playing 'the flowers of metropolitan night culture... women who belong, but not to themselves'.[32] Yet alongside such opulent examples of sexual display, Graham pits an equally powerful image of those less visible women, notable only for the mundane circumstances of their daily lives, for whom the West End offered a valuable means of self-assertion or escape:

Every bus halt has its hundreds waiting to get home. For now is the great demobilisation of pleasure - from the gay centre to all the humdrum suburbs and the stuffy box-spring beds.[33]

Cinema provided one focus for which these late-night commuters ventured into the West End or the local high street. As film historian Jeffrey Richards notes, the coming of sound in 1928 marked an upsurge in cinema building and attendance across the capital, pushing the appeal of the movies out beyond a core fan-base of young, working-class, female enthusiasts to an increasingly 'respectable' middle-class audience. And though the tastes of such constituencies differed significantly (with working-class viewers preferring the pace and ambition of Hollywood film to the stage-bound gentility of English productions), the impact made by the silver screen on all facets of social life, but especially fashion, was clearly in evidence.[34] The *New Survey of London Life and Labour* concurred, stating that

The influence of the films can be traced in the clothes and appearance of the women and in the furnishing of their homes. Girls copy the fashions of their favourite film star. At the time of writing, girls in all classes of society wear 'Garbo' coats and wave their hair a la Norma Shearer or Lilian Harvey. It is impossible to measure the effect the films must have on the outlook and habits of the people. Undoubtedly they have great educational possibilities which have so far been very imperfectly attained. But the prime object aimed at is not to instruct or 'uplift', but to amuse, and in this object the cinema has proved very useful.[35]

Clearly the popularity of film confused and disarmed its critics, for in a tangible way, though the content of the majority of productions seemed superficial and sometimes immoral, their hold on the imagination and aspirations of the audience had a positive impact on the ways in which the population of London presented itself to the world. As the New Survey implied, this effect was often attained at the expense of local traditions, imparting the glossy sheen of American manners in contexts which were far removed from the sunny environments of Los Angeles or Manhattan. But sometimes the connections between London and cinema culture were tighter than an enthusiasm for 'Garbo' coats might imply. Richards's comparison of the careers and appeal of English stars Gracie Fields and Jessie Matthews makes this very clear. Indeed, in promotional terms, the refining of Matthews's screen persona perfectly mirrors the development of London as a site for escapist entertainment during this period. Born over a Berwick Street butcher's shop to a working-class family with sixteen children, Matthews joined a line of 'independent, strong-willed working women achieving success in a hard competitive world' who might previously have sought fame on the Music Hall or Variety circuit. Her looks and aptitude for singing and dancing would, a generation earlier, have landed a role at the Gaiety. The technology of film, however, provided Matthews with a different setting. As Richards states,

Jessie's six vehicle films from Evergreen on were Art Deco fantasies, taking place in a highly stylised, high contrast, hermetically sealed black and white world of ritzy nightclubs, luxury hotels, ocean liners, newspaper offices, radio stations, theatres and mansions, where vast floor spaces were polished to a preternatural brightness. Chrome gleamed and angular metallic accoutrements spoke of the influence of modernism.[36]

This heightened hymn to artificiality offered an alternative response to the realities of the depression than that represented by the more realistic, northern milieu of Fields' cheerfully optimistic and community-minded 'mill-girl' films, one that sought solace in the hallucinatory attractions of metropolitan glitter and the material rewards of personal achievement. Matthews' embodiment of this individualist ethic chimed well with the emerging idea of the West End as a space where one might live one's dream and dream one's life.[37] And at its most ebullient, the tendency toward hedonistic escapism found its apogee in the attitude on display at the celebrated Gargoyle Club in Soho, one of many such venues famed for its relaxed morals and elegant clientele. Stephen Graham described its cosmopolitan attractions:

Among the many literary members there are Compton Mackenzie, Rebecca West... among politicians, Viscount Grey; scholars, Sir William Beveridge. There is, of course,

**❸❿** Jessie Matthews in a costume
designed by Joe Strassner for *It's Love Again* 1936 (British Film Institute)

a swarm of actresses, society girls and men about town…. There are always beautiful women interestingly dressed, and with them men with meditative brows and slow feet; low faces, professional faces, and some soldierly men, and dreamy young artists a whit unsteady. The walls are a glittering mosaic of seven thousand little square mirrors. Chinese curtains shut out the gloom of the Soho roofs and the London night. The low gilded ceiling looks like the lids of many jewel boxes… Pictures by Matisse add to the artifice… The music is as up-to-date as gramaphone records, say a month ahead of the barrel organs, and commonly a season behind New York, whence most of the smart jazz melodies derive… The ambition of the committee seems to be to combine the amenities of an artistic and social club with normal amusement. 'We want to make it a place where the Sitwells would not be ill at ease and not perfectly at ease', explained a member to me one night.[38]

Beyond the haunts of aristocrats and playboys, the demand for amusement was also discernible in the more democratic palais de danse of which the New Survey counted 23 in 1933. The best amateur dancers came from the Jewish East End, but the attractions of the dance-hall were broadly targeted and 'typists, shop assistants and factory girls rub[bed] shoulders in them'. Dressed in 'smart frocks' or lounge suits for the men, habitués valued the informality of such venues and it was reported that 'people drop into a palais after the day's work or on Saturday evenings as casually as they go to a cinema'.[39] Besides film and music, the life of the street offered its own attractions, presenting a tableau of modernity as striking as anything witnessed on screen. The New Survey recorded that cafes, confectioners and fish and chip shops (all businesses whose interiors were remodelled during this period in hygienic, streamlined styles) in the inner suburbs remained open until after ten o'clock in the evening, while the extravagant architecture of cinemas, fun fairs and theatres provided a dramatically lit backdrop for the carousing of the crowd. Of particular note was 'the modern practice of lighting up closed shops' which formed the focus for 'a new kind of attraction for Sunday evenings. The central streets… are then thronged not only with people going to and from some church, chapel, cinema or public house, but also with a large number of young men and girls who stroll about chatting and shop-gazing'.[40]

That the spaces of the cinema and the shop sheltered an electrifying sense of modern living in London between the wars is an experience caught most evocatively by J B Priestley in his novel Angel Pavement. Here, in an echo of the fraught urban scenes recorded in Alfred Hitchcock's early London films, the clerk Turgis becomes infatuated by salesman's daughter Lena Golspie to the point of murderous psychosis, seeing in the feminized surfaces of the West End's pleasure zones a reflection of his own overwrought passion. It is a passage that maps a landscape of consumption which would also have been eerily familiar to many of Priestley's female readers, acquainted as they were with London's ever-expanding luxury retail sector:

When he was pursuing her, though only in this strange, shadowy fashion, Lena and he alone were real, the only real human beings in a city that had been turned, with all its winter magnificence of lighted lamps and shop windows, golden buses, glittering night signs, and shining wet pavements, into an illuminated jungle… Everything he saw spoke to him of women and love. The shops he passed were brilliant with hats and clothes that Lena might wear; they showed him her stockings and underclothes; they were piled high with her entrancing little shoes; they invited him to look at her powder bowls, her lipstick, her scent bottles; there was nothing she wore, nothing she touched, they did not thrust under their blazing electric lights. The theatres and picture houses shouted to him their knowledge of girls and love. The hoardings were covered with illustrations, nine feet high, of happy romances. The very newspapers, under cover of a pretended interest in Palm Beach or feminine athletics, gave him day by day photographs of nearly naked girls with figures like Lena's. And in and out of the buses, tube trains, theatres, dance halls, restaurants, tea shops, public houses, taxis, villas, flats, went boys and their sweethearts, girls and their lovers, men and their wives, smiling at one another… clasping hands… kissing.[41]

# GOING SHOPPING

If Priestley is to be believed, the streets of inter-war London were strewn with the ephemera of the boudoir, confusing the unwary in a tangle of lace and a fog of perfume. Given such impediments, how might more measured or experienced consumers, the Dalloways and Minivers, have negotiated these eroticized vistas? The reality of shopping was of course less ripe than the novelist suggests, but tourist guides and magazine surveys still depicted a labyrinthine network of outlets in which the customer might easily lose herself. In the same way that the leisure zones of the city were demarcated by the registers of social class and the type of entertainment on offer, so the fashion shops of the capital subtly oriented their goods to particular incomes and tastes, laying traps for the naive. And in fairness to Priestley, the attitude of proprietors across this highly differentiated sector to issues of promotion and display conformed to a shared interest in sensual and opulent effects that seemed designed primarily to seduce.

In its upper reaches the London retail scene of the 1920s and 1930s benefited from the influence of both Paris and New York where the art of selling was at its most sophisticated. Representatives of French couture houses and American sportswear companies made their presence known in the West End and sometimes found London to be a highly profitable sort of city, especially when financial or political crises threatened business at home. Liberty invited Paul Poiret to collaborate with them for a season, and Worth installed Madame Champcommunal as a designer in their London branch. Maggy Rouff, Molyneux and Schiaparelli also traded from Mayfair premises. From the other side of the Atlantic New Yorker Marjorie Castle launched the first clothes shop on Berkeley Square, selling American 'hostess dresses'. Her compatriot Rose Taylor opened up in Grosvenor Street, dealing in ready-to-wear day dresses and pampering her customers with a beauty-bar where they could rest and reapply make-up.[42] But aside from their provision of items which held novelty value or extra prestige for British shoppers, such outlets also informed a style of interior design which combined the pared-down elegance of the French hotel and the sleek luxury of American modernism, all reinterpreted through the prism of a peculiarly English sense of theatrical decoration. Thelma Benjamin, editor of the *Daily Mail*'s women's page, recognized its dramatic appeal in the trappings of one prestigious exemplar:

Englishwomen have reason to be proud of the House of Isobel… which occupies magnificent premises in Regent Street and numbers some of the best dressed women in London's world of fashion among its clientele… A dress show chez Isobel is well worth visiting… the mannequins show off to great advantage as they pirouette on the black marble platform against a grey background, or slowly 'sail' up and down the handsome black marble staircase. Her Court dresses are always of particular beauty, and she maintains that an Englishwoman of taste can best dress an Englishwoman to advantage.[43]

The House of Isobel was typical of several Court dressmakers who, encouraged by the earlier commercial success of Lady Duff Gordon, pioneered a canny marriage between aristocratic associations and a gently risqué bill of fare. Situated in the golden rectangle between Regent Street, Piccadilly, Oxford Street and Park Lane, these elite businesses fronted the thoroughfares familiar to Mrs Dalloway and offered their wares to women of her class. American anglophile Paul Cohen-Portheim was alive to the atmosphere of the district in 1930, drawing attention to its localized nuances, its contradictory tendencies toward restraint and swagger. He described Bond Street as a resort for 'well dressed women and super-smart men with a…swinging gait you never seem to see elsewhere… It has conquered Hanover Square, a stronghold of dressmakers in the east, and is now seizing on Berkeley Square in the west'. By contrast, the new Regent Street suffered (in Cohen-Portheim's opinion) from a stolid respectability. It was 'reasonable, but without charm' like 'a woman whom people describe as 'really admirable' because she is worthy, but none too attractive.' Park Lane however, encapsulated all that was forward-looking:

It looks like the Brighton Parade facing a park instead of the sea… Now the biggest new houses of London are arising here, huge hotels, flats, clubs. Some of the private mansions survive but Park Lane is doomed to share the fate of all Mayfair. Flats and hotels are the headquarters of the rich of today, and here a new centre is arising for their benefit. It is bright and new and expensive-looking, and represents the post-war spirit with all its defects and its advantages. It is interesting because it is quite of the present, and there is so much that is old left in London that it can well afford an outburst of modernity.[44]

It was in the quieter streets moving back from Park Lane to the east that the most exclusive dressmakers had their premises, often hiding behind 'those magnificent old dwelling homes, the fine rooms of which make such delightful settings for lovely frocks'.[45] Thelma Benjamin recommended Hanover, Princes, Dover, Albermarle and Wigmore Streets as notable locations for the acquisition of fine gowns. Her fellow shopping journalist Elizabeth Montizambert related how, in the pale-grey rooms of Dover Street, Miss Phelps at Phelps-Paquin traded on a twenty-year association with the more genteel members of the London acting profession, boasting Ellen Terry as her first client. The Hon. Mrs Fortescue also pandered to theatrical tastes at Cintra in Sackville Street, its interiors decorated as 'a sort of Aladdin's Cave, with black floors and walls' where 'a golden ceiling and a gold-woven alcove lighted with jewelled lamps look down on… rich cushions, lacquered furniture and original bibelots'.[46] Set-dressing of the kind practised by Mrs Fortescue was considered a forte of London's high-fashion establishments, often linked by observers to the cult of domesticity with which English feminine culture was internationally associated. The skills of the country-house

*Feminine but efficient disorder*
(By courtesy of " Vogue ")

**❸❶** Madame Champcommunal at work at Worth by Francis Marshall, 1944 (Museum of London)

mistress, renowned for her ability to create a hospitable yet characterful ambience, here seemed to extend into the commercial sphere. The juxtaposition of old and new which marked the inter-war urban landscape was similarly identified as an inspirational influence, shot through with a vein of surrealism that also informed the fashion photographs of Cecil Beaton and Angus McBean. The fashion illustrator Francis Marshall recalled that 'there was an eclectic brilliance about it, a merging of baroque decor with Victorian charm that was fascinating. Behind it was the court ceremonial of many special occasions... This blending of historic royal functions with the modernity of the twentieth century was unique'.[47]

The eclectic aesthetic of the couturier's salon also drew on the precedents set by the specialist boutiques whose 'artistic' presence enlivened the shopping experiences of wealthy women. Thelma Benjamin described the traditional displays of the tea and coffee, ice and chocolate, perfume and linen shops in Bond Street and the Burlington Arcade with rapture. But it was the florist shops in particular, the specific quarry of

Mrs Dalloway, that endowed London's fashionable streets and businesses with their extraordinary character. By the mid-1930s the city supported a veritable cult of the bouquet and the button hole, and when Francis Marshall claimed that 'a milliner's shop in 1937 was like a flower garden in a mist' he did not exaggerate. Alison Settle provides more detailed evidence of the rustication of Mayfair:

Molyneux made what must have been a wild innovation when he introduced huge vases of flowers in every room, standing against the over-mantles of glass. Apple blossom, white lilac, roses, every woman looked at them appreciatively... In England Stiebel used flowers even more effectively. Constance Spry, that wizard with flowers, affixed temporary vases of white plaster shoulder high in his rooms and filled them with magical blends of flowers... it put the buying woman into a mood of content.[48]

Further west in Knightsbridge and Chelsea, the artistic impulse was felt even more strongly. Cohen-Portheim valued the 'anti-fashion', creative pretensions of the region:

I approve of Sloane Street, which has a feeling of modernity about it, and of a type of women who shop thereabouts, who are smart enough, though not necessarily grand or millionairish, like they are (or should be) in Bond Street. These streets do not depend so much on 'The Season'; the people you meet here seem to live in and belong to that part of the world, and you feel quite possibly some of them can't pay their bills... It is a young place in spirit, and it also has the advantage of not being a 'sight'.[49]

The bohemian credentials of the district were born out by the presence of eccentric entrepreneurs including Sheba at 1 Cadogan Place, which specialized in embroidered tea-gowns displayed in a panelled music room, and the neighbouring Mrs Reeves who dealt in bespoke head ornaments.[50] The sense in which the shopper in this area was forced to take on a more intrepid, exploratory attitude was born out in Thelma Benjamin's shopping guide produced exclusively for the American traveller in 1930. The Wearing Studio at Knightsbridge Green is described in terms that magnify its 'out-of-the-way' quirkiness:

At the top of Brompton Road, just opposite Tattersall's, the famous horse market, Knightsbridge Green consists of three fine trees which flourish exceedingly as they grow over an old plague pit... You go up and up, and then almost breathless and despairing you come to a chair on a small landing and an encouraging notice "Only twenty more stairs"... At the top you find spacious studios where real artists weave exclusive and delightful materials... There is now a definite revival of home-spun and the vegetable-dyed wools come out in colours like old Persian rugs.[51]

This taste for unique hand-made products sold in atmospheric premises was a particular speciality for which London could claim credit, and the presence of such shops had a demonstrable effect on local trends in fashion design, retail display and the social standing of garment workers during the period. Elizabeth Montizambert likened them to 'jewels

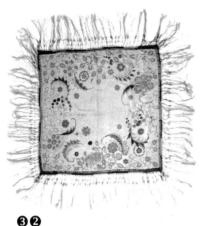

**❸❷**

Hand painted shawl by Gwen Pike,
c.1930 (Museum of London)

in the sober setting of the street' and noted how 'in many cases they are the result of the incursion of the amateur into the world of commerce'.[52] The Merchant Adventurers Store at 25 Sloane Street, for example, had grown from a small experiment in a Chelsea flat started by well-meaning aesthetes in 1919. It sold a mixture of antique and contemporary craft products including 'old lace, exquisite lingerie fit for a princess, brocade bags and unusual gifts of every description'. Montizambert claimed that 'the shop has been a great boon to the educated home worker, who may rent... shelves... on which to display their handiwork if it passes the high standard of quality exacted'.[53]

To some extent the content and approach of such concerns drew on the uniquely cosmopolitan culture of the city. They complemented the provision of embroidered peasant blouses and wooden ornaments at the Russian shop at 194 Brompton Road, blue glass and faience beads at the Palestine Art Industries sale rooms in Harrington Road, mother of pearl, carpets and Sinai necklaces at the Egyptian Produce and Industries Association on Holborn Viaduct, or lace and embroidered linen at the Italian craft shop at 116 Cromwell Road.[54] And they mimicked the profusion of exotic gewgaws to be found at the Caledonian Flea Market in Islington, the largest of its kind in the city, where there were 'acres of every imaginable sort of second-hand goods for sale, from broken plates to costly Chinese porcelain, from discarded stoves to Queen Anne silver... and miles of new cotton or wool stuffs, and thousands of housewives with newspaper parcels and nets and perambulators'.[55] But for the less intrepid and 'better-bred', the most concentrated incidence of 'artistic' shops were to be found in Beauchamp Place. Their ambience was informed more directly by the amateurish 'gaiety' associated with the world of the debutante or the E.F. Benson heroine than the immigrant trader or cockney housewife. According to Montizambert,

In Beauchamp Place... the dressmakers... are nearly quite as numerous as the antique sellers, and display their wares with equal skill. Their names sound like a jolly confraternity of frivolity - Coralie, Osra, Ena, Pique, Chica.... Ardinello, Fairies and Watteau... One of the prettiest shops... is called Thamar... The face creams and phials are arranged with so much grace that they somehow remind you of the bleaches and washes of fair Italian medieval women, and how entranced Isabella and Beatrice d'Este would have been at the sight of the quaint bottles and perfumes... more efficacious than their golden pomander balls.[56]

Nothing could have been further from the down-to-earth, practical ambience of Oxford Street, which in the inter-war years saw the process of corporatization initiated by Gordon Selfridge before 1914 come to profitable fruition and begin its long post-war slide into social and economic decline. Cohen-Portheim typically bracketed its attractions with those of the rather frumpy women who trod its pavements. In 1930 it was 'an impressive assembly of large stores and draper's shops, but it ha[d] a strangely suburban or provincial atmosphere, and always seem[ed] full of agitated spinsters holding hands while trying to cross the road, and red-faced stout women with many parcels bumping into everybody'.[57] The built styles of the emporia in which such visitors sought their bargains were, however, nothing short of spectacular, even if the range and presentation of the goods on offer frequently failed to inspire the admiration of newspaper shopping correspondents or other more elevated commentators.[58] Elizabeth Montizambert admitted that

In one of the great departmental stores like Peter Robinsons there is the perfection of detail that shows the skill and knowledge of the connoisseur. The ground floor is paved with unpolished blocks of marble after the fashion of the floor in Milan cathedral, and opposite the lifts the zodiacal signs are inlaid in a large circle. All the wood used in the building is walnut of a very fine beautiful grain, and as much care and ingenuity have been expended on the cash desks as if they were pieces of elaborate furniture. The lifts remind one of inverted tea-caddies, only with the lacquer inside instead of out - sealing wax red, with black bands picked out in gold. The doors are bronze faced round with pale green marble.

Her description weaves together a visual tapestry that incorporates the grandeur and scale of Gothic architecture, the glamorous trappings of modern travel and entertainment and a certain petite-bourgoise homeliness, indicated by the allusion to tea-caddies and sealing wax. But in the end all such artifice is deemed wasted, for 'with all this wealth of rich detail the imagination of the organisers has ended. There is no attempt to so arrange the wares disposed for sale in any other fashion than that of the conventional British shop'.[59]

**3 3**
Black silk chiffon cloche hat decorated with appliqued tambour work and embroidery, Dickins & Jones, Regent Street, c. 1930 (Museum of London)

With the exception of Selfridges, whose American management endowed it with a livelier image, only Marshall and Snelgrove rose to the challenge of Montizambert's desire for an imaginatively stocked and arranged Oxford Street department store. Likening its interiors to 'a cave of Aladdin', she approved of a policy which encouraged 'merchandise scattered about in lavish profusion... a riot of glowing colour... silks and cushions, gorgeous lamps and ornaments of jade and amethyst.. piled with an apparent carelessness that is the subtlest of temptations'.[60] Within their striking exteriors, most neighbouring department stores appeared to avoid 'vulgar' spectacle, catering instead to a middle-English concern for value, quality and 'no nonsense' service. Thelma Benjamin understood the 'conventional' leanings of her *Daily Mail* readership well when she advised that the tailor-made costumes at Debenham and Freebody in nearby Wigmore Street 'are cut and tailored by expert men tailors' and that 'personally, I always find their gloves particularly worthwhile... They have a remarkably good cut'.[61] Such opinions backed up the store's own modest claims that it was 'very English in its character and has maintained a personal atmosphere...The majority of the productions of the house are from the workrooms on the premises, and customers are assured of the highest standards... Prices are not necessarily expensive as there is always in stock a wonderful variety of really moderately priced ready-to wear clothes'.[62]

Away from the bustle of Marylebone, other large stores also set their well-crafted wares before the same discerning audience, backing up Benjamin's hunch that 'the Englishwoman has the reputation of being a tailor-made woman and that is why probably that for country and sports wear English models reign supreme'. [63] At Fortnum and Mason in Piccadilly, cardigans, tweed skirts and jerseys dyed to match, suede and corduroy golf coats, and garments for cruising were displayed in Winifred Maudsley's celebrated women's wear department on oak tables and benches which hinted at the ambience of the old moated manor house that many middle-class women of the period saw as their ideal domicile. But it was Jaeger, back on Oxford Street, who most successfully caught the imagination of bourgeois customers like Mrs Miniver. Following a period during which their sanitary woollens were associated with a dowdy crankiness, the store enjoyed a renewed fashionability in the 1930s - bolstered by the popularity of sportswear. A standard Jaeger advertisement of 1934 depicted a woman in a tweed cape alighting from a train, golf clubs slung across her shoulder. Its colloquial copy was a clarion call to the respectable provincial for whom London's streets were now within easy reach:

Plunder Jaeger's stronghold of besieging clothes. Dash straight to Jaeger House as soon as you reach London. Storm the fashion floor before you storm the town and you'll be a scintillating success wherever you go. Jaeger have the nation's divinest frocks and coats and hats and jumpers. So new that they've barely caught their breath. So blithely exhilarating, so wittily wearable, that they're worth coming a million miles to see. Miss the Albert Memorial, neglect the Tower of London, give the Houses of Parliament the go by, but forget to visit Jaeger and your trip's an arid calamity. Jaeger House is in Oxford Street, almost opposite Bond Street Tube Station... Obliging and trustworthy buses converge on it from all points of the compass. [64]

# SUBURBAN SAVVY

As the advertisement suggested, women did indeed converge on the West End of London 'from all points of the compass', sating their desire for modern, metropolitan commodities and entertainment. Many were foreign or provincial, but by far the most significant type of consumer to pay regular visits to the department stores and salons of the 1930s was the suburban visitor, hailing from the rapidly expanding fringes of the city and bringing with her an attitude which was to redefine the tenor of fashionable life both 'up West' and back home. The intensified development of the underground and suburban train network during this period both eased the passage of bodies across the metropolis and enabled the huge programme of house building which shifted the social dynamics of the capital in a profound manner. Between 1924 and 1947 tube lines established under the West End and the City before the War were extended out toward Edgware, Arnos Grove and Leytonstone, instantly opening up swathes of virgin territory to the house-building speculators of Middlesex and Essex, whose new semi-detached villas disgorged armies of workers and shoppers back into town on a daily basis.[65] The effects, as observed by the *New Survey of London*, were almost instantaneous:

Developments of this kind inevitably tend to standardise prices throughout the London area and to equalise the general quality of the goods offered. Incidentally, it may be noted that the travel induced in this way is cumulative in its effects. The large establishments require larger staffs, who have to travel ... [66]

The advertising images which accompanied such travellers on their regular commutes indicate the central role played by aspirational consumption in linking suburb to centre and forming a homogenous or consensual ideal of fashionable London living which was no longer limited to the exclusive activities of a wealthy minority. Many of these visual prompts employed both the stylistic apparatus of the avant-garde painter and designer and the sophisticated psychological armoury of a fledgling advertising industry. Critics such as Roger Fry were thus suspicious of the creation of an illusory culture of acquisition aided by the striking flourishes of Cubism, Futurism and Vorticism. In 1926 he complained that 'advertising has, in recent times, taken on a new complexion... It is tinged with a new poetry - a new romance.... It brings about a new relation between the public and the great limited liability companies... They produce in the public a non-critical state of romantic enthusiasm... More and more the whole thing takes on an air of unreality'.[67]

The Underground companies themselves (with the exception of the District Railway) encouraged the idea of a travelling community untroubled by social distinction through the abolition of class segregation in their carriages. This myth of equality was also promoted in posters which depicted crowds of customers whose difference was still marked by dress, occupation or interest, but whose access to the services of the Underground was unified by a standard ticket price and a coherent experience of the service. As early as 1913, F.C. Witney's poster *Underground for Business or Pleasure* contained the figures of theatre-goers in evening dress, mothers and children, men about town and a golfer, all united in their metropolitan freedoms. By the mid-1920s, emboldened by Frank Pick's reorganization of the management and corporate image of the London Underground, poster artists capitalized fully on the democratizing potential of travel, fashion and entertainment. Pick himself encouraged the adoption of striking visual solutions to marketing problems and 'justified advertising that was slightly above people's heads as being preferable to a descent to the lowest common denominator. A good poster, he believed, could be both inspirational and aspirational; images populated largely by the fashionable and the wealthy were not, therefore, aimed at those people alone'.[68]

The availability of off-peak travel reductions aimed at suburban women who might use the time and savings for shopping expeditions to the West End was publicized with a verve to match Pick's proselytizing vision. The imagery of such posters often utilized the rhetoric of the party invitation or the fashion plate, encouraging women to engage with the visual and sensual excitement of consumption promised in the designs. E. McKnight Kauffer's *Winter Sales* of 1921 presented an abstracted picture of urban energy in the raking lines, swirling raincoats and jostling umbrellas of a high-street crowd in full tilt. In Horace Taylor's *To Summer Sales by Underground* of 1926, the scene has been transported indoors where women in cloche hats and short-sleeved summer dresses rummage amongst patterned textiles. And a theatricalized sense of consumerist gratification is implied in Alma Faulkner's *Come Out of Doors in Your New Dress* of 1928, where a woman in her slip selects a flounced garment from the twin wardrobes of her suburban dressing room, as if preparing for a performance on the stage.

Following an afternoon's shopping, travellers were often encouraged to extend their visit by taking a meal at a restaurant or visiting the cinema or theatre.[69] Marc Severin's London Underground-commissioned *Why Go Home?* and *Why Wait Till Later?* of 1938 both utilize this image of the West End as a playground for suburbans, an idea that had been forcefully communicated in Paul Nash's paired posters *Come out to Live* and *Come in to Play* of 1936. In the first the dome of St Paul's and the bustle of the City are compared to the leafy gardens and tennis courts of a suburb in summer, while in the second the bright lights and nocturnal glamour of Piccadilly Circus are contrasted with the rainy monotony of wintery suburban streets. The dialectical attractions of domestic peace and cosmopolitan distractions was also a theme used

❸❹ *Come Out of Doors*, London Underground Poster by Alma Faulkner, 1928 (London Transport Museum)

to sell suburban living to potential home-owners. When the Hampstead Tube reached Edgware in 1924 William Kermode's *Move to Edgware* set the shabby terraces of the inner-city against the spacious villas of a bucolic Middlesex. And in Fred Taylor's wordless 1925 depiction of Edgware Underground Station rising amid the fields and scaffolding, the twin motivations of escape and connection are visibly made concrete.

The more complex realities of suburban life were another matter. For example, the *Guide to Edgware*, published in 1927, described the makings of a small town which - despite direct train connections to Broad Street, a daily tube service, electric trams to Paddington and a main road sharing the suburb's name bringing motor cars from Marble Arch - might have existed independently of the capital whose hinterland it was rapidly annexing. Its author - aptly enough a chartered surveyor by profession - suggested that

The development of Edgware since 1923 has been phenomenal. The contrast between Station Road - a rural thoroughfare with fields on both sides - as it was with what it is would greatly surprise any native who returned after spending a few years abroad. The approach to the tube station is a spacious semi-circular colonnade of remarkable dignity. Opposite the entrance, a very fine block of three-storied shops and offices have been erected on the Mall. Many of the best known firms have acquired premises here. At a moderate estimate there will soon be a population of 40,000 residents within a mile and a half from the Edgware tube station, so that the adjacent shopping centre can hardly fail to become one of great importance. [70]

Certainly the advertisers in the *Guide* presented an image of refined gentility, and seemed to be at pains either to differentiate their services from those that might be on offer in the smoky city, or to claim equal standing. Among the prospectuses for preparatory schools and master builders were puffs for Emile's Ladies Hairdresser who offered an 'efficient and courteous service, in centrally situated and beautifully fitted premises'. The Corner Café adjoining the tube station served tea, lunches and light refreshments 'daintily and quickly in homely comfort', their 'fresh unpreserved cream received daily from Devonshire'. And in a later public-information leaflet for residents of Mill Hill and Edgware of 1934 Leon's exclusive ladies' tailor and furrier of Finchley Road - 'late of New Bond Street' - promised that 'nothing can compare with well-cut tailored wear for smartness - every garment made is personally cut and fitted by myself, and being made on the premises under my constant supervision I am able to guarantee entire satisfaction'.[71] Venossi's Modern Ladies and Gents Salons similarly boasted its metropolitan credentials with 'expert West End staff in attendance' while Palmer's, the 'permanent waving specialists' of Colindale, appeared to be targeting a more reactionary clientele with its assurance of 'no cut-price mass-production work' and 'English assistants only'.[72]

In many ways the parochial prejudices of the independent shopkeeper, which mirrored those of his or her customers, defined the tenor of suburban fashion provision. In 1933 the *New Survey of London* dismissed the idea that such outlets were under threat from 'the growth of large-scale businesses and combinations', citing 'a recent attempt to estimate the proportion of small shops to others in a typical Broadway in the suburbs' which 'showed that out of a total of 187 shops, 130 were independent traders premises, 44 belonged to multiple companies, 11 were local department stores... and 2 were co-operative stores.'[73] More important still than numbers were the values embedded in the small traders' selling style:

His survival is due possibly to his robust individualism, which attracts his customers, as much as to the personal service he gives them. His prejudices and manners, his cheerfulness in the face of real adversity, and the sense of sportsmanship of the customer... as well as his own knowledge of local matters and the sympathy he willingly gives to tales of ill health and personal happenings, give him a hold on his public which is not easily destroyed by the big store, however highly trained in methods of salesmanship are its polite but impersonal staff. The independent trader has more time to give his customer, goods often of equal quality and price, and a clearer knowledge of his local market and its needs, than that possessed by the central or multiple stores.[74]

In answer to such competition the large department stores and multiples often adopted a tone of familiarity which belied the impersonal nature of their transactions. The Oxford Street store D.H. Evans, for example, which styled itself 'London's Most Modern Shop - Planned For Easier Shopping' wooed the conservative housewives of suburbia with complementary vans that travelled as far as Watford, Sidcup, Redhill and Slough despatching customer purchases. According to the delivery map enclosed with the mail-order catalogue for 1939 the more proletarian inhabitants of the eastern fringes were apparently denied this service, but it is doubtful whether the flowery selection of bed jackets and dressing gowns, maids' uniforms, afternoon frocks for the fuller figure, coatees and gowns for evening, tennis wear, deck slacks and beach frocks - many of them named after such sleepy British towns as Padstow, Gillingham, Gainsborough, Fleetwood and Rosslare - would have appealed much to them anyway. In Leyton and Chigwell tastes tended more toward Hollywood than Havering. [75]

Yet it is only through acknowledging that span of possibilities, between glamour and respectable conformity, that the vivid spectrum of modern fashion culture in inter-war London becomes visible. That the increased volume and choice were interpreted in several different ways is clear. The suburbans, for example, were often dismissed by a metropolitan elite as a tribe of unoriginal copyists.[76] As the humorist Charles Duff observed in his satirical *Anthropological Report on a London Suburb* of 1935 : 'They imitate each other in speech, dress and behaviour. They imitate each other in such habits as the angle of wearing a hat, the colour of a necktie and the kind of flowers grown in their gardens.... As I walked along, nearly every house presented the same phenomena: a man in plus fours, a woman in cotton, a dog a la mode, a car and a wireless set... '[77] At the same time the individuality and heightened class-consciousness of outer London's inhabitants also offered endless material for amused and loaded comment.[78]

**❸❺** Sutton High Street Shoppers by an unknown amateur photographer *c*.1930 (Museum of London)

Far from conforming, the partying suburbans on display in K.R.G. Browne's comical memoir *Suburban Days* of 1928 are a picture of lower middle-class status-seeking, their competitive idiosyncracies somehow bolstered by the increased opportunities for unfettered consumption. Here the author and his wife approach with trepidation the house of Mrs Grisley-Goole, the doyenne of Acacia Avenue, SW88:

My hair subdued, we… were admitted by a heavily starched menial, bereft of our outer trappings and shepherded into a large and recklessly illuminated apartment wherein was assembled all that is best and brightest in Acacia Avenue society. Among others we noticed our hostess, in a mauve velvet confection which had somehow the effect of increasing her width and decreasing her height; Mr and Mrs Wheelsmith, the latter in arsenical green, the former in a too tight collar and - though this is guesswork - those patent braces of which he is almost indecently proud; Mrs Thimbleton-Twigg, overpoweringly regal in alpaca and sequins; Mrs Edgeworthy, in jet earrings and her best teeth; the man Edgeworthy, in an odour of moth balls and a state of obvious gloom; the Edgeworthy twins, in puce; Mr Duckett, in elastic-sided boots; and a good deal of Miss Pank, in a garment which, on one of her years and physique, amounted to a public scandal. [79]

How very like, but also subtly distanced from, the clothing and attitudes that might have been on display at Mrs Dalloway's party are the guests of Mrs Grisely-Goole. The velvets and sequins are the quintessence of metropolitan chic, if worn a little too self-consciously. Arguably this equivalence reflected the social changes of the inter-war years which saw the confidence of an established upper middle class rocked by Imperial decline and economic disaster, whilst a newly enfranchised lower-middle class reaped the benefits of mortgages, hire purchase and stable employment in the public and leisure sectors. A 'levelling out' of the cultural and material landscape was perhaps inevitable in these circumstances, but the links between these two presentations of London's social life relate to influences that are also more specific than such generalized political and social developments. As this chapter has attempted to demonstrate, in shopping for her party clothes the London Hostess, of whatever class, was presented with a reinvigorated retail landscape that had expanded to incorporate all of the challenges which modernity proffered. A 'democratization' in dress habits may have been one outcome of this, but the rich influence of cinemas, boutiques and department stores in centre and suburb also helped to germinate the seeds of an individualistic resistance which would bloom in the bomb sites of the following decades. As Alison Settle predicted in 1937:

You cannot expect that the [young] girl will be contented with the old method of changing store stock twice a year and seeing the same merchandise in between. She wants her fashions snappy, both in time and style.[80]

# *The Teddy Boy:*

## LAMBETH, SOHO AND BELGRAVIA
### 1945-1960

It seems to me that the basic principles of our way of life have not changed much. We still like to be ladies and gentlemen and if fewer succeed in so doing then at least more attempt it than would ever have dared to before. But all are fighting to preserve something they believe in. The young man who has just left his public school or University dresses, when in London, in a neat dark suit, with well-pressed narrow trousers, cuffs to the sleeves of his jacket and possibly lapels to his waistcoat. Even if he doesn't indulge in such fashionable details, he would feel uncomfortable in anything other than a hard collar and a bowler hat. His more daring companions may flourish a flowered waistcoat and a velvet-collared coat; but if I mention too eccentric examples I may frighten the reader out of my argument. Let us agree, however, that the average young man of position tries to give an air of substance without being stodgy: of having time for the niceties of life. His appearance may be only demonstrating wishful thinking: that he has several thousand a year in the funds, and that income tax is only a shilling in the pound: that he is prepared to be a good father to a large family. But I think the wish is there all right.[1]

London couturier Hardy Amies captured the complacent, wistful and undeniably elitist tone of early post-war British fashion commentary in his autobiography *Just so Far* of 1954. Having made his name alongside Norman Hartnell, Amies belonged to a generation of designers who had flourished under the auspices of the Incorporated Society of London Fashion Designers as arbiters of a renewed and invigorated version of a distinct London style framed by the conditions of War. Founded in 1942, the Society had proposed to the Government that they design clothing according to Utility regulations that demonstrated how home-front restrictions need not preclude elegance. Through its combination of traditional references (function-specific formal garments) with an ostensibly more utopian, democratic direction (new synthetic fabrics and an expansion of diffusion lines), their ongoing work was broadly in tune with the dialectical tendencies of cultural production in 1940s and 1950s Britain which waxed nostalgically for pre-war certainties while setting its sights firmly on the testing concerns of national reconstruction. By time of the Queen's accession in 1952, with fellow Society members Peter Russell, Charles Creed, Digby Morton, Michael Sherard, Victor Stiebel and John Cavanagh, Amies and Hartnell fostered a highly tailored, Anglo-Saxon variation on the New Look which transported the romantic escapism of Dior's Paris confections from the Seine to the Thames. Countless promotional fashion shoots produced to promote British fashion featured immaculate models, whose rather imperious beauty hinted at an Albion unbowed by years of bombs and rationing. They typically graced the stage-set of a ceremonial and seemingly unchanged capital city in the boned corsets, high heels and frou-frou petticoats which announced an end to the frugal inconveniences of austerity. In the most familiar scenarios the patrician facades of Horse Guards Parade, Trafalgar Square, the British Museum and the club-land of St James formed the desired backdrops for an astonishing display of female dandyism.

This juxtaposition of London's Imperial topography with the silk and netting of the couturier's salon is an intriguing one, suggestive of wider concerns that the coming of a feminized and largely American-influenced mass-consumer culture would further weaken London's diminishing reputation as a political and economic centre of Empire. However, while the fortunes of the home textile and luxury-goods industries were clearly increasingly reliant on the important patronage of middle-class women in the boutiques and department stores of the capital - even as the docks and other traces of traditional masculine labour declined and the markets of the former colonies disappeared - London's enduring symbolic status as a man's city, spiritual home to the gentleman and all of his sartorial trappings, appears if anything to have been strengthened during this vital transitional period. Amies's pertinent reflections on the clothing of his own sex were underpinned by his growing interest in the potential of the menswear market as a field for creative and economic exploitation. By the end of the 1950s he was installed as consultant for the multiple tailoring firm Hepworth's, and almost in anticipation of this his description of the evolving dress code of the aspirant young man about town is far more redolent of a long-established code for London life than the more synthetic drafting of Parisian style onto the London scene that characterized the self-consciously patriotic activities of the Incorporated Society.[2]

The co-ordinates of what had become known as the 'New-Edwardian' look are clearly discernible in Amies's prose. This was a 'revivalist' style of masculine dressing displayed in its most self-assured and 'aristocratic' incarnation in Norman Parkinson's iconic photograph of 1950, titled *Back to Formality: Savile Row* which featured a group of English gentlemen elegantly conversing in the Mayfair sunshine.[3] Kitted-out in smoothly streamlined formal business dress they have rejected the more capacious and baggy 'one-size-fits-all' hang of the Utility and demob clothing that served its purpose in the drab circumstances of the recent past, opting for a swaggering return to the panache of early twentieth-century sartorial styles - styles that themselves paid conscious homage to the Regency London of Beau Brummell. Bowler hats, highly polished shoes and tightly rolled umbrellas provide a hint of the regimental glamour of the parade ground while velvet collars, embellished waistcoats, ticket pockets, covered buttons and turned-back cuffs recall the ostentation of the race track and the music hall.

**❸❻**

*Back to Formality: Savile Row*
by Norman Parkinson, 1950
(Norman Parkinson Estate)

In a deft example of synchronization Max Beerbohm - the last of the great English dandies - died in 1956, just as the dandy style was achieving a new notoriety on the streets of his home city. His diminutive but dapper figure and his biting wit had marked him out as a natural chronicler (through the miniaturizing lens of his writings and his caricatures) of the circle of Wilde and Beardsley in the 1890s, and during that decade he had produced a definitive essay (titled *Dandies and Dandies*) on the nature and history of dandyism. In this text Beerbohm set down the philosophy which governed his own attitude to life and to his wardrobe: a mask-like trick of expending great effort with the minimum of evidence on outcomes which themselves betrayed the utmost simplicity through their 'easy' surface sheen. Literary theorist Robert Viscusi illustrates how the dandy as idea, body and text conjoin in Beerbohm's lustrous life as in his publications: 'Dandies make themselves. Whatever they may be by birth and nurture, dandies are born anew as dandies when they dress themselves according to the dandy code. The dandy self, naked and fresh, is a figure in black and white. Completely dressed, almost completely monochrome, he is, to put it simply, a written thing.'[4] Elements of Beerbohm's wardrobe survive at the Museum of London. Dating from the golden Edwardian era, before he lived almost wholly in exile from modernity in the Italian Villa to which he had first retreated in the 1920s, the clothing, like the regular radio broadcasts which Beerbohm continued to make for the BBC, speaks of the formal grace of a largely forgotten London. An evening suit impeccably tailored in black wool and a soft brown (originally heather-coloured) smoking jacket trimmed with velvet and braid suggest a life lived permanently according to the stylish rituals of Mayfair before the First World War.[5] In their stubborn adherence to a set of rules which were soon to be swept away, and their strange timelessness, they also evoke the power of Dandyism to reinvigorate and renew while maintaining a seeming reverence for conservative or traditional values. The re-writing of the dandy code along new class-lines and recontested territories in the transformed and transforming London of the 1950s thus lend Beerbohm's 'hand-me-downs' a posthumous significance.

**3 7**
Swallow tail coat belonging to Max Beerbohm, c.1910 (Museum of London)

Smoking jacket belonging to Max Beerbohm, c.1910 (Museum of London)
**3 8**

As a city of concrete spaces and intangible atmospheres, post-war London figured as a crucible for such stylistic change and reinvention, but all in the context of continuity. Roy Porter alludes to the period as an Indian Summer, with all the hazy and nostalgic possibilities that the phrase suggests: 'the trams sailed majestically through pea-soupers; East Enders had their knees-up at the pub and went hop-picking in August; contented commuters... tended their herbaceous borders... variety enjoyed its swan song at the Hackney and Deptford Empires... The coronation of Elizabeth II in 1953, when chummy neighbourhood parties were staged in bunting festooned streets, was the high spot of London as a prosperous, well-integrated, secure, safe city'.[6] This is the London of sepia childhood memories, a paradise before the (to some commentators) hellish onslaught of sexual emancipation, global recession and social disintegration that marked later decades. Yet as the 1950s progressed, premonitions of an unsettling modernity were more keenly felt. Porter notes the destruction of Park Lane's Regency terraces in 1956 by developer Charles Clore, pulled down to make way for the Hilton hotel and setting a precedent for Richard Seifert's more intensive colonization of the city's eighteenth- and nineteenth-century skyline. As tower blocks shadowed church spires, new moral codes infiltrated the stuffiness of an official metropolitan culture still run on Victorian lines, leading to 'a rare alliance between youth culture and commerce, aristocratic style and a new populism'. This 'breath of fresh air' was felt nowhere more keenly than in the changes affecting men's clothing, and a tracing of its consequences in this field forms the basis of this chapter. Popular historian Harry Hopkins, writing ten years later, from the cool vantage point of the mid-1960s, pinpointed the social ramifications of a London-based masculine style revival, whose expressive and exotic appeal seemed as rooted in the post-war cityscape as the new juxtaposition of plate-glass and steel which jostled for space with 'the time-honoured observances of cornice and moulding, pediment and column':

And thus it came about that a brief, discreet fashion revival among young men about town in the West End in 1948... a very tentative riposte to the women's 'New Look'... crossed the River and, exaggerated - almost consciously guyed - became the defiant uniform of what the newspapers were soon calling the 'New Edwardians'. But most significant perhaps, was the Teddy outfit's function as the badge of a half-formed, inarticulate radicalism... A sort of half-conscious thumbing-of-the-nose, it was designed to establish that the lower orders could be as arrogant and as to-the-manor-born as the toffee-nosed ones across the River... The uniform's most important features lay, firstly, in the fact that... it was, in origin, English class-based, secondly in its cost which... might exceed £100... The Teddy costume conquered district after district in those years, making the fortunes of many a little corner tailor - and hairdresser - astute enough to 'humour the kids'. But, finally... the uniform gave way before the... gentler, more civilised, immensely variegated Italian and Continental styles which seemed to confirm and usher the opening society. And in England, where male fashions had always been one of those 'understood' things - essentially aristocratic, fear-edged, inhibition inlaid - nothing, it seemed, could ever be the same again.[7]

# THE MORALITY OF AFFLUENCE

Hopkins's account of the rise of the 'Teddy' style, which traces its origins as a whim of upper-class playboys in Mayfair, its migration to the deprived boroughs of south and east London, its symbolic importance as a mode of social resistance, and its rapid commercialization at the hands of a growing retail sector adapted to the desires of the teenager, has become an oft-repeated mantra of sociologists and historians of popular culture alike. In the rather unprepossessing frame of the newly fashion-conscious post-war adolescent, journalists, academics and style pundits have all been able to inscribe a range of narratives that position the Teddy Boy at the centre of debates whose subjects have been as various as the collapse of traditional working-class values, the inevitability of crime in a time of affluence and expanding state welfare, the homogenizing effects of American culture and the impact of supposedly new forms of teenage consumption on all of the above. It could be argued that in the rush to elicit significant meaning from hairstyles, postures and jacket styles, commentators have succeeded only in reducing a vibrant and ephemeral mode of sartorial behaviour to a rather generalized and mundane shorthand for social change, much of it negative in tone. In this version of history the Teddy Boy is pinned down as the first in a succession of subcultural stances whose fragile features have increasingly come to bear the crushing weight of late twentieth-century cultural analysis - teenage style deputizing in a postmodern world for the absences of old philosophies and religions.

It is not the overt intention of this chapter to place yet another level of interpretation over the exhausted frame of the New Edwardian. What is more necessary, in the face of readings which have too readily interpreted the teddy boy as a reactionary and racist dupe or a cipher for Americanized modernity, is a rather delicate act of excavation - the retrieval of fugitive attitudes and appearances from the street-dust and scholarly detritus in which they have laid buried or ignored. The Teddy Boy was indeed a significant actor on the post-war social scene, his features and actions taken up for immediate analysis by newspaper columnists, Picture Post photographers, radical and popular film-makers, even criminologists. But in the rush for explanations his more tenuous connections to place, his ghostly status as another London myth, and his temporal reliance on the city's sartorial and social infrastructures have perhaps been lost or overlooked. Once uncovered, these traces might offer important clues to London's enduring reputation as a site for testing fashionable boundaries at the level of the street and among the fugitive young.

The lecture hall dissections ensued long before the teddy-boy style was announced officially dead by that chronicler of nascent youth cultures Colin MacInnes, who in his essay *Smart Schmutter* of 1965 stated that 'though caricaturists (who really ought to start looking a bit - even the best of them) still draw dated Ted stereotypes, the style, in its authentic pure absurdity, is now only to be found in outlying holes and corners (I last saw it in a caff at Goring-on-Thames)'.[8] Sociologist T.R. Fyvel produced the first classic account of the mode in his 1961 text *The Insecure Offenders*. He identified its

English origins in an attempt by Savile Row tailors 'to regain the leadership in men's styles' in the late 1940s, relating this to a 'slightly pretentious revolt' by 'the young dandies who after the war strolled through the West End, wearing longer jackets, tighter trousers, curled bowler hats ... making a proclamation... against the despised social levelling brought in by the Labour government and the new mass culture from America'. Fyvel claimed that by 1950 'the Edwardian style in its full bloom had utterly and unexpectedly transported itself across the Thames to working-class South London, where its music-hall like exaggeration found an appeal amongst gang-members and petty criminals'. From there the uniform came to signify a sullen rejection of 'respectability' in preference for the easy attractions of a life passed on the borders between the legal and the illicit.[9] In Fyvel's case this signification bore material consequences which linked the Tony Curtis hairstyles, 'slim jim' ties and crepe-soled creepers adopted by the hoodlums who terrorized his own North London habitat to a generalized deterioration of the physical environment of the inner city and the passing of so-called 'traditional' proletarian family values for a selfish celebration of individuality and short-term pleasure. Here was a picture of decline visible from the window of his own top-floor maisonette :

*Teddy Boys in North Kensington* by Roger Mayne, 1958 (Museum of London) ❸ ❾

Each Saturday and Sunday towards dark... I could see the small dark figures of boys and half-grown youths... in twos and threes or larger groups... wearing the identical Teddy boy suits. All... made off in the same direction, towards the main streets beyond the big railway stations, an untidy area of converging streets and crowded traffic, of shops, cinemas, public-houses and bright lights, aesthetically a God-awful wilderness, but to the boys obviously representing life with a capital L.

I sometimes thought that one could see the social wasteland through which they wandered in actual visual terms. North of the Estate lay row upon row of squat nineteenth-century slum streets, with bomb gaps of fifteen years before still showing... Now they stood condemned and so were harshly degraded, like a whole way of life... together with memories of worn doorsteps, dark passages, mother at the sink and father shirt-sleeved in the kitchen with his newspaper...

To the young... it did not matter that in its back streets this was a dispiriting region of blank warehouses, untidy street markets and sleazy lodging houses. In the main streets at any rate, the young felt surrounded by a full tide of confident life... reflected in the ultra-modern layout of the chainstores; in shop windows crammed with radios, television sets, record players... This London, offering its pleasures freely to those with money, spoke with the only voice of authority that mattered. The importance of their homes had dwindled; work meant little.[10]

Like a well-meaning Victorian philanthropist, Fyvel proceeded to illustrate the destructive tendencies of urban modernity, and of capitalism in particular, through recourse to detailed case-studies of those 'delinquent' young men whose pleasures disturbed his evenings, listing their expenditure on clothing and other luxuries, grading their leisure haunts and analysing their social prejudices. His was a mode of investigation that (perhaps cynically?) drew great and evocative resonances from the textures of life which it aimed to describe, while reserving a palpable disdain for the material evidence which constituted the style itself (which was clearly assumed to be lacking in taste and unattractive). Thus the trappings of working-class dandyism, though spectacular in their expense and visual effects, symbolized little more than a false-consciousness, a naive trust in the power of consumerism to transform humdrum realities. Furthermore, this false-consciousness was seemingly so persuasive and pandemic that Fyvel felt it necessary to show how its consequences could be felt globally from the Soviet Union to the United States. London was simply one among many examples of a local culture in retreat from a general and coarsening vulgarity.

Later academic interpretations, predicated on an understanding of 'culture' as a constructed and mediated practice, rather than a universalizing instrument of value-laden comparisons, have taken a less totalizing view of the teddy-boy phenomenon. Texts including Paul Rock and Stanley Cohen's essay on 'The Teddy Boy' which appeared in Bogdanor and Skidelsky's 1970 collection *The Age of Affluence* have been more sympathetic to the idea that clothing and material culture might aid a negotiated sense of self-identification rather than disguising some older notion of authenticity. Yet in their clear celebration of the romantic ideal of the working-class rebel, Rock and Cohen came close to supplanting one weighted version of reality with another. Their concern was to highlight the way in which the trajectory of the Teddy Boy was as much a case of press hysteria, a process of journalistic misrepresentation, as it was a sequence of commercial and social transactions which placed the sartorial choices of slum dwellers on a par with those of West End socialites. In the end theirs is a discourse based on a premise of ownership, both of the image of delinquency as it was propounded by reactionary journalists, and of the practice of an attitude and philosophy which in their reading found its most compelling and novel incarnation on the deprived streets of Lambeth rather than in the louche bars of Mayfair. Dick Hebdige in his highly influential deconstruction of British subcultural styles, published in the late 1970s as Punk waned and Thatcherism promised to transform the social landscape, took a similarly proprietorial tone in relation to a selective trajectory of musical and fashion-related tastes - which for the author signified a rather utopian celebration of 'authentic' black popular cultures by white male working-class pioneers stretching back to the modernists of the early 1960s. For Hebdige the Teddy Boy, 'uncompromisingly proletarian and xenophobic', represented little more than a retrograde denial of the 'real' roots of rock and roll.[11]

It is left to Geoffrey Pearson to puncture this residual understanding that subcultural activities can be co-opted meaningfully to particular political and moral ends by their investigators. Such caricatures, he states, 'have offered a convenient metaphor of social change... The entrance of the dazzling war babies in their Ted suits, understood as harbingers of irresponsible affluence and rootless materialism, seemed to fit the bill precisely'. However,

What was and is totally submerged in the conventional understanding of the Teddy boys was that their style and demeanour was by no means unprecedented. Their rough fighting, territorial edginess, for example, is better understood as a continuation of earlier forms of gang-life in working-class neighbourhoods - rather than a sudden departure from tradition. So, too, the Teds had borrowed large parts of their supposedly unprecedented cultural equipment from earlier youth cultures... It is clear that the conventional picture of the sudden and unrivalled appearance of the 'affluent' and 'Americanised' Teddy Boys... must be seen as a gross distortion of the actual events.[12]

The phrase 'territorial edginess' stands out in Pearson's account as the most suggestive route by which further investigation of the Teddy Boy phenomenon might proceed, for in a basic geographical and temporal, as well as in a more conceptual sense, it is his location at the borders between north and south, central and inner, respectable and dangerous London, his emergence on the cusp of pre- and post-war social and cultural attitudes, and the sense in which he floats across the class, racial and sexual divisions of the capital that makes the Teddy Boy such a beguiling and evocative metropolitan figure. At the time of his notoriety, bohemian writers and artists as diverse as MacInnes, John Minton and the young Joe Orton were attracted by the possibilities which the bombsites of working-class London held for erotic adventure and self-transformation. The proletarian dandy emerged as a 'romantic' hero of those spaces - an attractive focus for desires and aspirations that seem to have persisted as a form of urban folk legend. A denizen of the edge, his shifting identities are so contingent on these historical, imaginative and spatial specificities that it is best perhaps simply to return to the scenes of his 'crimes' before attempting any more ambitious an interpretation of his elusive energies.

# WE ARE THE LAMBETH BOYS

When director Karel Reisz and photographer Walter Lassally produced their affecting portrait of the lives and fantasies of the members of a south London youth club in the film *We are the Lambeth Boys* in 1958 they were consciously attempting to portray their subjects in a manner which avoided the value judgements and pre-conceptions of the sociologist or the cultural critic. One of the most enduring examples of a series of films produced by Reisz and other young film-makers as part of the project 'Free Cinema', the *Lambeth Boys* aimed to challenge the orthodoxies which were deemed to be prevalent in cinematic practice and in society at large, re-emphasizing the social responsibilities of the artist and avoiding the distortions of commercialization. Most importantly, such films strove to stimulate a visual and emotional liveliness through the 'unmediated' directness of their technique, inspiring personal expression from all involved - author, subject and audience - by their recognition of the poetic significance of the 'everyday'. Laying aside the heavy idealism, which by contemporary standards appears impossibly naive, Reisz's tender evocation of a week's work and pleasure among the self-consciously fashionable working-class teenagers of Kennington (a district of Lambeth) provides a revelatory glimpse of a society in transition between the familial duties and work expectations of an older generation, and the more fluid networks of friendship and pleasure which the modern city offered. Most startlingly, the film is a snapshot of the Teddy Boy craze as it affected living and situated consumers. These are not the shadowy and threatening figures of Fyvel's nightmares or the partisan hooligans of Hebdige's thesis; instead, as they engage in a game of backyard cricket, exchange flirtatious banter with female members of the club, discuss the cost of modern tailoring, pose on the edges of the dance-floor or wheel their bicycles toward school assembly or first jobs, Reisz's Teddy Boys, resplendent in the requisite slim ties and pointed shoes of their cult and choreographed against a (slightly incongruous) soundtrack of modern jazz, represent a mode of citizenship with far more positive overtones - brimming with self-confident promise.

Other, competing representations of the south London mise en scene were not so complimentary. Ten years before, in one of several social and economic surveys of post-blitz London commissioned in the late 1940s, Harry Williams had portrayed a district be-devilled by poverty of spirit and a grim sense of ennui. 'Ugliness', he stated, 'was the dominant impression of our visit, tiredness the next. The white drawn faces of the women shoppers, picking over the rubbish on sale with dispirited fingers, the unnatural quietness of the children, the sullen brooding withdrawal of the men spoke of a state of affairs never approached during the worst moments of the war.'[13] This is a rhetorical account of austerity not so far removed from the dehumanizing reports on the East End poor which had characterized touristic writings of the late nineteenth century. Williams relied on the same dismissive terminology that had been employed by Mayhew, Besant and Booth to describe the cheap offerings of the countless street markets which had marked the territory for outsiders two and three generations before. Money, he implies, was not necessarily in short supply, though a 'tawdry' choice of goods and the lack of a will to spend compromised the desire to consume in any manner that would have made sense to a visiting middle-class journalist. More shocking still was the apparent lack of self-respect evidenced by the bodies of the locals: 'Taken all in all they are a poor lot. Some of the young girls are fine and upstanding - the women are notably better than the men - and a handful of athletic young men may catch the eye, but look closer at the herd. Bowed shoulders, spindly legs, concave chests, weak eyes... bad teeth... small frames... grey faces... Look for yourself and see.'[14] Though clearly damning in the most unsympathetic of terms, Williams's repulsed reactions shed some light on the threatened reactions which the 'alien' figure of the Teddy Boy aroused in observers who had perhaps come to expect only grey submission from the sad streets across the Thames; and his topography of dingy markets and dowdy local shops evokes a scenario in which working-class dandies might find copious and adaptable retail outlets for the purchase of their wardrobes together with a ready-made 'outdoor' theatre for their eventual display. Here was a long-standing and 'hidden' culture of the street corner and the crowd, a sublime and gritty setting for shameless acts of sartorial delinquency.

Delinquency was a subject which also concerned the respondents of a *Mass Observation Report* of the same year (1949) who aimed to record the habits of 'problem' juveniles in similar inner-London slum districts. The language of the report had not yet picked up on the Teddy-Boy terminology favoured by the newspapers, so that descriptions of the clothing and posture adopted by young gang-members were intriguingly free of the familiar references to aristocratic or West End modes of dressing, preferring instead to cite the influence of Hollywood or more localized sartorial characterizations as the source of a collective look - which in all other respects adhered to the flamboyant visual register of the dandy aristocrats of Mayfair. Bored and pointless acts of destructive energy were typically bracketed with transgressive sartorial tastes, making sense of a blitzed and jagged urban landscape in which the presence of violence was constantly referenced:

Two youths, ages about 18, are standing outside a dairy. They pick up between them a large crate of empty milk bottles and throw them in the road, breaking all of them... they run across the road and join a gang of youths numbering about 15 or 16. Most of them are dressed very flashily - striped flannels and 'house coat' style of belted jacket; large, loosely knotted, plain coloured ties; and several of them are wearing the wide-brimmed American style of trilby. Long 'side-boards' are a prominent feature with the majority of them.[15]

The standard wardrobe of these young men, with its belted jacket, loose flannels, bright tie and extravagant hat, paid clear homage to the enduring style of the gangster film, a source of inspiration to British adolescents since well before the war and not especially linked to London.[16] Certainly it was a look which lent some force to the swaggering demeanour of the dance-hall habitues noted by the mass-observers, its loose and flapping layers well adapted to a slouching, hands-in-pockets, collar-turned-up, street-corner posture.[17] More specific to the circumstances of working-class London was the choice of the epithets 'Spiv' and 'Dago' to describe an ostentatious flaunting of garish accessories, a combination of formal and casual items and what was interpreted as an 'effeminate' obsession with the hair:

Three youths of a 'spiv' type have sauntered in. They are all wearing grey pin-striped flannels and the 'house coat' style of jacket. Two of them are wearing white shirts with a vivid paisley tie, whilst the other is in a brilliant open-necked sports shirt. All these have carefully cared for hair - long with artificial waves, and a heavily greased 'Boston slash back' in two cases.[18]

Like the Teddy Boy, his predecessor the 'Spiv' was a figure rooted firmly in the realm of caricature, but whose extreme characteristics bore that sense of familiarity encouraged by an acquaintance with real versions on the street (caricatures generally drawing their power from a close observation of the living world). Harry Hopkins recalled his ubiquitous presence in the life of the nation as 'an abstraction'. The Spiv was 'a figure in a modern morality play. The convention was rapidly established by the pocket cartoonists... peaked shoulders, the wasp waist, the dazzle tie, the hoarse behind-the-hand whisper 'Nylons'.'[19] During the War and in the early years of the Welfare State the Spiv's flouting of the rules (circumnavigating the restrictions of rationing with a ready supply of black-market luxuries) positioned his conspicuous delight in display as a taboo. Again, like the Teddy Boy, he established his patch in the markets, pubs and backstreets of London's poorer districts and marked out his pantomimic role through excessive grooming.[20] But while the Spiv adopted the moustachioed glamour of the latin crooner as a fitting disguise - good looks aiding his professional role as a swindler and inveigler of female clients, the Teddy Boy called on an extensive battery of styling techniques that placed his prouder narcissism more firmly in the spotlight with no practical justification. As T.R. Fyvel remarked, hairstyles 'were a source of particular pride and attention to their wearers and were acquired by appointments with special barbers, which involved the use of dryers and hairnets and cost between 7s 6d and 15s for a setting, a considerable outlay for young wage earners.[21]

Thus by 1949, though *Mass Observation* doesn't name him as such, the figure of the Teddy Boy was rapidly emerging (sartorially) as a particular working-class London type: Anglo-Irish or 'cockney' in his associations in contrast to the continental and American preferences of London's sizeable Italian and Maltese gang members. Though he drew some inspiration from the 'spivvy' style which Colin MacInnes coined 'American Drape', which 'hit Charing Cross Road in the late 40's and constituted the first underground revolt against wartime uniforms and sackcloth and the whole 'Men's Wear' conception of English male attire', his evolving look was far more negotiated, deliberately differentiated and consequently even more subversive.[22] Rather than lifting an idea of sharp respectability straight from the movies or stealing it wholesale from memories of GI magnificence, the New Edwardianism of the Teddy Boy located its referents closer to home, in the grey grime of the inner suburbs, among the stilted hair-

**❹ ⓞ** *Charing Cross Road Shop Window* by Henry Grant, 1951 (Museum of London)

cut photographs and pots of brilliantine that gathered dust in the windows of high-street barber shops or the countless tailor's notices which simultaneously announced the ease with which trousers could be tapered to the latest style.[23] Almost parochial in their styled outrages against the accepted way of being, the young of Lambeth engaged in a struggle which ironically bound them closer to home. Local historian Mary Chamberlain recalls how the working-class culture south of the Thames positively encouraged the attention to surfaces and distinction, that proof of selfhood which the Teddy Boy's uniform so effectively communicated:

Those dreamy acres were far from 'monotonous' and far from monolithic. They were the battleground where a war of class and status was fought and defended. It mattered if you took in washing, visited the pawn shop, if shoes were unpolished and clothing torn. It mattered if you drank tea from a saucer, if the table was not laid, if the curtains were not washed weekly. It mattered because in those finer rituals and finer manners lay a definition of self, and a differentiation from the neighbourhood, a way of circumventing and resisting the threat of destitution which lurked forever round every corner of working-class neighbourhoods.[24]

# OUT OF MAYFAIR

Journalist and bon viveur Douglas Sutherland claimed to have encountered as barren and despondent a sartorial scene on returning to London's West End in 1945 as Harry Williams had stumbled across in Lambeth. The indignities of clothes rationing seemed to be designed deliberately to embarrass any pretender who sought re-entry into London's post-war social throng. Sutherland, however, was able to pass muster through his skilful adaptation of some cast-offs formerly belonging to an acquaintance who was in show business:

The two suits I took, not without some diffidence, to that most elegant of all tailoring establishments, Messrs Kilgour, French and Stanbury, in Dover Street. So it came about that, in shabby suited London, I suddenly blossomed into one of the best dressed men-about-town, such was the genius of Messrs Kilgour, French and Stanbury. It was also quite fun, when envious acquaintances used to inquire the secret of my sartorial magnificence, to flash at them the label sewn on my inside jacket pocket which still bore the name of Mr Oscar Hammerstein.[25]

This confident approximation of style gained through the author's privileged access to elite tailoring provision and his surreptitious borrowing from the shabby-genteel world of bohemia, is as good a summary as any of the factors pertaining in 'fashionable' late 1940s London which contributed toward the success of the Edwardian look and its variants in both 'upper-class' and avant-garde circles. The combination of constrained circumstances, a rather 'raffish' relaxation of moral and social codes, together with a nostalgic yearning for the leisured lifestyle of a pre-war fairyland effectively dictated a dress code which was by turns tightly controlled, impossibly presumptuous, often misleading and because of that rather tragic. Sutherland's passage through the louche mews pubs of Kensington and Chelsea, the patrician afternoon drinking clubs of Mayfair's Shepherd Market and the exclusive Thursday Club of Fitzrovia (whose membership included royalty, actors, painters, society photographers and literary editors) in the final years of the decade furnished him with a gallery of aristocratic rogues and losers whose singular appearance set the context for a look which never strayed far from the theatrical or the deceptive. The Star Tavern, behind Belgrave Square was a typical Knightsbridge destination, home to a collection of undoubtedly rich, if reckless, spenders of their inheritances [and] others whose financial backgrounds were less impressive but who nonetheless were eager to be regarded as young men-about-town of good social background…what they had in common was a certain vagueness about their social background coupled with an insistence that they had enjoyed a public school education. They also shared a liking for Savile Row suits, and such ostentatiously displayed gee-gaws as Cartier watches, gold cigarette lighters and recently hyphenated surnames.[26]

Savile Row, whose well-crafted products finally made their way (by one means or other) onto the backs of Sutherland's privileged Belgravian wasters, maintained a distanced froideur as the focus for a more respectable renaissance. Immediately before the war the environs of Old Bond Street had witnessed the maturing of a home-grown couture industry whose opulence almost rivalled that of Paris. Fashion journalist Francis Marshall described what was left in 1944, noting that 'the most famous salons are nearly all within a small area of the West End, many being in Bruton Street and Grosvenor Street. They range from elaborately decorated salons with the most modern decor of mirrors, glistening chandeliers, stuffed satin upholstery and baroque ornaments, to the dress shop which is little more than a small flat on a top floor of Brook Street'.[27] Hardy Amies's move to Savile Row and the ongoing development of the Incorporated Society of London Fashion Designers after the war continued the discrete glamorization of this quarter of the West End, and though the focus was predominantly on the marketing of a very English and aristocratic version of femininity, the rising importance of menswear made a significant impact on the tenor of its streets, not least through the influence of classic tailoring techniques on the style and 'hang' of London couture, but also through the reticent business culture associated with the world of the tailor. In 1953 The British Travel and Holiday Association produced a guide to shopping in the capital which asserted that 'Bond Street is to London what the Rue de la Paix is to Paris, but with this difference; whereas the Rue de la Paix is a broad and pretentious street that carries its distinctions with an… air of self importance, Bond Street seems to be concerned only with self-effacement'.[28] The good manners of the Savile Row suit thus lent a quiet restraint to the district and though the profound luxury of its finish was never in question, any ostentatious flouting of those qualities would have seemed impossibly rude.

As a symbol of tradition the suit maintained a powerful grip on definitions of Britishness in the post-war era. A.W. Allon of the tailoring-trade press stated in 1949 that 'in an age of tremendous industrialisation it is good to know that one craft at least retains its position in the general scheme of things - as solidly important as ever. Indeed the craft of tailoring has become more than just the means of making a living: it has become a fundamental part of the British way of life'.[29] In the context of a sartorial sense of Britishness, London played a distinctive role. An R.J. Pescod writing in the same tailoring compendium as Allon paid appropriate homage to the superiority of 'West End' cutting techniques which in the nineteenth century distinguished the clothing of the 'upper ten' from the provincial styles of the middle classes. A combination of factors, including a well-judged sharpness in the making-up of seams, creases and darts, high-quality textiles and a relaxed ease of wear, identified the Savile Row pedigree of a suit, and while distinctions had since become less easy to spot, to the trained eye of the artisan or the discerning consumer there was 'a difference - difficult as it is to define. There is a subtle quality about the suit which emanates from the West End today which sets its seal upon the place of its origin as the indisputable Mecca of good tailoring'.[30] Working against the odds Pescod attempted to delineate precisely what that quality constituted in terms of a specific style. The single-breasted waistcoat boasted 'narrow shoulders, deep armholes, and rather long points'. The single-breasted lounge jacket was marked by its 'gracefulness of outline' and 'comfort'. 'The waist is moderately defined and the hips are fairly close. A medium amount of drape is provided.' Finally in the evening-dress coat Savile Row saw its finest product. 'In no other garment... is there such scope for the cutter's skill... many of the finest examples of evening dress wear have come from houses in the West End; and London is proud of such work. The long sweeping lapels, the tapering skirt - these are the main points of style that should be noted.'[31]

Though essentially conservative and locked into a long tradition of understatement, it is clear that the components of the Savile Row suit in 1949 were adaptable to the subtle exaggerations that would constitute the New Edwardian style for the aristocratic equivalents of Lambeth's Teddy Boys. The editorials and letters pages of the trade journal *Men's Wear* traced the ways in which its more flamboyant components were a gradual response both to the enforced deprivations of textile shortages and to a desire for distinction and display among those who sat at the edges of the establishment or in the demi-monde which was as powerful as that felt by young working-class men whose world-limits lay across Waterloo Bridge or along the Mile End Road. In 1947 the frustrations of austerity were causing concern. Under the shocking header 'Burlington Arcade had pyjamas at 11s' a correspondent reported that

"The East End has come to the West End". In these words a representative of Noble Jones, hosiers and shirtmakers in London's exclusive Burlington Arcade, W1, described the appearance of considerably cheaper than usual lines in West End hosiers' windows. A 'Men's Wear' reporter saw utility pyjamas at 11s, ties at 4s 6d and shirts at 9s 11d in the famous shopping thoroughfare... "We can't get much else" a leading hosier said..."It is a complete stalemate" he went on. "People with taste just won't buy this stuff, and yet it is the only type of thing we get these days." [32]

Five years later, as the spectre of clothes rationing faded, London's resurgent social calendar dictated a greater degree of formality, and an attention to self-presentation among men which bordered on the extravagant. In April 1952 the headline boasted 'Men now Dress-Clothes Conscious at West End Restaurants says Berkley West, Men's Wear Style Critic'. The article continued:

Eighteen months ago London's Savoy Hotel put a ban on admittance to its restaurant in the evenings unless one wore dinner jacket suit or tails. Within six months the ban was lifted. The attempt to restore pre-war sartorial standards failed... partly because it was made too soon after the end of clothes rationing; and partly because it was impractical to enforce the rule on foreign visitors... Only a few of London's West End hotels, restaurants and clubs now demand tenir-rigeur. Perhaps it is for this very reason that men now, quite voluntarily dress for dinner in the West End, even when unaccompanied by ladies... At private parties too, men's styles are attracting... more attention than women's gowns. When the Spanish Marquis Pardo de Santayana gave a party recently at his Hyde Park Gate flat, men's styles were so outstanding that they were commented on by several consumer newspapers. Reason, on this occasion, was the array of coloured and embroidered waistcoats worn with single breasted dinner-jacket suits. [33]

Throughout the coronation year *Men's Wear* journalists continued to hail the return of formal styles of dress and the much needed boost they gave to those in the business who relied on the sale of accessories. Commentators associated features such as the embroidered waistcoat or the turned-back cuff with 'the top end of the trade', although by the autumn of that year the wider take-up of the trend was gathering pace. In October 'a Pathe pictorial film in Technicolour, featuring the clothes worn by sporting, stage and radio stars' was released with great anticipation. As *Men's Wear* proclaimed, 'the four minute feature, entitled 'Man About Town'... will focus the attention of millions of cinema goers on men's clothes... designed and styled both for comfort and appearance, and not just produced to standard patterns... Filmed at the Victoria and Albert Museum, among the treasures of the past, the picture suggests... that the colourful male costumes of bygone days have not given place completely to body covering which has no creative genius, but, rather, that they have been succeeded in this age by a new and modern conception of styling'.[34] The lubricating effects of show-business and celebrity played a crucial role in both popularizing and to an extent neutralizing a masculine look that veered dangerously toward the louche and the stagey, for in its theatrical incarnation the New-Edwardian style was rapidly coded as sexually subversive. In its most extreme variations the tightly tailored bodies of Savile Row's camper followers paid allegiance to a dandified philosophy of life in which elegant repose and a certain withdrawal from the humdrum bother of modern living could be summed up in the placing of a button hole or the height of a shirt collar. Cecil Beaton and Kenneth Tynan produced a typical celebration of the arch 'Edwardian' outlook in their publication *Persona Grata* of 1953. As an apt example the theatrical entrepreneur Hugh 'Binkie' Beaumont sprawled in profile on a chaise longue across one of Beaton's photographs. Tynan's acerbic prose described the effect :

Beaumont, who is forty three years old... is the eminence grise of English Drama. Out of self defence he has become an enigma, and it suits him, his was never an emphatic personality, and he has little truck with personal wealth or imperatorial whim... His social manner is flawless, twinkling without smugness, shining without slickness; the gestures are soft and self-effacing, inducing a gentle hipnosis... as he talks he smokes, insatiably but smoothly, never in nervous sucks... His trick of holding his cigarette between the middle two fingers while wearing a monogrammed signet ring on the little

**0 0** *Binkie Beaumont* by Cecil Beaton, 1953 (Sothebys)

one, represents his only homage to dandyism. Vocally… favouring a lazy, glazed, leaning tenor, which irons out its sentences as if they were so many silk shirts. 'Terrible' is the universal epithet.[35]

Ultimately it was Beaumont's body as much as his clothing which marked him out as a 'true' dandy, the softness of his voice deputizing for the luxury of silk shirts. But perhaps this was the logical destination for a sartorial practice which lost its visible and refined potency at a moment when refinement, modernity, outrage and all those other dandified preserves were opened up to a teenage market on an unprecedented commercial scale. In such a context distinction could only be marked by rather than on the body. As pop journalist Nik Cohn stated almost twenty years later, 'the Edwardian look... lasted 'til about 1954, by which time it had been taken up and caricatured by the teddy boys, who made it so disreputable that even homosexuals were embarrassed to wear it. Nothing could have been more ironic: having started as an upper-class defence, Edwardiana now formed the basis for the first great detonation of male working-class fashion'.[36] In confirmation of Cohn's analysis Men's Wear had anxiously attempted to retrieve what had been a tailoring godsend from the hands of the hooligans. In an extended article of October 1953 the debate was a semantic one, aiming to differentiate the sartorial slang of south London thugs from the received pronunciation of Savile Row. In July of that year a stabbing case on Clapham Common had aroused the interest of the press, largely on account of the dress codes of the perpetrators. During the trial in October the Daily Mirror reported of the ringleader that 'he took great pains to look like a dandy. Like most of his companions, nearly all his money went on flashy clothes and just before the murder he borrowed twelve pounds from his uncle to buy a suit... This man was a born coward beneath his... gay dog clothes'.[37] Though the term 'Teddy Boy' was not used by the newspapers at this stage Men's Wear both recognized and tried to refute a connection:

Mention of Edwardian-suited youths in the recent... trial... at the Old Bailey has created the impression... that this style has been adopted generally by that section of young men who parade in groups around the streets. Inquiries I have made reveal that nothing could be further from the truth. The broad shouldered, draped jacket suit, usually in gaberdine remains the mode. Those who chose Edwardian suits for their visits to Clapham Common did so because they wanted to be different from the rest, whose main concern is to dress like their favourite screen tough guys.[38]

The article went on to note how local tailors and outfitters close to the Common either expressed indignation at the suggestion that they specialized in 'Spiv' clothes, or freely admitted that they catered for local teenage taste. Mr Leonard Rose, the manager of tailoring chain 'Maxwell's' defended his customers, claiming that 'the general run of lads in Clapham are no worse than anywhere else. They believe in colour and appearance'. That this more parochial taste for 'colourful apparel' fell short of Men's Wear's definition of the Edwardian was avowed by a Mr Harry Avoner who traded on Clapham High Street: 'We notice that a few of our younger customers drift to shops outside the locality which specialise in 'more fashionable' styles, but the phase soon passes and they come back.' It was the Edwardian look's expensive reliance on a tight fit and expert tailoring that more than anything else protected its direct appropriation by 'undesirable' constituencies, though even the bespoke trade could not retain copyright in Mayfair forever. During the same year the ready-made industry was beginning to respond to the inevitable shift in taste that followed such events as the International Wool Secretariat's show of men's apparel at the Festival Hall in May 1952 and the aforementioned Pathe documentary Man About Town. Men's Wear noticed some hesitation on the part of mass-manufacturers to jettison the more standardized drape coat for the intricate sizing demanded by Edwardian lines, but the potential for renewal hidden in the new style, its bridging of modernity and tradition, positioned its clean silhouette as a symbol for London's returning confidence.[39] As Berkley West announced,

1953 was the turning-point in reviving clothes-consciousness. At the beginning of last year, the influence of the original Edwardian outfits was beginning to be felt in every section of the trade... Criticism of Edwardian styles from the magisterial bench, which suggested that such styles symbolised the juvenile delinquents, came too late to have adverse effect on the influence of Edwardian trends. This trend was the greatest single factor in re-awakening style-consciousness in men, because it had repercussions in every branch of the industry. An American style shirt or a jazzy tie could not be worn with an Edwardian suit. Result has been that even in the case of those who confined their Edwardianism to narrow trousers and natural shoulders to the jacket, it was necessary for appropriate accessories to be purchased. A slow return to formality in all forms of men's apparel was evident, even in such things as leisure wear and beach wear.[40]

# AFTER DARK

London now has many more large floor show entertainments and cabaret shows to offer the visitor than has Paris, and at prices well below those which the capital of France has been able to demand in the past. The man largely responsible for this change of front is Percival Murray, pioneer of floor show entertainment in England as well as proprietor of the world famous Murray's Cabaret Club. His policy and lead in the 'glamour plus' type of floor show has been very ably followed by many of his colleagues... Edmundo Ros, for instance, the celebrated band leader, owns and personally welcomes visitors to his exclusive club in Regent Street. Bob and Alf Barnett control the highly succesful and lush Embassy Club in Bond Street - established there since the early 1920's and Jimmy O'Brien is personally responsible for the destiny of that gay spot with its delectable show the 'Eve' in Regent Street.[41]

The juxtaposition of elite display and street violence which echoed the dual meanings of Mayfair hauteur and Lambeth bravado was perhaps not as stark as *Men's Wear* journalists liked to claim. London's social geographies in the 1950s actively encouraged a kind of sartorial miscegenation, promoting scenarios whereby players from both worlds could rub shoulders and borrow some of the glamour that attached itself equally to aristocratic profligacy and underworld criminality. Alan Markham's leisure guide for visiting roues revealed a sparkling night-time map of burlesque bars, casinos and dance halls which traced those streets that during daylight hours gave themselves over to the luxury and sartorial trades. Plush interior spaces like these provided a platform for display well removed from the bomb-sites and grey austerity which marked open-air London. In the gilt and candlelight of the nightclub the elegance of Berkley West's 'new formality' could be shown-off to greatest advantage, whether the wearer hailed from Park Lane or from Peckham.

Part of the attraction was clearly sexual. Douglas Sutherland recalls how 'the years immediately after the war saw the heyday of London as the vice capital of Europe... In the West End, when the lights went up again, the prostitutes lined the streets'.[42] In this context Cohn's comments on the transition of New-Edwardianism from SW1 playboys to 'homosexuals' to petty criminals takes on an extra resonance, though it is likely that the style transference which he claims as a linear and socially-declining one was in effect more simultaneous, cutting across class constituencies in a dangerous and exhilarating manner. Frank Mort has provided a detailed analysis of the years preceding the Wolfenden Report, when the nature of vice in the West End (both hetero- and homosexual) penetrated the rigid structures of London life far more profoundly than in a simple libidinal sense, linking the political, the social and the cultural in a radical metropolitan geography of barely disguised desire.[43] In a material form these connections manifested themselves in examples such as the pornographer John S. Barrington's easy movement between social groups and photographic genres, facilitating his priapic and professional adventures along the length of the Charing Cross Road and encouraging a relish in self-reinvention that saw him adopting a series of outrageous sartorial disguises ranging from the bohemian to the dandified.[44] Similarly on tin-pan alley the manufactured personas of early English pop-stars such as Adam Faith, Tommy Steele and Cliff Richard played on the gold-lame camp of 'revue culture' and an eroticization of the working-class lad which were the daily bread and butter of the Savile Row-clad impresarios and entrepreneurs whose financial clout and underworld connections re-formed the sprawling pleasure-zone south of Oxford Street.[45] In other words illicit carnal activity had something of a lubricating effect on the social networks of post-war London, forging, behind a facade of respectability, channels through which new fashionable identities could emerge. The attendant frisson of life 'Up West' clearly acted as an incentive for the gang members of South and East London to chance their arm in more glamorous territory, their own engagement with the centre bolstering its edgy reputation. *Mass Observation* singled out Jack, the son of a bookmaker and a shoplifter as a typical denizen:

Jack, aged seventeen, no occupational training... has never had a job since he left school... His clothes are made for him by an expensive West End tailor, and he also wears hand-made shoes. His mother meets these bills and invites more. 'About time you got yourself some new clobber, ain't it Jack?' she has said almost every time I have met her. In spite of his almost dandyish appearance he has no respect for these clothes and is quite frequently involved in typical West End 'rough and tumbles'... His days are spent lounging about the West End back streets with the 'boys', evenings in pubs and cheap West End clubs - billiard and pin-table saloons.[46]

The mythical streets of Soho formed the epicentre for aimless boys like Jack, though Daniel Farson's homage to the bohemian credentials of the district suggests that the attractions for young libertines were hollow: 'the few places to go in Soho were wholesome to the point of boredom with a whiffle of skiffle on the washboard and a hiss of frothy coffee from a clean machine'.[47] Certainly the more familiar mythology of

**❹ ❷** *The French House* by Daniel Farson, *c.*1953 (Daniel Farson Estate)

Soho appears to favour its reputation as a haunt for public school drop-outs, slowly pickling their artistic and literary talents in smoky upstairs drinking dens and fiercely exclusive members clubs. The brash and commercial concerns which fronted its pavements may have added local colour, but largely signified only 'vulgarity' to its self-appointed chroniclers. In 1966 Frank Norman and Jeffrey Bernard could cite the 2i's coffee bar at the Wardour Street end of Old Compton Street as a fairly long-standing feature of the Soho scene, though their sense of alienation at its fashionable 'show-biz' surfaces is clear.[48] Run by ex-stunt man Tom Littlewood and ex-wrestlers Paul Lincoln and Ray Hunter, the café launched the career of Tommy Steele and touted all the credentials from criminal connections, through a well-defined 'pop ambience' (capitalized upon by the makers of the television music show *Six Five Special* who used its downstairs dance floor as a filming location) to its reputation as a meeting place for resting rent-boys, to qualify as a significant influence on the emergence of a recognizable, if highly romanticized London 'youth style'. Yet the impact of such venues has arguably been written out of histories which aim to produce a spuriously 'authentic' version of Soho's 'bohemian' past. Even Dick Hebdige seems to favour an analysis which annexes the 'materialist' gratifications of music, fashion and sex that drew the Teddy Boys across the bridges:

Subcultures were in fact literally worlds apart. The college campuses and dimly lit coffee bars and pubs of Soho and Chelsea were bus rides away from the teddy boy haunts deep in the traditionally working-class areas of south and east London. While the beatnik grew out of a literate, verbal culture... and affected a bemused cosmopolitan air of bohemian tolerance, the ted was uncompromisingly proletarian and xenophobic.[49]

Dick Hobbs, in his more astringent study of entrepreneurship and working-class style in the East End of the post-war period presents perhaps the most convincing account of the haphazard ways in which the collision of classes and attitudes in the West End of the 1950s resulted in those bizarre new codes of cultural and sartorial behaviour that marked the following decade. These were codes which were also locked into older patterns of consumption and social habit that raise the context and status of the New-Edwardian suit and its wearers above the narrow and reductive connotations of posthumous interpretations. As Hobbs states:

Important in the formation of style was the cultural overlap of the East and West Ends of London that occurred... as a result of alterations in gambling laws, the resultant indiscreet manifestations of East End villains in West End clubs, and the fashionable 1960's notion of classlessness. Conversely show-business personalities and members of the aristocracy flirted with East End pubs and drinking clubs, and a cockney accent became de rigueur for acceptance into bourgeois society as pop stars, hairdressers, and photographers rediscovered their humble roots. For young East Enders, this opened up a privileged and exotic domain.[50]

It was this potential for reinvention and transformation that invested the neon lights of Soho with such promise, drawing acolytes from both ends of the social spectrum. Hobbs quotes former criminal John McVicar, who in his autobiography recalls his fascination with the actors in this twilight scenario of billiard hall, coffee bar and public house: 'their rakishness, their flamboyant clothes, their tough, self-reliant manners, their rejection of conventional attitudes to sex and money... I unconsciously modelled myself on the more successful representatives of this new society'.[51] This productive crossing of boundaries between the respectable and the dissolute, the bespoke and the commercial, the elite and the popular, the East and the West clearly fuelled the emergence of a highly loaded and varied register of London-specific masculine styles which dominated the fashion scene between the end of war and the beginnings of 'the affluent society' that burgeoned in the 1960s. The complex patterns of its formation endorse

Angela Partington's recent call for a fashion history of the period which rejects the simple logic of 'trickle down' theory for an understanding that 'post war culture is not one in which distinctions and hierarchies collapse', but a 'horizontalized one in which differences multiply'. [52] And its chameleon-like character anticipated, indeed made possible, Colin MacInnes's 1966 observation that 'a vogue for camp, rather too pretty garments.. has also spread from shoplets in north west Soho into the most unlikely places. And the pop-drainpipe line of Spitalfields is suddenly echoed, Chelsea-wards, by fawn 'cavalry' twill slacks you have to amputate both feet to get into... As has often been noted by dress sociologists, 'top' and 'pop' clothing are usually closer in style (and influence each other more) than either is to the wide intermediate ranges of bourgeois and petty bourgeois dress'. [53] Most importantly, we should recognize that the seemingly conservative beginnings of this 'menswear revolution', as represented by Hardy Amies and his ilk, led inexorably if ironically through Mayfair, Soho and Lambeth to a cultural moment which Roy Porter sees as one of London's finest:

A culture materialised that was irreverent, offbeat, creative, novel. Politically idealistic and undogmatically left-wing, it broke through class-barriers and captured and transformed many of the better elements of traditional London: its cosmopolitanism and openness, its village quality, its closeness, its cocktail of talent, wealth and eccentricity. There was a rare alliance between youth culture and commerce, aristocratic style and a new populism. It was a breath of fresh air. [54]

# The Dolly Bird:

## CHELSEA AND KENSINGTON
## 1960~1970

For a whole decade, until about 1965, all the youth of England was on fire, and silken dalliance did not lie in the wardrobe, it lay upon their backs as a badge and symbol of their revolution. In the last eight years there have been signs that the movement has lost its impetus. Some pop idols have been declared bankrupts, espresso bars have disappeared, the Beatles have disbanded. But much of what they stood for has passed deep into the fabric of British culture, and for ten years at least 'Swinging London' was the envy of the world.[1]

In 1973, as it prepared to move from Kensington Palace to the purpose-built modernism of the Barbican, the London Museum (now the Museum of London) held a retrospective exhibition highlighting the achievements of the women's-wear designer Mary Quant. More than any other figure associated with the previous decade, Quant had come to symbolize a moment when the city rediscovered its confidence following the devastation wrought by war and a period of grinding austerity. Through a playful and highly significant engagement with processes of conspicuous consumption, personal enlightenment and sexual revolution, her generation overturned pre-war strictures of elegance and restraint in dress. By the early 1970s the idea of 'Swinging London' encapsulated in Quant's work had lost those connotations of excitement and new possibilities which had marked its heyday. In the face of economic uncertainty, international turbulence and social unrest, the shine attributed to the recent past was dismissed by many pundits as little more than the surface polish of media hype, its effects dulled by a pervading sense of collective guilt for the naive and selfish pursuits of youth.[2]

The Kensington Palace exhibition took no such stance, preferring instead to document the positive changes which the infamous events of the 1960s had effected on the material and cultural landscape of the capital. This bracketing of clothing design with other examples of social flux was an innovative step for the curation of fashion, and it is notable that the accompanying catalogue essay paid minimal attention to the output of Quant herself, preferring instead to present a contextual montage of architectural, theatrical, journalistic and folkloric scenes which paid homage to the progressive and modernizing tenor of the times. As John Hayes, Director of the Museum stated, 'no exhibition which did full justice to [Mary Quant's] achievement could fail to be about London life as well as about fashion... it seemed fitting, on the eve of our translation to a modern building, that our last exhibition at Kensington should be about contemporary life'.[3] Following in this vein, it is not the intention of this chapter simply to rehearse those debates that have since raged between commentators on the left and right concerning the moral merits and political legacy of the swinging phenomenon.[4] The emphasis here will instead centre on exploring the relationship between those glossy images of a rejuvenated city which have defined our subsequent understanding of the period as a real and an imagined cultural watershed, and the lived networks set up between designers, entrepreneurs, writers and consumers which inspired and furthered such representations - for this confluence arguably rerouted the course of London fashion and global style in unprecedented ways.

## QUANT AND THE CHELSEA ATTITUDE

The Quant exhibition was careful to set its chronological boundaries outside of the measure implied by the duration of a standard decade. Though the notion of Swinging London has come to be recognized as a defining theme of the 1960s, its power as a relevant descriptive term was already on the wane by the time of its infamous appropriation by *Time Magazine* in April 1966. Furthermore, many of the influences which informed its hegemony were in place by 1955. This was the year in which Quant opened her first boutique on the King's Road in Chelsea, amidst a sea change in social attitudes and consumption practices which were to be formally identified by Colin MacInnes (among others) by 1959.[5] In an article for the journal *Twentieth Century*, the novelist and keen observer of London's contemporary popular cultures cited the comments of Nancy Mitford, who on a recent visit to London had declared that

Working class girls and boys are incomparably smarter than the others... Compare the publics in Oxford Street and Bond Street of now and of however far your memory goes back, and the present superiority of Oxford Street is startling. You will also observe there - as in any proletarian district of the capital - the lavish, colourful eruption of gay stores selling 'separates' to the girls, and sharp schmutter to the kids: shining, enticing shops like Candy-floss. But the transformation of the working class to power and relative affluence means that these styles... are no longer working class at all.[6]

Though Chelsea in 1955 still bore traces of an artisanal past, its bohemian credentials disqualified it from any claim to be properly 'proletarian' in the sense that the more accessible Oxford Street was. And Quant's new shop (named Bazaar - a title replete with associations of the exotic souk and notions of the extreme or unusual) charged prices that were way out of reach of the average working-class pocket. However, the broad direction of her assault on received and genteel ideas about fashion were clearly in tune with Mitford's suggestion of a more democratic turn in the evolution of English style. Beyond this, the appeal of her project was certainly rooted in a childlike abandonment to ephemerality, novelty and pleasure, summed up in Mitford's perceptive use of the term 'Candy-floss'.

Quant's preternatural autobiography (published only ten years after the foundation of her business, but seeming to contain the summation of several lifetimes' achievements) demonstrates how the deliberately naive and 'classless' appeal of her brand was underpinned from the outset by an acute understanding (largely provided by her husband Alexander Plunkett Green and her business manager Archie McNair) of the commercial potential residing in Chelsea's shifting social and creative milieu. McNair, though a lawyer by training, ran a photographic studio in the King's Road and sought (unsuccessfully) to persuade Plunkett Green to back a neighbouring coffee-bar venture. McNair's hunch that the rich and well-connected clientele of his photography business would form a niche market for further 'lifestyle' outlets proved to be prescient, and it was on the basis of this that Quant and Plunkett Green entered into the retail trade. Self-consciously extricating herself from any accusation of exclusivity or social elitism Quant enumerated her co-revolutionaries and future clientele as 'painters, photographers, architects, writers, socialites, actors, con-men and superior tarts. There were racing drivers, gamblers, TV producers and advertising men. But somehow everyone in Chelsea was that much more... go-ahead'.[7]

Recalling her school days in Chelsea during the 1950s, Alexandra Pringle offered a less spectacular version of the King's Road and its inhabitants as they existed before the changes inaugurated by Quant and the 'Chelsea set' took hold. 'With its tall plane trees, squares of white fronted houses and red coated pensioners' the district offered the traditional London vistas that would continue to form an important backdrop and counterpoint to a coming fashionable modernity, but in its range of amenities and retail outlets the local landscape clearly belonged to a previous and more provincial era. Pringle remembered 'Jones the grocer, where there were glass-topped biscuit tins, Timothy Whites (chemist), Sidney Smith's the drapers, and the Woolworths with its counters piled high with sweets... There were also quite sedate expeditions... to the Kardomah Coffee House following missions to Peter Jones for dress patterns or fabrics'.[8] Behind this respectable facade of familial cosiness, however, Chelsea also boasted a reputation for louche raffishness. This was earned largely through its long-standing provision of cheap studios and bed-sits, which were essential for the survival of artists, theatricals and other low-earning but socially ambitious creative types who had crowded into the district since the mid-nineteenth century. Furthermore, attendant myths of debauchery and the availability of stylishly shabby accommodation proved attractive to later generations of trust-funded drop-outs from neighbouring Belgravia.[9] It was among this transient community of bohemian incomers that Quant and Plunkett Green, themselves recent graduates from Goldsmith's College of Art, found a natural kinship. Their social world revolved especially around The King's Arms in Fulham

Road, an establishment colloquially known as Finch's, whose liminal atmosphere was still intact in 1966, when it was listed as a notable venue by cult architectural critic Ian Nairn:

With all the charades that are put on in London for people to posture in and think themselves odd, it is more and more difficult to provide for the real thing. This place is really odd - naturally odd and eccentric - and feels quite different from the pubs that are trying it on. For one thing it is still rough; and for another, the local cockneys haven't been driven out. They coexist with the wildest avant-garde, and with yours truly... scribbling these notes in an uneasy no-man's land. (No. That's unfair. No-man's land, certainly, but not really uneasy. This pub has got the secret of live-and-let-live.)[10]

The 'anything goes' nature of Quant's new-found bohemia was central to the success of Bazaar in several ways. In his notes on 'home' published in Len Deighton's celebrated *London Dossier* of 1967, Nick Tomalin distinguishes between the left-wing Hampstead coterie established by Jewish intellectuals in the 1930s and the more materialistic concerns of the post-war Chelsea rebels who 'gathered in coffee bars and boutiques rather than Kaffeeklatsches or comrades demos'. Setting themselves against the constraints of austerity and the collectivising tendencies of a nascent Welfare State they were 'anarchists rather than communists'.\Political revolution and a concern with the social good were therefore less important to Quant's new patrons than the freedom to express their sense of individuality without censure. As Tomalin rather dismissively put it, 'they fled from Tunbridge Wells, Wilton House or Alice Springs rather than Auschwitz... The tyrant they defied was Daddy, not Hitler'.[11]

Such priorities were closely met by Quant's finely-judged stylizations of Art Student outrage. Jazz musician and raconteur George Melly was well aware of this when he attributed her genius to her daring 'to throw a custard pie in the face of every rule of what, up until then had constituted British fashion'.[12] Generational rebellion certainly fuelled Quant's drive to create, but this was also inflected by a rather disingenuous, meritocratic belief in the irrelevancy of the class system (which disregarded the privileged backgrounds of most of her peers and clients) and a receptiveness to the energy of the urban life around her. She rationalized her own success through her insistence 'that the secret of successful designing is to anticipate changes of mood before they happen'. 'I get new ideas all the time,' she assured Jonathan Aitken as he chronicled the activities of the new 'youth' entrepreneurs of London in 1967. 'Going to night clubs, seeing colours in the streets. It's a sort of flair within me. I'll keep in alright.'[13] Such tenacity had brought significant press recognition, positioning Quant as a fashion pioneer and setting a template for younger acolytes. Brigid Keenan of the *Daily Express* recalled that

Suddenly someone had invented a style of dressing which we realised we had been wanting for ages. Comfortable, simple, no waists, good colours and simple fabrics. It gave anyone wearing them a sense of identity with youth and adventure and brightness. No wonder the young journalists raved.[14]

Yet this official line rather obscured the haphazard nature in which Bazaar established itself on the Chelsea scene. Quant's wide-eyed enthusiasm for the project almost seemed to will its existence in the face of planning problems, subsidence, complaints from the Chelsea Society regarding 'architectural vandalism' and an attitude to stock-control and supply that was disorganized in the extreme. (Early items in the shop were constructed from fabric bought expensively at Harrods and made up unsystematically by Quant on a sewing machine in her flat.) Such cheerful amateurism succeeded in spite of itself, imprinting a brand identity that grew organically out of the local culture. Quant's recollection of this period lends the venture a flavour not dissimilar to that of children planning a grand adventure in the Enid Blyton tradition: 'It was to be a bouillabaisse of clothes and accessories... sweaters, scarves, shifts, hats, jewellery and peculiar odds and ends. We would call it Bazaar. I was to be the buyer. Alexander inherited £5,000 on his twenty first birthday and Archie was prepared to put up £5,000 too.'[15]

From such shaky foundations Bazaar gradually became a national then an international institution, presenting a prototype of chaotic creativity underpinned by a steely acumen, that by 1964 was being replicated across the capital and further afield. Quant was adamant about the very visible role the shop would play in the life of the community, claiming that 'we wanted Bazaar to become a sort of Chelsea establishment'.[16] This strong street presence was partly achieved by an attitude toward window display that prioritized visual impact over the necessity to make sales. The boutique window as pop-art

Mary Quant's Bazaar Shop, The King's Road, c.1965 (Hulton Getty)

installation was to become a familiar feature of the iconography of 'Swinging London', but in the late 1950s Bazaar was already offering such surrealist extravaganzas as 'the model of a photographer strung up by his feet to the ceiling, with the most enormous old-fashioned camera focused on a bird also suspended at the most incredible angle'.

Or, 'figures in bathing suits... with madly wide stripes... all strumming away on white musical instruments... with bald heads and... wearing round goggle sun-specs which... were incredibly new'. In knowing homage to the figure of the nineteenth-century Parisian dandy, that precursor of modern urban fashionability, one mannequin was 'beautifully dressed and leading this lobster on a gold chain' and in a further bracketing of nostalgic 'retro' referencing with a brazen avant-gardism that suited the Chelsea mood, Quant (aided by her shop-workers Suzie Leggatt and Andrew Oldham[17]) 'hired beautiful girls to act as sandwich men. These girls, elegantly dressed and looking tremendously chic, walked in the gutter along the King's Road and Brompton Road carrying the traditional type of sandwich boards with the announcement "Come to Bazaar - MAD Reductions' printed in beautiful old playbill type. They were a sensation'.[18]

Alexandra Pringle and her generation were clearly thrilled by such innovations. She recalled that by the early 1960s

Local residents stared and pointed as young women catwalked up and down... They wore big floppy hats, skinny ribbed sweaters, key-hole dresses, wide hipster belts and, I believed, paper knickers. They had white lipsticked lips and thick black eyeliner, hair cut at alarming angles, op-art earrings and ankle-length white boots. They wore citron coloured trouser suits and skirts that seemed daily shorter. They rode on miniature motorbikes. They had confidence and, it seemed, no parents.[19]

Such exotic creatures may well have given the impression of hailing from nowhere, but Quant acknowledged the increasing role played by the media in nurturing and circulating what had by now become the stereotype of the 'Chelsea girl', her appearance and attitudes based to a large extent on the ethos purveyed by Bazaar. 'Chelsea', she claimed, 'ceased to be a small part of London; it became international; its name interpreted a way of living and a way of dressing far more than a geographical area'.[20] Pulp novels such as Paul Denver's *Black Stockings for Chelsea* of 1963 revelled in this shorthand for permissiveness, providing lurid images of parties where 'the first floor bulged with beatniks and jumped with jazz, West Indian percussion and the socked out beat of rock and roll.... The party was getting hotter by the second. The second floor landing was jammed with girls in tight blouses, wide skirts and knee-high cavalry boots. A dishevelled girl who an hour ago had looked like something out of a fashion supplement was hammering frantically on a bathroom door... Nobody was giving a damn.'[21] In the *New York Herald Tribune*, John Crosby gave the Chelsea Girl a more glamorous, if still objectified and reactionary gloss, suggesting that he would like 'to export the whole Chelsea Girl with her "life is fabulous" philosophy to America... to spread the word that being a Girl is a much more rewarding occupation than being a Lady Senator'.[22]

In effect the image of the Chelsea Girl, 'leather booted and black stockinged', presented a robust challenge to the sexual and social status quo, and Quant found herself held responsible by many commentators, who variously described her look as 'dishy, grotty, geary, kinky, mod, poove and all the rest of it', for a perceived state of moral decline.[23]

Yet even the publicity-hungry founder of Bazaar knew that she could not claim all the credit, admitting that 'in fact, no one designer is ever responsible for such a revolution'.[24] Those in the mainstream British fashion industry, which was concurrently reorganizing itself as a formidable player in the revitalized post-war manufacturing economy, were indeed sceptical about her prominence as an innovator. From the hindsight of 1969, when the Swinging phenomenon had lost its glossy currency, various representatives from the rag trade were cruelly dismissive of Quant's contribution to any turnaround in the sector's fortunes. A couturier stated that 'although I think [she] is witty, and some of her designs quite original... she has lowered the standard of mass-produced clothes, both from the point of view of making and from the point of view of graciousness'. Others were even more vitriolic in their assessments, focusing on her personal life. A fabric designer imagined that 'she must be rather masculine as a person - quite kinky', while a vendeuse suggested that 'the harshness and coarseness of her clothes bring out nasty reactions in men'. Much of this antipathy can be put down to professional jealousy. For example, the owner of a madam shop (the genteel ancestor of the boutique) clearly envied Quant her youthful market, arguing that 'she is a success because she is grotesque without taste - the kids have a vast amount of money, and the more grotesque a garment - the more they like it'.[25] Yet regardless of its underlying causes, the ferocity of the backlash clearly revealed the power to shock and provoke that still resided in the Chelsea 'look'.

At an organizational level, Quant's success in promoting her vision was also reliant on a broader restructuring of London's supply chains and publicity networks, which remain obscured in her own account. This process had been initiated in 1950 when eight major British wholesalers came together behind the leadership of Leslie Carr-Jones to form the London Model House Group. The Group looked to the robust American fashion scene for inspiration; seeing in the corporate efficiency of Seventh Avenue's clothing giants a more appropriate model for modernization than the patrician elitism of the existing Incorporated Society of London Fashion Designers. By 1955 the Model House Group was itself in the throws of reorganization, building on a new sense of prestige to attract further members and capitalize on the arising publicity. The emerging Fashion House Group of London put its energies into the organization of promotional events such as the twice-yearly London Fashion Weeks. These were launched in 1958 under the chairmanship of Moss Murray with an unprecedented budget of £40,000 a year. Buyers and department-store executives in Europe, the United States and the Commonwealth were encouraged to attend and by 1963 the shows were being exported to Paris. In an echo of the Beatles tour, the itinerary was extended to North America in 1966, when as Murray recalled 'we sailed on the Queen Elizabeth with a party of eighteen model girls, manufacturers and twelve top British journalists. We were a wow! It simply wasn't done for a big store not to have British fashions'.[26]

The Group subsequently fractured along the fault-lines of design, manufacture and marketing. Young designers eager for autonomy set up the Association of Fashion Designers, and the established trade oriented itself toward the Government-sponsored

Clothing Export Council following the lobbying of the Board of Trade by the high-street stalwart Aquascutum. However, despite their decline in influence, the commercial and organizational initiatives set up by London wholesalers and suppliers in the late 1950s were integral to the success and profile of the Chelsea style. Indeed, it could be argued that they supported a brief twenty-year interlude of unchallenged productivity in the history of British fashion, that was not marred by the more familiar story of falling orders and bankruptcies. Michael Whittaker, who produced the shows for the London Fashion House Group in the mid 1960s was adamant that 'high as we've got in the business, there would be no Mary Quant - or any of the others like her - without the original promotions of the Fashion House Group of London'.[27] Quant's lucrative forays into the American market (she entered into creative partnerships with New York-based J.C. Penney in 1962, and Butterwick and Puritan Fashions in 1964[28]) and her British-based wholesaling arm the Ginger Group, established in 1963, certainly shared more closely in the 'wheeling-dealing' business rhetoric of international corporatism espoused by technocrats like Carr Jones and Murray than in any effete sense of bohemian creativity as symbolized by the King's Road.

It was, in fact, a combination of commercial know-how and the ability to promote her unique vision of King's Road permissiveness more widely through licensing deals that secured Quant's place at the apex of the London fashion scene. The direct inspiration for this came from McNair who, on realizing that the manufacturing side of the business (based in nearby Ives Street) was draining profits, advised Quant to concentrate on designs which could be sold on to international buyers in the form of aspirational products (including cosmetics and hosiery). McNair's motto became 'Money is the applause: If you do something well, if you make dresses people want, money is the applause.'[29] The future impact of this shift away from a Fordist understanding of clothing production toward an interest in anticipating and meeting consumer desires was evoked by journalist Roma Fairley, who in 1969 asked her readers to

picture a huge warehouse in a dreary warehouse district. There is a steady drenching drizzle which has replaced the old pea-souper as London's speciality. Outside is an advertisement for staff. Inside, beyond the grubby 'Enquiries' window, you catch your breath at what seems a huge, splendid wardrobe for an enormous harem.[30]

Fairley was describing the day-to-day realities of the mass-manufacturing fashion business at a moment of transition; a time when these two cultures (of supply-led production-lines and the inspired modernity of design) came together. The dreary warehouse represented a post-war world of predictable monotony interspersed with spectacular flashes of ephemeral colour (in this case a consignment of garments for the Susan Small label - a mid-market competitor to Quant).[31] This was all very different from the rarefied notion of creativity and craftsmanship associated with the traditional model of fashion, where style percolated slowly down from Paris. Yet these opposing systems shared a certain energy. As Fairley observed: 'A wholesale collection is just as electrifying as couture. But there is no creative hysteria, just the hard selling reproductions digested and formulated into the firm's price range.'[32] The dual prerogatives of accounting and circulating novel styles may have given rise to a degree of schizophrenia. The director of high-street multiple Wallis revealed as much to Fairley when 'in a big light room, with hundreds of sketches on the walls he waved an arm [indicating]: "the swinging look for Chelsea, Jolie Madame for Knightsbridge... mainstream of Wallis clothes all over the country" '.[33] But schizophrenic or not, George Melly acknowledged the unique manner in which Quant had reconciled such contradictions to great effect in her hybrid assault on complacency in all its forms:

Quant chucked lady-like accessories into the dustbin, recognised the irrelevancy of looking like a virgin, took into account that pavements and restaurants were not muddy hunting fields nor parties and dances the antechambers of morgues. Innocent and tough, she attacked the whole rigid structure of the rag trade and won hands down and skirts up.[34]

## SWINGING DOLLIES GO SHOPPING

Melly suggests that Quant's victory was a cultural *and* a material one. He claims that Bazaar 'was a banner, a battle cry, a symbol of the new sophistication, and above all news. It was also the one true pop manifestation between rock and the Beatles'.[35] Nowhere was this more visible than on the streets of London, especially those in Chelsea. Though from 1957 the emphasis of the Quant business shifted upmarket to Knightsbridge (where a new store was opened), and into the international market through its licensing deals, the impact of its legacy in the King's Road was nevertheless profound. Vidal Sassoon, the celebrity hairdresser who was so instrumental in fixing Quant's image on the public consciousness, was adamant that its place was at the heart of those physical and psychological changes affecting London life during this period: 'I always said that the King's Road was Mary's atelier... it was one marvellous show. You could go to the King's Road, outside Mary Quant's, and there you had the young people - it was wonderful.'[36]

Certainly by the mid-1960s the particular 'pop' chemistry of Bazaar was being replicated with gusto across the metropolis. Jonathan Aitken, identifying (with a certain patrician aloofness) the emergent boutique ideal as 'a small shop of flamboyant atmosphere specialising in original and colourful clothes, usually at low prices', estimated that there were '2,000 of them in Greater London' by 1967.[37] In the King's Road itself their presence was beginning to impact on the very social tenor of the area, and Aitken noted the manner in which 'King's Road clothes get way-out as you get way-up'.[38] Peter Jones department store at Sloane Square, where Alexandra Pringle had endured stifling shopping expeditions for fabrics with her mother, remained a bastion of respectability behind its Modernist glass and concrete facade (graciously incorporating a few nominally swinging concessions when the quality and prices were commensurate with its standing as an 'establishment... where Peers' daughters have their wedding lists[39]'). A hinterland of supermarkets and coffee-bars (themselves harbingers of new American and continental modes of retailing) was then interrupted by Bazaar before Top Gear and Countdown ('for the briefest of mini-skirts'[40]) announced the incursion of a new wave of innovative fashion outlets. Owned by designer James Wedge and his model girlfriend Pat Booth, these two concerns were computed to hold up to £20,000 of stock at any one time, attracting a turnover of £1,000 per week. The product of an Essex secondary modern school, National Service and Walthamstow Art College, the 30-year-old Wedge, who claimed to work a regular seventeen hour day, fitted precisely the model of the new working-class entrepreneur - dressed unobtrusively 'like a prosperous undertaker'.[41]

The cool repose of Wedge's investments were as nothing, however, compared to the voluptuous success of the men's boutique Hung on You, which established itself a little off the main drag of the King's Road in Cale Street. Famed for its psychedelic window installations, considered by Aitken to be 'worthy of a dipsomaniac's nightmare', the store also boasted the requisite 'faces' as customers and staff. Dressed in 'a lace shirt

Hung on You, *c.*1967 (Hulton Getty) ❹❺

and orange jeans too tight for him to move' the 18-year-old American assistant Irving Fish was aided by Londoner Barbara Allen who sported 'a mini-skirt so short it would not even have afforded coverage over a pigmy's buttocks' and a transparent smock. In an interior modishly fitted up with rush matting, William Morris wallpaper and oversized cane chairs, Aitken was desultorily shown 'a dozen billiously coloured shirts and a few sequinned jackets, all of which were being made for special customers'.[42] Aitken's surprise at the laid-back service revealed his psychological distance from the boutique scene, which tended to operate like an extended and exclusive family. As one guide for the London shopper warned: 'not only is there no hard sell, it is sometimes difficult to get any attention at all. The girls who work in them are invariably depressingly pretty... They sit at the back somewhere reading magazines, entertaining their friends, or telephoning interminably about special autumn orders of astrakhan mini spats'.[43]

The proprietor of Hung on You was Michael Rainey. Rainey featured in *Time Magazine*'s infamous April 1966 issue, accompanying socialite Jane Ormsby Gore at Dolly's Discotheque in Jermyn Street where they were pictured drinking Campari and Soda, 'the right drink... because it is red and tickles'. Tightly networked into London's moneyed and entertainment crowds, Rainey produced theatrical styles for the pop aristocracy. As he revealed to Aitken, the store had been a success since its opening in December 1965 through selling to Donovan, The Who and the Beatles and accruing enviable media coverage. As for the stock itself, independent stores like Hung on You clearly inspired a cautionary note from the shopping guides who stated that 'boutique clothes are not mass-produced and are therefore expensive... They usually come from small collections produced by new designers whose heads are seething with fresh and astonishing images of elegance. They are sometimes very badly made and somewhat experimental in shape, so it is inadvisable to shop in boutiques if you are looking a mess and feeling indecisive'.[44]

Evidence of the insecurity engendered by boutique culture sits rather awkwardly with the inclusive, democratic emphasis put upon the swinging phenomenon by many journalists. A scratch beneath the surface reveals the competitive cronyism that sometimes underpinned the 1960s style revolution. Nowhere was this contradiction more evident than in the World's End boutique Granny Takes A Trip. One of the flagships of the emerging counter-culture, this was perhaps the most politicized of Chelsea's new fashion outlets. Owned by Nigel Weymouth, an economics graduate from the University of London, John Pearce, a tailor trained at the London College of Fashion, and Sheila Troy, a former film extra ( a 'tuned-in' trio representing the perfect cross-section of Swinging London's supposed meritocracy), the shop's policy seemed to undermine and critique the shiny consumerist rhetoric put in place by Quant while covertly pursuing its own version of her remunerative supply and display strategies. Nigel Weymouth recalled that

We used to go down to Church Street Market and Portobello Road, collecting these old clothes, and we thought it might be a good idea to open a shop with all these things...

We started off exclusively with old clothes: rather nice beaded dresses, blazers, all that sort of camp nonsense. That was fun… The whole point was just to keep it change, change, change. Then we decided we'd design our own clothes… Once we did that I began to lose interest in… the rag trade. I lost interest in playing shops. [But] we really did pioneer… disposable clothes… the ethos of the new dressing up… not taking it seriously.[45]

This studied ennui reflected a rising tide of cynicism about the benefits of consumerism affecting London's youthful constituencies in the later 1960s, alongside a shift in the registers of metropolitan taste: from pop to psychedelia, mod to hippy, and in terms of drugs use, from 'uppers' to 'downers'.[46] The contents of the shop itself also illustrated a confusing diversity, a harbinger of postmodernity. In 1967 Aitken observed 'Charleston dresses… Victorian bustles… Boer War helmets, African fezes, Arab head dresses, Chicago gangster suits… military uniforms, blown-up photographs of Edwardian chorus girls… antique swords, glass walking sticks… feather boas… [and] an early gramophone'. This was set 'alongside a mass of with-it accoutrements such as mini skirts, op art shirts, gold-rimmed sunglasses, floral ties, velveteen breeches, yellow suede jackets, pink PVC jackets and so on ad hallucinationem'.[47] For unwary visitors such as drama student Jonathan Meades, this profusion of exotic goods, presented without guidelines, was intimidating if not a little sinister. His encounter with Granny Takes a Trip was

the first time I realised this extreme snobbery based on clothes, speech, mannerisms, and not so much vocabulary but lack of vocabulary. It was all extremely excluding… I remember Nigel Weymouth sneering at me - you could hardly see his face through this mass of Afro hair… He obviously thought I was a joke… wanted me moved out of the way, because I was an extremely bad advertisement for his shop.[48]

Meades's paranoia was not entirely mis-placed. Publications such as Karl Dallas's *Swinging London: A Guide to Where the Action is* revelled in the production of alienating lists of 'in' and 'out' venues, implying the existence of a hidden hierarchy of places and people arranged to weed out the 'naff'. As its editorial stated (before going on to list two dozen of London's self-appointed style elite, their favourite clubs, restaurants, hairdressers, clothes shops, drinks, cars and cigarettes): 'there are only a limited number of people who can make things happen. They are the ones who can make a place in… They can, by their choice of car or length of skirt… change the very face of our cities'.[49]

Behind the laconic front, Weymouth certainly set out to change just that. Granny Takes A Trip represented the extreme edge of the Chelsea boutique renaissance, both psychically, chronologically and geographically. It insinuated itself into the crumbling tenements of the World's End, where bohemian, elitist Chelsea met grey working-class Fulham, presaging the process of gentrification which would gather pace in the 1970s. Mocking the Union Jack patriotism of the neighbouring British Legion headquarters in its display of nostalgic memorabilia, Granny's bright purple fascia bore the provocative sub-Wildean legend 'One should either be a work of art or wear a work of art'. In Weymouth's words 'our shop, in pop jargon, would be described as very camp. Camp is kind of taking the mickey out of sex by being theatrical. Sort of playing out fantasies in real life. It's a romantic dream world we're catering for'.[50]

As Susan Sontag suggested in her influential 1967 essay on Camp, such playfulness carried a subversive, even destructive kick, whose power it was advisable not to underestimate.[51] To some contemporary commentators it seemed that London itself had come under its delusional spell. In June 1966 Anthony Lewis of the *New York Times* had reported that the atmosphere in the capital 'can be almost eerie in its quality of relentless frivolity. There can rarely have been a greater contrast between a country's objective situation and the mood of its people'.[52] For Christopher Booker, although 'there were more boutiques in the King's Road than ever before,... the idea of 'Swinging Chelsea' had become a Frankenstein's monster... fallen to a glittering, commercialised invasion, dominated by large fashion chains and other external interests. And it was somehow symptomatic that by the summer of 1969, even Bazaar had been sold, to become a chemist's shop. Already it was itself the symbol of a Chelsea that was almost gone'.[53]

## SWINGING STEREOTYPES

Booker's doom-laden critique of British popular culture in the 1960s is also full of picturesque but pointed references to the state of the weather. It is as if the quintessential national obsession with the fleeting effects of the elements inflected a collective inability to see beyond the mists of hype. We are informed that 'the rain poured down almost unceasingly' during the summer of 1965, while the following year 'the temperature had risen into the eighties' gilding the city in a 'strange orange afterglow' and encouraging 'a sense of hedonistic detachment'. Between these meteorological extremes Booker suggests that Londoners came to read their city and its economic and social development through the prism of public relations and media rhetoric rather than by trusting the less spectacular evidence of their own eyes. Instead of looking through the window for guidance on the carrying of an umbrella, it seemed as though the population preferred to rely entirely on the exotic language of the shipping forecasts. This is not to imply that the material environment of London was in stasis during these years. Booker paints a vivid picture of the changed landscape which awaited a time traveller of 1955 transported forward into the city of 1965:

as he sped along the curving M4 motorway from London Airport below the unfamiliar howl of jet airliners, there would have been soaring new glass and concrete blocks breaking the skyline, the tallest of which, the GPO tower, had only just been opened... Next, perhaps, he would have been struck by the change in appearance of the young... Nothing would have surprised him more than the exhibitionistic violence with which these fashions grabbed at the attention - the contrasts, the jangling colours, the hard glossiness of PVC, the show of thigh... curiously impersonal, like the expressionless stare that so often went with them, or the throwaway generic terms - 'birds' or 'dollies' - that were used to describe their wearers…. Our visitor would have found the same visual violence everywhere; in the ubiquitous neon lighting, on shop fronts, on advertisements, in the more garishly decorated restaurants… If he had opened a fashion magazine, he would have been amazed by the blank harsh photography and the awkward, even ugly contortions of the models. And if he ventured into one of the discotheques, the sensation of a strange alienating harshness would have struck him more forcefully than ever.[54]

TIME Map by R. M. Chapin, Jr.

But the speed with which such change was being interpreted and fed back to its metropolitan audience by the machinery of an overbearing fourth estate left little time for impartial assessment or critical reflection, lending credence to the theoretical suppositions of such contemporary luminaries as Guy Debord and Marshall MacLuhan that style was superseding substance in a logical conclusion to the late capitalist project.[55]

The infamous issue of *Time* magazine which appeared on April 15 1966 is generally held up as the key example of this myth-making process. It was the culmination of a series of articles which had exercised a normally solipsistic American press since the American journalist John Crosby had submitted a piece titled 'London: The Most Exciting City' to the British *Daily Telegraph* Colour Supplement a year before. The emphasis here was on eroticism. Crosby described a 'kaleidoscope of young English girls who were appreciative, sharp tongued and glowingly alive, who walk like huntresses, like Dianas, and who take to sex as if it's candy and it's delicious'.[56] This sexual element was also a factor which informed the commissioning of the *Time* assignment. Andrea Adam, who was on the staff of the magazine at the time, remembers that 'London was special, it had a kind of mystique. But what prompted the bloody cover story was not a fascination with a socio-cultural phenomenon, it was the fascination amongst the senior editors for mini-skirts... Any opportunity to put legs, tits or bums in the magazine and they would do it'.[57] Underlying motivations accepted, the April edition also offered an effective shorthand version of change and innovation that would come to stand in for the more nuanced material experiences which the city had to offer. This was a generalizing approach which carried powerful consequences for London's subsequent development as a world fashion centre whose importance was symbolic rather than economic.

❹ ❻ 'Swinging London Map' from *Time Magazine,* 15 April 1966 (Time Magazine)

Pre-empting Booker, the publisher's letter which introduced *Time*'s 'Swinging London' edition also made great play of the physical and cultural changes which had affected the capital since the 1950s. It related how, on a previous visit, one of the magazine's editors 'looked at the bomb sites' and visited the Tower of London 'where she remembers having a dreary serving of watery mashed potatoes and brussels sprouts'. Undeterred, the same journalist had come again in 1965 'to find a better England. It was L'Etoile and Ad Lib and the trattorias in Soho - and a place on King's Road (*sic*) where she could buy a pair of bell-bottom slacks by Foale & Tuffin that made her something of a trend-setter back home in New York'. Inspired by those experiences the magazine had commissioned seven staff writers in their London Bureau and five American and British photographers to indulge in four days of 'the most concentrated swinging... that any group of individuals has ever enjoyed or suffered'.[58] The iconic collaged cover by Geoffrey Dickinson caught some of the freneticism. It incorporated Big Ben, a red Routemaster bus, a Rolls Royce, a Mini Cooper, dolly birds, peacock males, Union Jacks, a discotheque entrance, the recently redesigned road traffic signs, the fascia of a bingo hall, roulette tables and caricatures of Mary Quant, Harold Wilson, The Beatles and The Who in its melange of high and low, 'trad' and 'mod' signifiers.

The article itself adopted the format of a story-board for an imaginary film constituting five varying London 'scenes'.[59] These included an aristocratic evening with the son of a peer in Mayfair, starting at Jack Aspinall's Clermont Club, an exclusive casino situated in an eighteenth-century town house on Berkeley Square, and ending in Annabel's nightclub nearby; a Saturday afternoon's shopping in Chelsea and the Portobello Road, taking in the Guy's and Doll's coffee bar in the King's Road in the company of Mick Jagger, Cathy McGowan and an anonymous teenager in a black and yellow PVC mini-skirt; a concurrent Chelsea lunch party in Le Reve Restaurant with Terence Stamp, Jean Shrimpton, Michael Caine, Vidal Sassoon, David Bailey and Doug Haywood, where the conversation centred on the evils of Apartheid and the current form of Chelsea football team; and an early evening cocktail party at Robert Fraser's Mayfair Gallery, attended by Jane Ormsby Gore in a red Edwardian Jacket, ruffled lace blouse, skin-tight black bell-bottoms, silver-buckled patent-leather shoes, ghost-white make-up and 'tons of eyelashes', designer Pauline Fordham in a silver coat, and starlet Sue Kingsford in a two-piece pink trouser suit which revealed her naked waist. As we know, Ormsby Gore was later to join Michael Rainey at Dolly's discotheque. The final scene focused on dinner with Marlon Brando, Roddy McDowell, Terri Southern, Francoise Sagan, Barbra Streisand, Margot Fonteyn and Warren Beatty in the Kensington house owned by Hollywood star Leslie Caron. After an excellent meal 'of chicken, claret and Chablis' these international jet-setters 'danced till dawn'.

The accompanying colour photo essay, credited to Derek Bayes, Ben Martin and John Reader, presented a group of 'dolly birds' in bright PVC raincoats disporting themselves on the King's Road, the gaming table at Crockford's gambling club in St James's, Foale & Tuffin's shop close to Carnaby Street, and schoolgirls and a 'unisex' couple browsing in the same vicinity. Mavis Tapley was pictured in her Pimlico boutique Hem and

Fringe, an exotic dancer cavorted in a Soho striptease joint and a bowler-hatted City gent paused on Tower Bridge. Finally, the cocktail party at Robert Fraser's and Scotch's discotheque of St James's were shown to be buzzing with swinging types. This idiosyncratic mix of images endorsed an editorial claim that 'there is not one London scene, but dozens. Each one is a dazzling gem, a medley of chequered sunglasses and delightfully quaint pay phone boxes, a blend of 'flash' American, polished continental and robust old English influence that mixes and merges... The result is a sparkling slap-dash comedy.'[60]

Readers of *Time* were not so quick to recognize the satirical flavour of the article, and the letters page of the magazine was home to an earnest debate on its merits and veracity over the next few issues. Correspondents likened Swinging London to the amoral city of Thackeray's *Vanity Fair*.[61] One argued that 'that's a hell of a test by which to measure a city's greatness: its ability to appeal to the moronic fringe, the smart alecs and the social climbers'. He substituted an alternative vista of 'mist along the river, the cries of the street markets and the smell of old books' in a bid to reclaim the capital's patrician self-respect. Another suggested that the style renaissance held as much promise as rumours of the returning health of Britain's manufacturing base, stating that 'you have managed to look decadence in the face without seeing it.... All the turned on young men and women will burn out as quickly as a light bulb of British manufacture'.[62] The following month letter-writers were still contesting the worth of the article with two Londoners representing opposite views. A young woman enthused that 'as a dolly from the scene I say cheers for your gear article on the swinging, switched-on city of London and boo to all the American geese who call it humbug'. Her counterpart complained that 'visitors still find the same old dingy streets and grimy restaurants... Girls, except for women street cleaners, do not wear plastic suits. Carnaby Street is not a new phenomenon: it has catered to the chorus boy type for years'.[63]

Besides stoking the growing frustration expressed by contemporary readers with the apparent superficiality of journalistic analyses of London's transformation, the April issue also set in motion a succession of diatribes aimed at the hollow excesses of the new fashionable elite.[64] In 1970 John Lennon famously told *Rolling Stone* magazine that 'the class system and the whole bullshit bourgeois scene is exactly the same, except that there are a lot of middle-class kids with long hair walking around London in trendy clothes... nothing happened except that we all dressed up'.[65] In the same year Bernard Levin railed against a decadent 'colour supplement' sensibility, 'an increase in the artificial, the pre-packed,' and a world in which 'the harmless word 'trend' suddenly took on new meanings as the practitioners of this kind of turnover worship began to hunt more and more frantically for the latest gewgaw... with which to tempt the increasingly jaded palettes of their readers'.[66] In his much later survey of British film in the 1960s, Jeffrey Richards takes a similarly condemnatory view of the apolitical and hedonistic qualities of the Swinging London 'bubble'. He bemoans the fact that cinema in the period 'had been mainly London-centred, male-centred, style-centred, fatally self-indulgent'. The issues of class, race, region and gender had taken second place to the exaltation of a classless consumerist self. Interestingly, in order to support his thesis he cites the ideas of sociologist Bernice Martin, who proposed that the tenets of Romanticism were manifested in the swinging phenomenon:

Romanticism seeks to destroy boundaries, reject conventions, undermine structures and universalise the descent into the abyss and the ascent into the infinite. Its matrix is material prosperity that releases people from the immediate disciplines of survival and that concentrates their attention on their 'expressive' needs - self-discovery, self-fulfilment, experience and sensation.[67]

Martin's analysis is arguably less value-laden than the negative verdicts of Lennon, Levin, Richards et al. Indeed its optimistic eliding of avant-gardism with the 'expressive' potential of consumer culture opens up some space for a closer consideration of the positive benefits associated with perhaps the most persistent stereotype of Swinging London, the 'Dolly Bird'. The new West End landscape of boutiques and discotheques provided an arena in which some young women certainly found the freedom to 'destroy boundaries, reject conventions and undermine structures'. And though this may have appeared undisciplined and threatening to a reactionary old guard who utilized the dolly image to denigrate, titillate and dismiss, to many young working-class male, female, black and gay consumers London's revitalized fashion scene was clearly a psychological revelation, full of tantalising possibilities. As Sheila Rowbotham, then a young college lecturer based in Hackney, recalled: 'Swinging London... was always an external definition and regarded as a joke. It did catch something that was happening though, some process of interaction.... The creative mix resulted in an alternative way to be which was no longer simply marginal.'[68]

# DOLLY TRIUMPHANT

As Jonathan Green suggests, the Dolly Bird 'was not strictly a Sixties invention - the phrase had described a slattern in the eighteenth and nineteenth centuries and had referred to a pretty young girl since the early twentieth'.[69] Colin MacInnes identified a more recent precedent for the newly confident figure of the London Dolly in his sharply-observed description of the appearance of the smart working-class teenage girl of the late 1950s:

She's hatless, her hair is 'elfin' or 'puffed' and probably tinctured. Her face is pallid - 'natural make-up with a dash of mauve or creamy 'rose cameo' and, in either case, mascara round the eyes as if under artificial light at noon. Cotton décolleté blouse (with short blazer jacket if it's chilly, or she wants some pockets). Short voluminous skirt with rattling paper-nylon petticoats - or if it's cooler, one of buttock revealing tightness. Seamless stockings and pointed light-coloured shoes with stiletto heels, both very flattering even to legs that are recalcitrant. Light hanging bag. General air (from the age of thirteen upwards) of formidable self-possession.[70]

❹ ❼ Jean Shrimpton by Terry O'Neill, *c.*1965 (Terry O'Neill)

Many of the identifying features of the classic 1960s Dolly Bird are included in MacInnes's sketch, from the pallid make-up and heavy mascara to the provocative air of self-possession. But in some important respects the allure of the Dolly's predecessor was of a very different order. First, the original look strove for an adult sophistication which was at odds with the infantilizing tendencies of the Swinging version. The teased hair, sculptural skirts and stiletto heels all borrowed from an idea of soignée sexuality much promoted by a generation of masquerading matinee stars such as Alma Cogan, Connie Francis, Brenda Lee and the young Shirley Bassey. Secondly, as this roster of role-models implied, the style tended toward an international register of manufactured glamour that was American in origin. These second-hand trends were, however, enjoying a diminishing appeal by the early years of the next decade. The success of approachable home-grown stars like Helen Shapiro (proudly hailing from Hackney and rapidly followed by Dagenham-bred Sandie Shaw and Kilburn-raised Dusty Springfield), together with increased access to a new stable of British teenage magazines including *Rave*, *Teen Scene* and *Petticoat*, offered young women in London and other British cities an alternative range of attainable idols.

George Melly identified the London fashion model Jean Shrimpton as the prototype of the newly emergent Dolly Bird. Her distinctive yet softly unthreatening looks were highly adaptable to mass dissemination and reproduction so that 'her imitators... were almost interchangeable. All had long clean hair, preferably blonde, interchangeable pretty faces, interchangeable long legs' and, in their casual and interchangeable sense of beauty, their presence signalled a passively accepting attitude to easy pleasure that for Melly was vaguely unsettling: 'They represented girls as objects to an extraordinary degree. They produced a kind of generalised rather half-hearted lust, triggered off by their ever-shortening mini-skirts.'[71] Contrary to relaxed appearances, such laid-back panache was not attained without a degree of effort - yet even schoolgirls in Liverpool became proficient in replicating the effect. Maureen Nolan and Roma Singleton recalled the attendant rituals:

Clothes and make-up were as inspired as the music. The new fashion for tights hitched hemlines higher and higher, and two pairs of knickers were required, one over and one under the tights to give a tanned bare-leg effect from a distance... I spent most of my time trying to replicate those Twiggy eyes. White powdered eye-shadow was first applied... Next one of up to three pairs of false eyelashes... Black eyeliner was indispensable, for this was where the real artistry came in. First the false eyelash line had to be elongated into a Cleopatra type sweep.... Then ever so carefully, under the false lower lashes thin black lines were drawn in their shadow. The effect was spidery and stark. Finally, the eyebrows having been plucked away... [were] drawn in a brief but deep arch, reminiscent of Jean Harlow in her prime. A very black waterproof mascara would finish the look, blending false eyelashes with real.[72]

The extreme metropolitan version of the Dolly's toilette is boldly laid out in the Christmas 1965 edition of Mark Boxer's short-lived magazine *London Life* (a title characterized by Booker as symptomatic of the solipsistic attitude of the Swinging era[73]). Amidst quirky articles on children's party entertainers, futuristic Moon travel, the Ortonesque love letters of a Brixton prisoner, and a preview of the new James

## Spoil yourself at least once a year

Simple white jersey. Add glitter, jewels, furs to spell luxury and a special way of life. A life every woman dreams of and may possibly attain at Christmas, when there is an excuse to dress extravagantly to fit the party-time mood. These clothes are chosen simply to make *any* woman feel marvellous . . .

White ribbed jersey for a softly tailored suit with squared-off seaming around neckline, and diamanté and silvered buttons, from Maxine Leighton at 59 guineas. Big gold watch with white strap from Dickins & Jones at 4½ guineas. Silver court shoes with bow £3 19s 11d from Elliott Narrow Fitting Shops. The Afghan hound wears a silver and diamond American collar and lead (her own)

Maxine Leighton, 28a High Street, Hampstead, NW 3 (SWI 9214) and 22 Conduit St, W 1 (HYD 1174)

Dickins & Jones, Regent St, W 1 (REG 7070)

Elliott Narrow Fitting Shops, 48 Brompton Rd, SW 3 (KNI 0333) and 76 New Bond St, W 1 (MAY 3844)

22

**4 8** *London Life,* 25 December 1965 (Corporation of London)

Bond movie are two articles foregrounding the increasingly stylized adornment of the Dolly's body. 'Pop Eye' details the trend for elaborate eye make-up. In it actress Francesca Annis, designer Sarah White and model Jill Kennington are pictured with their brows encrusted in feathers and sequins or painted like tropical fish, and John Kennedy, proprietor of the Ad Lib Club, is reported to be 'amazed to see eyes in the smoky gloom growing gradually larger and brighter, like so many coloured lights on a

Christmas tree'.[74] This sense of Felliniesque decadence is extended to a fashion shoot extolling readers to 'spoil yourself at least once a year'. In this a model sporting a platinum-blond wig sprawls voluptuously across soft sheepskin in anticipation of Roger Vadim's 1968 sci-fi heroine Barbarella. She is dressed in variations of white jersey, glittering crochet, costume jewels and fur, all sourced from London shops.[75] Representations such as these segued seamlessly with the eroticized environment of Chelsea and Kensington, ensuring that the Dolly Bird was implicated in a broader consumerist *mise en scene* which held deeply subversive ramifications. Marianne Faithfull gave voice to what Angela Carter has described as 'the inexpressible decadence of the Sixties'[76] in her evocation of this sensual, enticing, but illusory landscape:

Harrods looming up like a great liner, Walton Street with dozens of seductive boutiques. Shop windows filled with bright smartie colours. Mini-skirts, sequinned gowns, slinky thigh-high boots, brass earrings.... [77]

Subsequent post-feminist readings of the Dolly scenario point up its glaring paradoxes. In her work on the 'Single Girl' (a less loaded descriptor of the Dolly Bird type), Hilary Radner indicates that though this ideal prioritized the positive characteristics of youthful energy, emotional independence, economic self-sufficiency and especially unfettered mobility, the extent to which such freedoms came under the control of young women themselves is debatable. Representations of the Single Girl, particularly those expressed through the newly kinetic medium of fashion photography, seem to Radner to have limited the capacity of young women to break through established constraints, particularly those set up by capitalist institutions.[78] As she argues, 'both in appearance waif-like and adolescent, and in goals to be glamorous and adored by men while economically independent, the Single Girl defines femininity outside a traditional patriarchal construction. At the same time [she] establishes consumerism as the mechanism that replaces maternity in the construction of the feminine'.[79]

Other interpretations also flag up the contingent nature of the consumerist freedoms the Dolly Bird's figure seemed to symbolize. Patricia Juliana Smith shows how the fantastic stage persona of Dusty Springfield both celebrated and camouflaged a discordant sexuality, for 'in the... ethos of Swinging London... one generally could be almost anything, no matter how extreme or incongruous, except oneself... particularly if one's own true self were queer. As a result Dusty Springfield paradoxically expressed and disguised her own unspeakable queerness through an elaborate camp masquerade that metaphorically and artistically transformed a nice white girl into a black woman and a femme gay man, often simultaneously'.[80] Yet despite its origins in the bleak politics of sexual and racial oppression, such masquerading offered the tools to construct something fresh and optimistic. The Dolly Bird with her borrowed finery and faux innocence epitomized that diffuse 1960s concept of the 'look', a notion which Radner suggests 'tended to undermine a concrete definition of style as ownership, something achieved through assembling a set of objects. The 'look' also emphasised the element of surprise, of the unanticipated, of the continually new, as an attribute of the stylish'.[81]

Crucially, the Dolly's 'look' was capable of cutting across the social and class constituencies which still marked London's new 'style meritocracy'. Thus on the television show *Ready Steady Go* Dusty Springfield could survey the studio audience and, peering through her panda eyes, discover that a fan wearing the same 'off-the-peg' Marks and Spencers dress as herself was cause for celebration.[82] Similarly Carol Denny, the proprietor of the boutique at 430 King's Road, could boast unreservedly that 'our biggest source of regular customers are the dolly birds, which to be slightly snobbish about it means working-class girls... It must be at least half their wages going on clothes'. This revelation was also a sign of changing times and priorities, for as Jonathan Aitken commented: 'Dolly birds may economise on their lunch-time eating habits to do it, debutantes may borrow... factory girls may work extra overtime... the point is they're all doing it.'[83]

# FIN DU SIXTIES

Everybody was so very rich, you see, due to sponging off the state or, I don't know, cornering the market in tie-dyed underpants... Or. But at that time Britain was a low rent, cheap food economy with relatively low wages and high taxes - most people I knew lived on very little.... Second hand furniture, old houses, old clothes were dirt cheap in the sixties, or else free. You could strip a derelict house, nobody else wanted the stuff. Oh God, those vast, whitewashed rooms with bare floorboards and a mattress in the corner with an Indian coverlet on it.... The pure asceticism of the late sixties.[84]

As far as the 1960s were concerned, the final destination of the drive toward a London style economy, which had been pushed through the King's Road on the back of the Dolly Bird's infamy, lay a couple of miles north of the World's End, at Barbara Hulanicki's Biba stores in formerly 'respectable' Kensington. Angela Carter describes above the counter-cultural and politically-aware influences which informed their febrile aesthetic meter: the retro, orientalist, recycled ephemera which gradually replaced that earlier fetishization of uncomplicated novelty which had marked Bazaar and the first boutiques. But a comparison of two items from the Museum of London's collection fixes the transformation in a more material sense. A navy-blue rayon culotte mini-dress by

**49**
Ginger Group Dress by Mary Quant, 1967 (Museum of London)

Mary Quant's Ginger Group of 1967 bespeaks the sophisticated minimalism of Quant's Knightsbridge. Apparently a scaled-up version of an infant's play-clothes, the simple front-fastening zipper and unconstricting cut prioritize a stripped-down modern functionalism which is underlined stylistically by a strikingly extended 'Peter Pan' collar, its edges picked out cleanly in contrasting white stitches, and the placing of a minimum of seams on the body of the dress. That this is little more than an adult romper suit is a jokey suggestion heightened by the childlike graphics of the swing tag, where the smiling face of a small girl in a sun hat announces the style of the garment as 'Big Toe'.[85] First appearances imply that a white and navy-blue Biba ensemble (sleeveless jacket and straight skirt in bonded rayon and cotton organza blouse) of two years later follows the same basic design principles. Its simple boldness and superficial similarity of construction (the jacket buttoning down the front, the plainly cut short skirt functional in the extreme) are also redolent of childhood. But there is perhaps less of a sense of innocence in the Biba product. The jacket and skirt sit at rakish slants on the hips and are lined in a provocative cerise. The long sleeves of the paisley-patterned blouse with its integral flowing neck-tie are set in tightly at the shoulders with just-discernable puffs - gently swelling out again as they reach the cuffs with their pretty pearl buttons. Lacking the overt playfulness of the Quant, there is in the more sophisticated Biba suit something of the sulky self-awareness of the adolescent's special-occasion frock or party dress - its apparent formality hinting at a barely contained desire to transgress.[86]

**5 0**

Suit and Blouse by Biba, 1969 (Museum of London)

Alexandra Pringle, who as a teenager moved from Chelsea to Kensington in the mid-1960s, was well aware of the constraining atmosphere of the latter district: 'a place of self-control and respectability with no sense of the raffishness and cosiness of Chelsea'.[87] Yet Biba seemed to undermine all that, inducing Kensington to 'lose its stuffiness' and finally subsuming 'that bastion of old ladyhood - Derry and Toms'.[88] In her memoir of the period *From A to Biba*, Hulanicki, who had trained as a fashion illustrator, shows herself to have been early attuned to the aesthetic of poverty and dereliction identified by Carter as the stylistic signature of the late 1960s. In 1964 she opened the first Biba shop in a decaying Chemist's store on Abingdon Road W8:

There were lots of black and gold signs left and the windows were painted half way up with scratched black paint with gold leaf edges. The woodwork outside was covered in marvellous peeling blue grey paint…. [Inside] a friend lent us two bronze lamps with huge black shades. We made long curtains in a plum and navy William Morris print with a plum dress fabric lining. I refused to have the flaking woodwork outside painted.[89]

Having established a cult following at this rather obscure location, Biba moved in the following year to bigger premises in an old Grocer's shop on Kensington Church Street where, as Jonathan Aitken observed, 'amidst the Victorian splendour of a massive panoply of burgundy coloured wall paper and heavy mahogany wardrobes, all the flamboyance of the swinging fashion cult stands exposed'.[90] At this stage in the store's development stock was simple, but plentiful, constituting 'everything from luminous pink socks to sombrero-sized felt hats and pop art jewellery', the majority of it designed and manufactured by an in-house team.[91] By maintaining a tight control over Biba's products, Hulanicki could tailor to an ideal customer whose attributes were closely aligned to the Dolly stereotype:

She was very pretty and young. She had an upturned nose, rosy cheeks and a skinny body with long asparagus legs and tiny feet. She was square shouldered and quite flat chested. Her head was perched on a long swan-like neck. Her face was a perfect oval, her lids were heavy with long spiky lashes. She looked sweet but was as hard as nails. She did what she felt like at that moment and had no mum to influence her judgement.[92]

In practice the ideal appealed to a broad constituency of consumers, composed of actual shop visitors and many mail-order clients.[93] Aitken estimated that '3,000 dolly birds each week push[ed] through the heavy Victorian wood and brass doors, intent on dissipating their last shillings on the tempting… baubles of the Aladdin's Cave… within'.[94] And though these included famous clients like Cathy McGowan, Julie Christie, Cilla Black, Sandy Shaw and Twiggy,[95] the majority of customers were 'working girls of slender… incomes' who spent an average £7 per week on Biba clothes and accessories. As Hulanicki boasted: 'the high expenditure rate never ebbs since after a month's wear a new dress is an antique, and the worst economic freeze does not touch the pockets of secretaries'.[96]

Biba's successful retail recipe supported the forging of a partnership with the high-street chain Dorothy Perkins, and a further move into the old Cyril Lord Carpet Company Warehouse on Kensington High Street in 1969. A final metamorphosis into 'Big Biba', based at Derry & Toms from 1973, announced a dissipation of the firm's original ideals and a damaging descent into bitter conflict with new corporate owners British Land before inevitable closure in 1976.[97] Yet these commercial developments disguise a profound recasting of the Dolly dream in the twilight years of the 1960s which symbolize more powerfully than boardroom strife an end to the swinging myth. Alexandra Pringle noticed the shift in tone:

As it moved from a back street to the main thoroughfare of Kensington, a certain lasciviousness, a sort of voluptuousness crept in. Crowded into dimly lit communal dressing rooms, now proud of the leanness that made every garment fit me better than those around me, I tried on clothes for the sinful and louche : slithery gowns in glowing satins, hats with black veils, shoes stacked for sirens. There were… evening gowns to make Betty Grable sigh, make-up - chocolate and black - for vamps and vampires. And for real life there were raincoats to sweep the London pavements, tee-shirts the colour of old maid's hats, dusky suede boots with long zippers.[98]

Pringle's memory concurs with Hulanicki's recollection that this conscious change of direction opened up the possibilities for self-transformation, possibilities that had been so constrained for the classic King's Road Dolly, and which eventually exposed the limitations of the over-determined idea of the swinging boutique: 'Once she was inside Biba the music thundered, the lighting was soft, and she became more mysterious. It was extraordinary to see how people applied… my dream image to themselves. I felt we gave them the basics that they could then interpret in their own way'.[99] In assessing the long-term significance of the store, historians such as Elizabeth Wilson have interpreted its style as an active influence on the emergence of Punk in the late 1970s, opening up a space 'for experimentation and subversion'.[100] Though the darker strictures of Punk threw into question the central tenets of those philosophies and aspirations which had defined the 1960s, highlighting the hypocrisy and vacuity of the preceding decade, it is perhaps no coincidence that its protagonists haunted the same London streets, taking over those spaces in the World's End and Kensington High Street that had formerly accommodated the desires of the Dolly Bird.

# *The* **Student:**

## CAMDEN MARKET 1970-2000

It's algae all the way from Camden Town tube station to the canal. Leather jackets, bootleg tapes, gutter T-shirts, more leather jackets, toxin burgers, all algae. No sane person would try to get any further up the High Street than Ryman's on a Saturday or Sunday. Each weekend there are 200,000 other people in the way.[1]

**5 1** Camden Market by Peter Marshall *c.*1990 (Peter Marshall)

At various moments during the final quarter of the twentieth century Camden Market in north-west London came to represent all that was streetwise and edgy about the capital for the rest of the world. Admittedly, its 'edginess' ebbed and flowed over twenty- five years, but for many younger visitors to the city its crowded pavements, eclectic merchandise, and particular smells and sounds offered a sense of 'connection' to underground trends and urban 'cool' that easily surpassed in scale and concentration the previous offerings of Carnaby Street or the King's Road. For older local inhabitants and more cynical observers the Camden experience was often less inviting. Journalist Marek Kohn likened the act of browsing among its stalls to the dubious pleasure of swimming in the dank canal that cuts across NW1's heartland. Certainly by the early 1990s Camden Market's attractions were waning. The forces of unchecked expansion and free-market competition meant that what had originally functioned as an alternative venue for the selling of craft or vintage goods to the 1970s counter-culture was submerged in a sea of cheap designer rip-offs, cloying junk-food aromas and aimlessly wandering tourists. However, setting aside the Market's recent association with the banal and seedy, it is clear that its vigorous ad hoc growth and romantic reputation as an arena for rebellion and innovation still mark Camden out as an apt symbol of London's struggling yet vibrantly creative fashion economy in the new Millennium.

For myself, as a student newcomer to London in the mid-1980s, billeted twenty minutes' walk from Camden Town in a Holloway bed-sit, the market signified all that was new and mysterious about an unfamiliar metropolitan culture. In 1984 it occupied just a third of its current territory and only imposed its noisy character on the district at weekends. According to memory, visits to its record, bric-a-brac and second-hand clothing stalls always took place under a perpetually leaden winter sky and brought with them the sensations particular to market-browsing of frozen hands and hot sweet tea. Coming as I did from the narrow horizons of South Somerset, the gritty atmosphere of the grey North London streets opened up a whole vista of self-transforming possibilities for me. The gothic presence of Camden's Irish pubs and working-men's hostels, its cut-price supermarkets, crumbling repertory cinemas, fly-blown Cypriot restaurants and old-fashioned barber-shops formed the back-drop to those 'Withnailesque' fantasies of tortured alienation which preoccupied much of London's student population.[2] For this was a time of Miner's Strikes, Greater London Council-sponsored anti-capitalist festivals, Clause 28 marches and Smiths' LPs. It was a moment before the massed hedonism of the rave, when the ephemera of an 'alternative' culture laid a monochrome ground against which the bright colours of 1990s club-style would glow with a heightened intensity.

The self-consciously serious pose of the 1980s fresher was aided by a wardrobe constructed largely from market-wares: if not all from Camden, then from similarly down-at-heel stalls in Bell Street, Brick Lane, Greenwich and Portobello, or sourced among the organized chaos of such canny importers of Americana as Flip and American Retro in Covent Garden. Narrow-lapelled three-button suits from the 1950s and early 1960s, sagging and rubbed Levi's 501 jeans worn with bulky turn-ups, heavy Harris Tweed or ex- RAF and Army overcoats (these latter from the strange warren of military surplus showrooms at Lawrence Corner near Euston Station - a long-standing emporium for cult clothing), collarless 'grandad' shirts or arrow-point collars and Jazz-style silk ties, Tootal brand paisley or polka-dot cotton scarves, reconditioned leather-soled brogues or ox-blood Doctor Marten shoes, thick woollen hiking socks, battered leather satchels, peaked flannel caps and lapel-pins from the communist Eastern bloc; all of these frayed echoes of earlier decades constituted a uniform that set itself in opposition to the glossy smartness of South Molton Street and St Christopher's Place in the West End or the corporate blandness of an emerging 'label' culture.

## MARKET CULTURE : A PREHISTORY

There was of course little that was original in the sartorial make-up of this anti-Thatcherite undergraduate posturing. The retro-styling of the early 1980s which segued so smoothly with Camden's nostalgic decay, had precedents in every preceding post-war decade - from the reactionary panache of New-Edwardianism to the camp opulence of Glam-Rock and the do-it-yourself kitsch of Punk. Similarly, the market's status as a mecca of well-sourced second-hand goods was underpinned by a long history of trade in old clothes in which London featured as a global hub.[3] In my own tentative attempts to dress in a recognizably Camden style, I was engaging (albeit unwittingly) in a long-established sartorial discourse with distinctly Londonate inflections. During the eighteenth and nineteenth centuries Rag Fair in Houndsditch had played a pivotal role in sustaining the clothing economy of the country and serving the sartorial needs of the poor. The spectacle of its trestles, loaded down with exotic cast-offs, also inspired several sentimental essays on the transience of wealth, taste and life by eminent writers.[4] Viewed as the province of the immigrant, the second-hand trade passed in the early twentieth century from Jewish to Irish hands and it remained under the control of Camden and Kilburn matriarchs until its decline in the 1950s. This was precipitated by the relocation of the 'shoddy' industries (the recycling of rags into textiles) from West Yorkshire to Northern Italy and the growth of the affluent society with its valorization of the new and mass-produced. The old-clothes dealer also found his business purloined by the rise of the Charity shop whose humanitarian ethos removed the shame associated with the buying of worn goods. Yet as the epithet 'nearly new' attained the ring of respectability in thrifty middle-class circles, 'top-end' second-hand clothing also enjoyed an unexpected revival in the early 1970s, through the inflationary endeavours of the Mayfair auction-houses and the revivalist interests of the counter-culture - and it was at this juncture that Camden Market established its prominence.

However, in order to locate the market's nearest ancestor, both in terms of its geographical location and its distinctive atmosphere, it is necessary to consider the influence of the famous Caledonian Market. 'The Stones', as the market was known among its traders, provided a clear blueprint for Camden's sublime scale and international renown. Shortly before the First World War the wide-open space of the metropolitan cattle-market situated just north of King's Cross between Agar Town and Barnsbury was given over on Fridays to second-hand dealers. By 1914 the market numbered over 700 stalls and had attracted the interest of a fashionable as well as a local audience. Its popularity necessitated the setting aside of Tuesdays as a further day for the selling of scrap goods and by the 1930s three and a half thousand pitches were available over the duration of the two-day jamboree. In her guide to the street markets

**❺❷** Caledonian Market by Cyril Arapoff, 1935 (Museum of London)

of London of 1936 (beautifully illustrated by the photographs of Moholy Nagy) Mary Benedetta characterized the 'Cally' as 'the happy hunting ground of hundreds of cheap jacks' where 'the old clothes women have their pitches mingled among the junk merchants. A few of them are rather grand and have improvised stalls, but most of them pile their clothes on the pavement or on strips of newspaper. The conversations that go on around them are often very amusing, if you can bear being in such close proximity to some of the old clothes'.[5]

Historian Jerry White has identified the London street market as one of those forms of semi-legal enterprise in which the informal skills of the local proletariat found ample potential for the making of a reasonable living. Mini-cab driving and used-car dealing have furnished similar examples of modern 'cockney' entrepreneurship which, in their mythological status as a staple of popular comedic representations of London life, trace a lineage back to the illicit activities of Mayhew and Dickens's amateur rogues and crafty costers. These trades 'offered scope for independence and advancement by exploiting wit, charm, shrewdness, a quick tongue and courage - qualities readily available as birthright in the London working class and largely untouched... by schooling'.[6] In a milieu such as the Caledonian market, such rough skills overlapped productively with the polite accomplishments of connoisseurship and an easy sociability based on a knowledge of the gradations of taste which furnished the success of 'shabby-genteel' stall holders such as the middle-class Jane Brown who, forced by economic circumstance, traded on 'the Stones' during the 1920s and 1930s. In her memoir of those years, Brown vouched for the democratic yet slightly risqué attractions which the market held for dealer and punter alike:

Visitors from America, the Colonies and, in fact, every part of the world, came to the market and took back, not only souvenirs bought at the pitches, but stories of the bustle, and freemasonry, and glamour, and above all of the incredible bargains that the lucky buyer might find - a rope of pearls bought as a string of cheap beads, an old master bought as a dust-covered frameless canvas. A visit to the Caledonian Market... was like buying a ticket in a sweepstake.[7]

But it was among the 'totters', or sellers of old-clothes, that Brown found the most compelling culture, and this community clearly bequeathed its colourful traditions to the later incarnation of the 'Cally' spirit in post-war Camden:

The 'tot' stalls usually comprise four poles on the corners of the pitch, with a clothes line running all round, and another line strung across the middle. Dangling on hangers along these lines are incredible arrays of second-hand or even tenth-hand evening dresses, looking very sad and tired as they flap in the wind; men's dress clothes, mostly purchased by waiters; suits of clothes, odd coats, odd trousers, dressing gowns and so on. As if the effect of these is not sufficiently grotesque, a hat is perched on the top of each... You find yourself at the point of feeling that these worn, derelict outfits may have a poor travesty of a life of their own... With few exceptions, the owners of these stalls are women; all types and kinds of women, but with one thing in common, their jewellery. They all wear heavy gold wedding rings... snake or gypsy rings... brooches and bracelets, and, if they can afford it, a gold muff chain as well... They are usually quite well-off and a number of them own considerable property. Normally they trade in nothing but clothes, but once in a while, one of them will buy some china, glass or trinkets.[8]

If the totters provide a premonition of later forms of market enterprise, then some of their customers also foreshadowed the bohemian browsers of Camden Lock. As Brown suggests, the totters' stock still serviced a predominantly working-class clientele searching out work-clothes or cheap alternatives to the ready-made, but other more 'pretentious' visitors found in the melee a stock of quirky aesthetic statements which marked their 'avant-garde' distinction from the herd:

A type that tests one's tolerance to the limit is the interior decorator, complete with neophyte being initiated into the mysteries of the trade... He... usually has a pale complexion... a tendency to baldness, flannel bags, sports jacket and an open-necked, coloured shirt. The shirt may be dark and worn with a red tie, or replaced altogether with a roll-necked jersey. If it is a she, bare legs, bare head, and a skimpy dress, or slacks and tunic over an American shirt-waist, is the uniform rig… 'Primrose yellow will look simply gorgeous with a touch of hyacinth blue.'… It is difficult to be patient with such poseurs.[9]

The Caledonian Market was bombed during the Second World War and in 1949, those traders who now styled themselves as antique dealers established a 'New Caledonian Market' close to the south side of Tower Bridge in Bermondsey. It would be a further twenty-five years before the totters found a site which offered the huge returns they had enjoyed in Islington, its location barely a mile west along the Regent's Canal.

# IN CAMDEN TOWN

On the surface, Camden in the 1960s and 1970s presented an inauspicious venue for the revival of a Rag Fair and the development of what would become a global tourist attraction. Its plain side streets of neat terraced houses and broad but unexceptional main thoroughfare were planned in the early nineteenth century as a facility for servicing the aristocratic terraces of Nash's nearby Regent's Park. However, the railway boom which so altered the face of North London from the opening of Euston Station in 1838 ensured that Camden's ambitions to emulate its wealthy neighbours were thwarted by a blight which would last for a further century and a half. The construction of lines from Euston, King's Cross (1852) and St Pancras (1868) threatened and obliterated swathes of residential property and those large houses which did survive were broken up into lodging rooms for a transient population of building labourers and navvies. The canal system which bisected the rail-tracks also brought its own grimy hinterland of wharves, warehouses, factories and stables to disturb any semblance of domestic respectability, so that by the 1880s Camden Town was synonymous with a down-at-heel seediness, the stain of which the district could not shift. In 1913 Compton Mackenzie capitalized on the depressing reputation of the area in his novel *Sinister Street*:

When the cab had crossed the junction of the Euston Road with the Tottenham Court Road, unknown London with all its sly and labyrinthine romance lured his fancy onwards. Maple's and Shoolbred's, those outposts of shopping civilisation, were left behind, and the Hampstead Road with a hint of roguery began… Presently upon an iron railway bridge Michael read in giant letters the direction Kentish Town behind a huge leprous hand pointing to the left. The hansom clattered through the murk beneath, past the dim people huddled upon the pavement, past a wheel-barrow and the obscene outlines of humanity chalked upon the arches of sweating brick… A train roared over the bridge; a piano organ gargled its tune; a wagon load of iron girders drew near in a tintamar of slow progress… He caught sight of a slop-shop where old clothes smothered the entrance with their mucid heaps and, just beyond, of three houses from whose surface the stucco was peeling in great scabs and the damp was oozing in livid arabesques and scrawls of verdigris.[10]

Other upper-middle-class creative types also looked to north-west London for the sense of banal degradation that Mackenzie found so repellent and so fascinating. During the early decades of the twentieth century, Camden's grubby aura titillated a generation of artists: it appeared to signify an alienating modernity equal to anything on offer in the capitals of continental Europe. In 1905 the painter Walter Sickert moved to Mornington Crescent, his choice of domicile vindicating William Rothestein's recollection that 'Walter Sickert's genius for discovering the dreariest house and the most forbidding rooms in which to work was a source of wonder and amusement to me. He himself was so fastidious in his person, in his manners, in the choice of his clothes; was he affecting a kind of dandyism 'a rebours' ?'[11] The murder of part-time prostitute Emily Dimmock in St Paul's Road (now Agar Grove) during the late summer of 1907 sealed the notoriety of the district. It aroused significant tabloid interest and provided Sickert with the subject of four canvases. The double-life of the victim, who masqueraded during the day as the respectable wife of a railway cook, and the fact that the main suspect in the case enjoyed an upstanding career as a commercial artist, heightened the suburban bathos of a case which would find echoes in the subsequent arrest of patent medicine salesman Dr Crippen for the murder and burial of his wife Cora, a retired music hall performer, at their home in Hilldrop Crescent off the Camden Road in 1910. In the popular imagination Camden thus became inextricably linked with the perversity and humdrum horror that bubbled up from beneath the surfaces of contemporary urban life.

An atmosphere of malignant decay still hung in the air fifty years later, until challenged by those processes of development and modernization which both hastened the demise of Sickert and Crippen's Camden Town while

*Gallery Box at the New Bedford Music Hall* **❺❸**
by Walter Sickert, 1914 (Museum of London)

also benefiting from the romantic potential of its negative associations. The industrial infrastructure of the goods yards, sidings and towpaths which had sustained employment opportunities for generations of Irish migrants since the 1840s limped into the post-war era. During the 1950s Camden Lock sat at the centre of a dwindling concentration of packing and haulage companies. Working against the economic tide T.E. Dingwall took over a large warehouse on the Lock in 1946, importing timber, building wooden crates and shipping them out to clients. But competition from rail carriers and road haulage firms, rising import prices and government initiatives to move heavy industry out of central locations to the Lea valley and Essex hinterlands spelt the end for Camden's water-based trades. The Great Freeze of 1962 seemed to seal the fate of other local employers including Gilbey's Gin, Carreras Tobacco, the Aereated Bread Company and Moy's Engineering, whose barges were ruinously impounded by ice for weeks; and by 1973, when Dingwall's finally relinquished their lease, their empty Victorian sheds overlooked the still black water of a silenced canal.[12]

The industrial decline of Camden Town was accompanied by the spectre of transport planning, invoked in 1969 by the Greater London Development Plan (only partially realized) to encircle the centre of London with a six-lane motorway running through the inner suburbs of Dalston, Bow, Denmark Hill, Brixton, West Kensington and Swiss Cottage. Years of planning proposals, consultations and public enquiries, accompanied by the compulsory purchase or more nebulous 'safeguarding' of broad swathes of land, had the effect of stalling investment in affected areas and impeding profits. In the depressed Camden of the early 1970s the consequences were particularly harsh, exacerbating the movement of an old working class out of the borough and creating a ruined landscape of empty houses and boarded-up shops.[13] For some, however, the resulting low property prices and ready supply of large early-Victorian family houses (whose dilapidated state after generations of use as bedsits and lodging houses only increased their appeal as blank canvases for sensitive reconversion) offered the potential for colonization similar to that which had faced the adventurous urban middle classes in Islington during the late 1950s. Camden thus became a target for those employed in the media and higher education-sectors who spearheaded a familiar process of gentrification in NW1. Journalist David Thomson, a gentrifying pioneer who had moved into such a house on Regent's Park Terrace with his wife Martina in 1956, looked back on this transformation in the borough's architectural fortunes and the character of its population from the vantage point of 1980:

When I first saw the faces in Bosch, Breughel, Hogarth - alive as they are - I thought they belonged to the past... Then gradually I began to see those faces on buses, at auctions, in markets, at fairs. For me it has been the same with Marc's cartoons. When I first saw them I thought Simon and Joanna String-Along were brilliant inventions, but now... I see the String-Alongs and their friends everyday. I suppose we are String-Alongs too in our way, or at least we are on the fringe of that noticeable tribe, but neither of us ever felt we belonged to it... And then, we came to Camden Town long before Marc made us look so funny. It was far less swish in the 1950s while gentrification was slowly tightening its grip. There were numerous cheap boarding houses in Gloucester Crescent, only one of which has survived, and half the houses in Regent's Park Terrace were occupied by several families… It was the hopscotch chalk on the pavement, the young mothers with prams, the crowds of children playing on the lawn that confirmed Martina's eagerness to live in the terrace. She saw all the favours of tenement life without the squalor.[14]

The Thomsons may have tried to deny it, but in many ways their privileged idealization of the effects of poverty segued perfectly with the attitudes lampooned in those astringent Mark Boxer cartoons from which they attempted to distance themselves. Simon and Joanna String-Along's antics were featured during the 1960s in Boxer's *Listener* series 'Life and Times in NW1', emerging again in *The Times* during the 1970s and 1980s. Obsessed with the trendy trappings of the 'alternative' lifestyle, and desperately paying heed to the latest dictates of fashionable political and sexual discourse, this pair of metropolitan grotesques, with their modish haircuts and heavy-rimmed spectacles, were portrayed in their Camden habitat attempting to stay one step ahead of the crowd. In the strike- and inflation-torn spring of 1975 Marc pictured them ascending the iron-railed steps to their house, rubbish swirling around their feet, bemoaning that 'if it gets any worse we'll have to find a permanently unfashionable area to move into'. In another scene, set in front of the window of a charity shop, Joanna remarks to a friend 'do you remember when we really liked buying second hand clothes?'[15]

**5 4** *The String A-Longs* by Mark Boxer (Mark Boxer Estate)

Introducing a collection of Marc cartoons published in 1978, James Fenton reflected on the relationship between the caricature of the String-Alongs, the pessimistic attitudes of the decade's avant-garde elite and their stultifying concern with nostalgia, pinpointing the symbolic and material convergence of all three in the environs of NW1. Thus 'if the Seventies may justly be called the Age of Revivals, it has been noteworthy that the supply of things to revive has dried up. Hence the dreary stalls at Camden Lock, piled high with tat. Hence the cult of junk… Hence the second-hand clothes stalls where young girls persuade young girls to buy foxes. Hence the fact that, whereas all over the rest of Europe children dress smartly, in London they look like the traditional Dutch boy in patched trousers'.[16] Through this negative assessment Fenton inadvertently anticipated the central role that the residents of Camden Town would come to play in fixing the referents of London style culture in the following decade. Inner-city deprivation and bohemian aspirations thereby provided the most favourable conditions for what has subsequently come to be known as the familiar process of urban Renaissance.

# THE RISE OF A MARKET STYLE

In 1971 entrepreneur Bill Fullwood, surveyor Peter Wheeler and promoter Eric Reynolds joined with architect John Dickinson as Northside Developments Ltd in a bid to capitalize on the potential of the empty land and buildings formerly belonging to Dingwall's at Camden Lock. Having generated some profit from the earlier development of property on Clapham Common Northside (hence the company name), they purchased the last seven years of Dingwall's lease for £10,000. The cobbled yards and warehouses of the site were cheaply converted into open-air and covered units which served as craft workshops during the week and market-stalls on weekends. These were situated around a central double-storey stable block whose sound-insulating thick walls and minimal fenestration made it an ideal rock-music venue.[17] Opened to the public in 1973 by local MP Jock Stallard, the Lock's first commercial tenants gravitated there from the London Art Schools, especially Hornsey and Camberwell, finding the low rents, industrial spaces and community atmosphere conducive to the production and retail of ceramics, glass, metalwork, textiles and furniture. They were soon joined by the antique and vintage-clothing dealers, health and world-food caterers and alternative therapists who have since lent the market its particular character. Writing in the year of its birth, journalist Nick Tomalin commented that

The whole scene is a fine example of how nice north west London is at this moment… Provided the site developers behave themselves, keep the pleasant relaxed shoestring atmosphere of the place, and don't overdo the rents and the rebuilding, it should be a blessing to everyone. An odd paradox of urban politics: the best way to make a neighbourhood interesting is to afflict it with planner's blight. True of Covent Garden. Once true of Camden Town. The Cypriots and the Irish colonised the place: so did the middle classes. Now there are nasty signs that with no smoke and no motorway threat property men may wreck the delicate ecological balance.[18]

As Tomalin suggests, Camden was not the only London borough to benefit from this form of 'grass-roots' anti-corporate development activity in the period. The slow closure of the old Covent Garden vegetable market from 1964 had threatened to kick-start a massive state and commercial rebuilding scheme which would have obliterated the traditional working atmosphere of the streets between the Strand and New Oxford Street. This was challenged in 1971 by the formation of the Covent Garden Community Association who fought to retain the historical personality of the area by protecting the housing rights of local residents and promoting the retention of small workshops and specialist retailers. By 1974, aided by conservationist campaigns in the Press, the unique social and architectural heritage of Covent Garden was temporarily saved from the grasp of over-zealous property managers and chain stores - the new vibrancy of the area captured in the orientalist melange of the tea, incense and textile importer Neal Street East.[19] Similarly, even as the Westway (one of the few segments of the Greater London Development Plan to be built) edged its way over the roofs of Ladbrook Grove, the lower end of the Portobello Market re-established itself amidst the concrete pylons as a weekly emporium of hand-me-down 'Deco' and 'Victoriana' whose variety rivalled the stock of Biba.

All of these community-based schemes were, ironically, underwritten by the political and aesthetic affiliations (the consumption practices) of those gentrifying middle-class pioneers whose economic and psychological investment in blighted locales brought closer their inevitable co-option by the very forces of mainstream commercialism which they so feared and despised. Jonathan Raban was alive to these contradictions in his perceptive examination of the labyrinthine meanings of contemporary urban culture, written in 1974 from the vantage point of a north-London suburb dimly recognizable as one of those bordering Camden Town's fringes, and favoured as a residence by those polytechnic lecturers whose habits he submits to a fascinating scrutiny. His observations are worth quoting in full:

Just as Mayhew found it convenient to classify his street folk by the objects they sold, we may need to label ours by what they buy. For the modern city, at least in its middle-class quarters, is a temple of useless consumption. If a class of non-producers distort and swell its social structure, its commercial life is correspondingly inflated by the trade in objects whose sole function is to enhance the identities of their purchasers. A list of shops on the nearest block in the inner London suburb where I live illustrates this quite dramatically... Of these, two are pubs and one a wine bar. Six are foreign restaurants, ranging from a smart Italian pastiche of a Venetian trattoria to a low curry cavern which serves business lunches; there is a fish-chicken-and-chips take-away, and a coffee bar with a downstairs folk cellar; shops selling leather goods and craft objects; a stripped-pine and Japanese lampshade furniture showroom; a cupboard-sized antique boutique; a continental supermarket, a delicatessen, a chain grocery, and a fancy greengrocer's (with avocadoes more in evidence than carrots); a tobacco kiosk, a store which sells camping equipment for hikers; two travel agents, three fashion boutiques; a radio, TV and electrical shop; an off-licence; a dry cleaner's and a launderette. An ordinary chemist's at one end has just been turned into a bistro full of rubber plants and dessert trolleys; while the newest venture is a shop that sells only white-painted Moroccan birdcages.

In the unlikely guise of the Moroccan birdcage, Raban found a powerful emblem of gentrification and the clout possessed by renegade middle-class taste-makers for transforming the character of unforgiving inner-city environments:

No urban planner, puzzling out the rational requirements of a new city development, would ever have arrived at the Moroccan birdcage shop. Yet of all the businesses on the block this is the one which is most typical of the peculiar big-city flavour of the quarter.

It is an example of pure bedsitter-entrepreneurism; you import a functional object from a distant place or period, make it both useless and decorative with a lick of paint, then sell it at a fancy price as a status-enhancer... The market in fashion is omnivorous in this improvisatory, make-do-and-mend way; it transforms junk into antiques, rubbish into something rich, strange, expensive and amusing... The Moroccan birdcage syndrome is a useful model for a certain kind of urban industrial process - a process which both supplies a demand for commodities whose sole feature is their expressiveness of taste, and becomes, by virtue of its laws of economic transformation, the ultimate arbiter of that taste. The stylistic entrepreneurs who make their living out of this curious trade go, along with gangsters and dandies, into the bracket of people possessed of a special kind of city knowledge.[20]

**5 5** Camden High Street, c.1977 (Camden Libraries)

While the values of bourgeois bohemianism were clearly reflected in the tatterdemalion quirkiness of all that was 'authentic', 'vintage' or 'ethnic' in the emerging market culture of NW1, with its hand-made jewellery, ephemera fairs and imported kaftans, Camden Lock's influence also spread to affect the more utilitarian retail ecology of a pre-existing High Street. Indeed one might go so far as to claim that by the end of the 1970s the Moroccan birdcage syndrome had entrapped the length of old Camden Town's main drag, from Mornington Crescent up to Chalk Farm. Two outlets in particular, whose history was strongly bound up with the needs of Camden's original Irish population, found their formerly unglamorous stock-in-trade taken up by those stylistic entrepreneurs for whom the exotic trappings of manual labour represented a new kind of street credibility.

A.H. Holt at 5 Kentish Town Road, almost next door to Camden Town Underground Station, had opened in the late nineteenth century to provide stout working boots to local navvies and builders. In the post-war era its proprietors Victor Blackman and Alan Romaine achieved a degree of notoriety through their links to London's thriving live-music scene. Romaine, who worked in the shop from 1962 until his death in 1994 was a member of the Johnny Miller and Billy Cotton dance bands and naturally encouraged the activities of the Rock On independent record shop when it opened in adjacent premises in 1975. From a room above Holt's, Rock On's recording and management arm Chiswick Records also orchestrated the ska and two-tone revival which would make Camden synonymous with popular bands such as Madness, whose combination of Jamaican, Irish and cockney music-hall influences translated local passions for a wider teenage audience.[21] During the late 1970s and early 1980s Holt's was central to the creation of a sartorial register for the white working-class subcultures who gravitated toward the pubs and clubs of the district, earning itself an international reputation as the first British retailer of Dr Marten's shoes and boots.

Besides Holt's, Alfred Kemp's of 20 Camden High Street also connected the activities of the Lock to a longer history of retailing in the borough. Specializing in second-hand men's suits it too relied on the patronage of Irish working men in search of the sober two-piece which would supply the appropriate image at church or in the pool hall. David Thomson described its old-fashioned attractions in 1980:

Most old clothes shops are rancid, their goods reek of urine and stale sweat in dingy chambers where you cannot see to choose. But Alfred Kemp's is spacious, well aired and lit, and smells when it smells at all of floor polish. All the clothes I have ever handled in it are spotless, revived and freshened by the cleaner. Most London clothes shops have wheelbarrows and cartwheels in their windows : anything but clothes. Kemp's has suits, jackets, trousers, shirts and shoes, hung one above the other and all along, filling all the window space. You can get a good look at them from outside the shop before you summon up the courage to go in, and by the cash desk on your left when you do go in…you see… a narrow sentry box which Mr Kemp inhabits when he is not buying or selling. On it there is a card in red and black to threaten you with the police. By a secret as sure and hidden as an invisible ray, they and every trader in Camden High Street are roused whenever you attempt to steal one of Mr Kemp's garments… His verbal politeness towards customers is superior in the old fashioned 'take it or leave it' manner of the most exclusive firms. He told me that in his father's time there were more than five hundred shops of this kind within two miles - he and Moss Bros are the only survivors.[22]

Like Holt's, by the late 1970s Kemp's attracted a younger clientele who found in their eclectic stock similar affirmation of cutting-edge taste to that on offer further up the street in the market. Madness's lead-singer Suggs remembered it as 'a fantastic shop… I got a brilliant green tonic suit in there and loads of other great stuff… It was one up from an Oxfam shop in that they had these old salesmen in there, who treated you really well. It was like you'd gone into an old fashioned tailor's and you were a gentleman, even though you were buying second-hand clothes'.[23] Such attitudes were further validated by the do-it-yourself philosophy of Punk, and, in a more localized sense by the masquerading tendencies of New Romantic club culture. These were framed by the ornate spaces of the nearby Camden Palace, which had been erected at the turn of the century to provide uplifting theatrical entertainment for the local population (complementing the established Bedford Music Hall on the other side of the road, whose star turns and rowdy audience had attracted the painterly attentions of Sickert). In 1977, having endured an interim decline as a flea-pit cinema and a BBC recording studio, the Palace enjoyed a short-term incarnation as the Music Machine, an alternative live-music venue with a reputation for violence, before its transformation in 1982 as the new home of Steve Strange and Rusty Egan's opulent Club for Heroes, the exhibitionist's

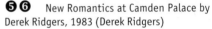
**5 6**　New Romantics at Camden Palace by Derek Ridgers, 1983 (Derek Ridgers)

paradise founded in Soho in 1978. The imaginative dress code of its followers (a surreal combination of the amateur dramatic wardrobe, transvestism and Weimar decadence) mirrored the trend for retro-outfitting that now dominated the stock of the shops and stalls outside, marking Camden's transition from a space of gentrification and counter-cultural agitation to one of slickly commodified 'pop' outrageousness. In this context the innocent 'folk-style' of Holt's and Kemp's truly belonged to another era.

## STREET-STYLE HIGH NOON

The atmosphere [of Camden Lock] is calm and relaxed with a vaguely Parisian air reminiscent of the concourse of the Pompidou Centre... Here weaving, jewellery making, knitting and many other skilful craft activities are carried on, and the market, in terms of its merchandise, largely takes its lead from this example. The market at Dingwalls is absolutely fascinating... but unfortunately there has emerged within the last few years a kind of Camden syndrome, throwing up images of women in Indian dresses with anaemic-looking babies strapped to their backs clutching whole-food rusks; and men with wispy beards and national health spectacles... the very type of seventies throwback often found in an area which has suddenly had a man-made 'ethnicity' thrust upon it... The clothes [on sale] are interesting in that they are either genuinely second-hand or are new and designed to look as if they've been well-worn. It's all very popular merchandise but pretentious in the extreme - a pretentiousness that surrounds the whole area.[24]

Kevin Perlmutter's irritable description of Camden Market, produced for tourists in 1983, is not unique in its misanthropic tone. The allure of the ever-expanding Lock attracted an equal balance of enthusiasts and detractors during its 1980s prime. As renowned for its crowds as for its merchandise, the market and its hinterland came to symbolize the quintessence of a north-London sensibility to the world. London's main listings magazines *City Limits* and *Time Out* (themselves a product of the same counter-cultural impulse which had inspired the development of the Lock) saw their own values reflected among the clutter of the stalls, and their pages provide a rich resource for recreating the precise 'looks' that came to be associated with London street-style in the period. Coinciding with the eclectic 'Hard Times' and 'Buffalo' attitudes promoted in early editions of *The Face* and *i-D*, the market's expansion offered an alternative to the matt-black, padded-shouldered, yuppie stereotypes peddled by bland high-street chains such as Next. In this parallel fashion economy *City Limits* could report that 'Tim and Sarah... make up their own versions of men's and women's 1950s clothes using old fabrics: gargantuan print skirts, blouses and... baggy trousers, all costing £2-£10'. Other dealers offered 'a mish-mash of old, new and everything in between : primary coloured espadrilles, dark denim jeans, pale green plants...' And beyond the market area, up the Chalk Farm Road, fixed shops such as Tonto now sold 'a wide selection of 1940s and 1950s authentic Wild West clothing imported from the USA. Hawaiian shirts from £7.50... Western trousers with press stud pockets in wool and gabardine £12.15. Most interesting buys are 1950s circular skirts and dresses individually decorated with heavy embroidery ric-rac and glitter'. The creepily named 'Crippen' was stocked 'for those, male and female, who are seeking the quintessential English gentleman look... Complete brace suits £57, fashion detailed wing collared shirts from £7.50'.[25] NW1 was rapidly being transformed into a giant postmodern dressing-up box.

By the mid-1980s the inexorable expansion of the market either side of Camden High Street and Chalk Farm Road was giving some cause for concern to the local authorities. In February 1986 the Development Control Sub-Committee of the London Borough of Camden turned down applications by the London Enterprise Property Company to continue the use of the upper floor of the former horse hospital near Dingwall's as an antiques market, by Petticoat Lane Rentals to continue the use of 192-8 Camden High Street for market purposes, and by Castle Rock Properties for the continued use of the Electric Ballroom at 184 Camden High Street as a Saturday market. The only application to win support was one relating to Hawley Wharf, and as the committee noted: 'This is certainly one of the better run markets in the area... The market operator has pointed out that many of the stall holders rely on this market as their only source of income and some were previously unemployed.' Bearing in mind Camden Council's reputation as a socialist stronghold, it is unsurprising that the rights of the unemployed should have taken precedence over the profits of property-based speculators, but an appendix to the committee minutes also makes clear that other practical matters were increasingly dictating planning policy:

The proposed Borough Plan Policy for markets states that legally established or approved off-street markets will be maintained, but that extensions or new markets will be resisted where they adversely affect local retailing, traffic and environmental conditions. The use of land in the Camden Lock area for markets will be resisted where such use is or will be detrimental to the amenities of residents in the locality. The change of use of vacant industrial premises to use as markets will not be permitted nor will the joint use of occupied industrial premises for industrial and market activities be permitted where the use for market activities may prejudice the full use of the premises for industrial purposes.[26]

In practice, the power of the Council to control the market's expansion was limited. For as an internal news-sheet noted in 1983, the London County Council General Powers Act of 1947 for the administration of street-market licences only had jurisdiction over stalls set up on public land, and as most of Camden's pitches had set root on private property this meant that the Council's ability 'to make them safe for the estimated 100,000 people who visit them every weekend' was severely compromised.[27] Yet despite its impotence, the Council acknowledged the difficulty of maintaining a balance between authoritarian control and the supporting of a fragile market economy whose output provided valuable promotional benefits to the district. In an echo of the tensions which simultaneously inhibited and encouraged the development of London's emerging status as an alternative fashion capital to Paris, New York or Milan, a report of the borough's Planning and Transport Sub-Committee from July 1987 reported portentously that

Open markets require a balance of flexibility, particularly with regard to type and size of stall structure and control - of numbers and operation, loading and unloading. Too little flexibility destroys the character of a market and its dual role as a community focus. Too little control results in problems of over-crowding, access, inadequate pedestrian safety and litter.[28]

By October 1989 Camden Market found itself on the brink of that slide into over-crowding, danger and litter that would spoil its reputation in the 1990s. A comprehensive report by feted pop star and club personality Vaughan Toulouse in that month's *i-D* magazine captures the character of a market on the point of implosion. Its visitors were an uneasy mix of international backpacking tourists such as 'Natalie and Caryn on a shopping holiday from Brussels' who came 'to London regularly to acquire the goth image [they] find so hard to create in Belgium' and the local stalwarts such as Eddie who bemoaned the fact that expansion and over-exposure were 'just turning the place into a creative graveyard. A lot of the people who've had stalls here for years are moving on already as rents go up and commercial shops like CCC's and Office Shoes move in... It's becoming like Covent Garden'. The stall-holders endorsed Eddie's view that mis-management of the market by developers and the Council was undermining its capacity to challenge the homogeneity of the encroaching chain stores. In the Stables, Toulouse interviewed Linda, a long-time dealer who dealt in 1960s second-hand clothing, 1950s accessories and kitsch knick-knacks:

The thing that is most worrying is that the Lock has been sold to developers and we all know what that means. They want to change the site into a nice little primary coloured, separate units affair where people can wander down from Hampstead, browse and wander back up there again. The kind of people the market attracts aren't wanted by the council.

In the Electric Ballroom, small-time entrepreneurs selling their own designs also noted a levelling-off of customers whose idiosyncratic tastes had helped to support the emergence of the market in the first place. At a stall called 'Ravish Me' Tori sold his own T-shirts, Sweat-shirts and underwear which he also wholesaled and supplied to West End avant-garde fashion emporiums Bazaar and Jones. He observed that 'the market is changing all the time. It's now nearly all tourists and they're not buying as much… Years ago it was really happening, but a lot of the really good stuff seems to have moved on - the market is living on its reputation'. Fiona, who sold student designs from her stall agreed that any attempt to capitalize on the market's unique character would 'yuppify the area and kill off a lot of creativity. It's one of the only places in London where young people can set up cheaply'. And 'Big Nigel', who conveniently overlooked the irony of his own presence 'selling T-shirts, pillowcases and baby accessories using designs based on Batman and Bazooka Joe', was able to predict the future with remarkable accuracy: 'It used to be more creative… Now it's almost like a mail-order catalogue.'[29]

**❺❼** Iggy Pop T-Shirt, purchased at Camden Market, *c.*1983 (Museum of London)

## CAMDEN AND CREATIVITY

During the same years that Toulouse formulated his gloomy prognosis, sociologist Angela McRobbie also turned her attention to the culture of Camden market. While all around the evidence of a corporate take-over of Camden mounted, McRobbie chose to focus on the continuing function of the market as a forcing-ground for new fashion ideas. She drew attention to the multivalent character of the crowds, celebrating their capacity for finding pleasure in the holiday atmosphere. 'The whole point is to amble and look, to pick up goods and examine them before putting them back. Public-school girls mingle with doped-out punks, ex-hippies hang about behind their Persian rug stalls… while more youthful entrepreneurs trip over themselves to make a quick sale.'[30] In the context of the economic and media revolutions of the 1980s, Camden emerged both as a symptom of and an antidote to free-market philosophies. In the obsession which its members displayed over questions of style, the crowds offered a living example of the postmodern consumerist turn to find significance and completion in the shifting surfaces of fashion. As McRobbie noted, 'young people go there to see and be seen if for any other reason than that fashion and style invariably look better worn than they do... in the shop windows. Here it is possible to see how items are combined with each other to create a total look.'[31]

This was a phenomenon also noticed by other commentators. In its richness and diversity Camden Market provided magazine editors, stylists, photographers, students and designers with an unprecedented degree of inspiration. In 1986 the French designer Jean-Paul Gaultier told Andy Warhol's *Interview* magazine that 'I feel closer to the streets of London than the streets of Paris because I hate the poorness of Paris streets. By 'poor' I mean not rich in imagination. Everybody wants to be like the other one... they want to be anonymous. In London I don't really get my inspiration. I get my energy'.[32] Similarly, Christian Lacroix saw in London's market culture a romantic sense of freedom. In 1992 he reflected that:

Besides its urban landscape... and bizarre characters... London has for a long time been for me an inexhaustible mine of old clothes, of textiles of all sorts... I have the impression now that opportunities for real finds are a good deal scarcer... but it is still possible to discover rare pearls among the dross... perhaps heaped on a tatty bit of lino or laid out on a stall that would be more at home in a fairground than in an antique market. And on the streets there is less of the wild intensity and richness of invention than there used to be, much of it having succumbed to that spuriously 'continental' elegance favoured by yuppies and the Thatcher generation... Nonetheless, there will always be those moments to treasure, when you suddenly glimpse a hat sprouting a crazy collection of flowers, a pair of shoes hovering somewhere between fluorescent and sugar pink, curious proportions, ethnic details or a hairstyle in all the colours of the rainbow.[33]

Though such commentaries clearly engage more closely with a mythic imagining of London as a bizarre repository of extraordinary sartorial experiences than they do with the more mundane circumstances that supported Camden's creative fecundity, they do help to magnify a moment during which the street market appeared to generate products and ideas at an extraordinary rate. McRobbie linked this state of affairs to broader shifts in the relationship between a London-based style medium, the objects of its focus, and the forced trajectory of their labours:

The implosionary effects of the mass-media mean that in the 1980s youth styles and fashion are born into the media. There is an 'instantaneity' which replaces the old period of sub-cultural incubation. The relentless forces of consumerism now operate at the style-face with teams of stylists being sent out by the magazines each month to scour the market places and end-of-term fashion-shows for commercial ideas. Students who start off working on the stalls move, often to their own labels, within a year of leaving college, with the help of the Enterprise Allowance Scheme and a bank-loan. They provide magazines and journalists with strong images and lively copy and the whole system reproduces itself at an increasingly frenzied speed.[34]

The design-partnership of David Holah and Stevie Stewart, who launched their Body Map brand while still enrolled as fashion students at Middlesex Polytechnic in the early 1980s, epitomized this aspect of the market's character and broader influence. Their stall in the Lock originally sold 'army surplus and cotton flannelette pyjamas dyed in a series of colours'.[35] But following their graduation in 1982 and the purchase of their entire student collection by Robert Forest, the buyer for the prestigious South Molton Street store Browns (a transaction that would quickly become a rite of passage for leading fashion graduates in succeeding years), Holah and Stewart quickly developed a signature style which combined the clubby kookiness, innovative cutting, pattern-making and use of unusual materials, and an understanding of media values that united a new generation of young London-based avant-garde designers. In March 1984 Angus McGill reported on their launch collection, shown at that year's London Fashion Week at the Commonwealth Institute in Holland Park:

**❺❽**
Body Map, Spring-Summer 1986 (Body Map)

Body Map calls its show 'Cat in the Hat takes a Rumble with the Techno Fish' so you will see at once what it is all about. The clothes are almost all black and white and made of the cotton I now learn is called sweatshirt. They are all pull-on, comfortable (said the model), crumpled, the girls with lots of holes and baggy, billowing tops and skirts that suddenly flare, the boys distinctly Genet.[36]

The following year the theatrical promotion of their collection 'Barbie Takes a Trip Around Nature's Cosmic Curves', with its 'trippy lights, models dressing at the side of the catwalk and shiny swimwear that looked like rubber', caught the attention of the American press, inspiring *Women's Wear Daily* to describe London as 'a teeming fashion marketplace buzzing with ideas. They bounce off the streets and out of the prodigious art colleges'.[37] The show's deliberate amateurism and unorthodox approach to conventional notions of beauty drew heavily on the shared values of a creative community with strong links to Camden market and the twilight world of North London squats and underground gay clubs. Thus in one catwalk scenario a journalist reported that 'male models wear skirts and long, leg hugging knickers over thick, coloured tights' and in another 'sequins, frills, fringing, plastic and the ceaseless clash of Dayglo-bright colours on blatantly fat models and silver haired women in their fifties' defied all expectations.[38]

Yet despite the fact that their client list included a large proportion of the commercial pop chart and the belated realization that their vision was commercial enough to inspire several unlicensed high-street copies, by 1986 the company faced its first liquidation. While the financial pages uniformly put this down to a lack of capital and a dearth of backers prepared to underscore the precarious but vibrant British fashion scene, the underlying factors forcing Body Map's untimely collapse were perhaps more closely related to Stewart and Holah's emotional and creative investment in an anarchic Camden mind-set that valued the sensations of a spectacular decadence above mundane management considerations and monetary achievement. Body Map carried the banner for a roll-call of talent which now reads like an obituary for the wasted potential of that decade's fashion, clubland and media communities. Richard Tory, Rachel Auburn, Scarlet, Pam Hogg, Demob, Christopher Nemeth, Helen Storey, Bernstock & Spiers, Stephen Linnard, Leigh Bowery, Trojan, John Richmond, Boy George, Helen Terry and Michael Clark all, among others, shared in their experience of rising fortune and swift decline. And although Holah and Stewart attempted several relaunches over the following years, their output and mode of operation always struggled to break out of the kitchen-table, friendly amateurism which sustained the continuing cult success of their B-Basic market-stall line.[39]

Other 1980s Camden Market traders, notably Wayne Hemmingway and his Red or Dead label, achieved a more sustained expansion into the commercial mainstream of British fashion than the art school entrepreneurs studied by McRobbie and feted by the style press. Hemmingway embraced a very different tradition of creativity, revelling in his outsider status as a geography graduate (from nearby University College) and a northerner. He remembered travelling down to London from Morecombe as a sixth-former 'with some mates; we all knew what we wanted to do - walk down the King's Road and buy clothes from Vivienne Westwood's Seditionaries store. But when we got in the door we were stunned... I felt so betrayed. I thought this isn't what Punk is supposed to be - it's just middle-class people wearing expensive clothes. I was totally disillusioned. I wanted to go back with bags laden with clothes, but I couldn't afford anything.'[40]

Once he was ensconced in London, Hemmingway found that Camden offered a more egalitarian setting for an assault on the elitist attitudes he observed among an impenetrable metropolitan 'style coterie'. The informal structures of the market also offered the freedom to empire-build in the tradition of the 'cockney' entrepreneur and Hemmingway tellingly adopted the colourful persona of the second-hand car dealer rather than the hauteur of the artist designer. From 1981 Hemmingway and his partner built up a network of 16 stalls selling relatively cheap second-hand and mass-produced streetstyle to a predominantly student-based and tourist clientele. Their wares were initially sourced from jumble and car-boot sales, charity shops and warehouse clearances, and though buying policy tended to follow rather than anticipate trends, Hemmingway's accumulated knowledge of popular style rapidly became a valuable business commodity. Moving in on Holt's traditional market, Red or Dead, as the stalls became known by the mid-1980s, began to focus on the selling of Dr Marten's boots and shoes. This relationship developed into a commercial and creative arrangement whereby Hemmingway advised Dr Marten's on the look of new products, leading to the launch of a factory manufacturing quirky Red or Dead lines in shoes and garments. In 1986 the company opened its first permanent shop in Rupert Street and by 1989 Hemmingway had produced its first catwalk show. Such was the scale of profit that by 1996 Hemmingway had sold his share of the company twice.[41]

At the time of writing, Red or Dead is a fading memory, its trademark platform boots and gauche retro-prints a reminder of childlike innocence. Hemmingway, now a successful brand in his own right, sporadically returns to the limelight, commentating on the kitsch carnival floats that accompanied the Queen's 2002 Golden Jubilee Procession for the BBC, or launching publicity-seeking attacks on the moral and aesthetic bankruptcy of the international fashion establishment. Though he would probably retreat from any direct comparison of his career to the more chaotic trajectory of Body Map, these two concerns, whose original stalls were only metres apart, reveal the capacity of Camden to generate potent myths of London fashion. Fashion theorist Caroline Evans has written persuasively about the internal contradictions and surprising revelations of the capital's fashion mythology in the late twentieth century. Looking to the practices of a later generation of London designers (specifically the Central Saint Martins graduate Shelley Fox) in the artisanal and bohemian environment of the East End, she links the architectural context, aesthetic direction and business methodology of Fox's work to the underlying connections between place and capitalist endeavour that sustain London's delicate fashion ecology. She states that

**5 9**

Red or Dead boots designed by Mila Lazaro, 1993 (Museum of London)

In architecture the interstices are where the problems start: moulds grow and fungi flourish. However in the business of fashion the interstices provided fertile growing space for a singular, small-scale and quirky style of London design and production.[42]

Camden-based furniture designer Ron Arad echoed Evans's celebration of the dark corners of London's creative landscape in his valedictory comments on a Camden market whose rough edges were by 1999 in danger of being smoothed away by the homogenizing effects of globalization and increasingly restrictive planning legislation. His valorization of a sublime market culture which combined beauty and ugliness in equal measure is a fitting epitaph to a moment of extraordinary productivity in the history of London's unlikely fashion spaces:

**6 0** Re-cycled knitted silk sweater by Buzy Body, purchased at Camden Market, 1995 (Museum of London)

It is easy to take a place like this and sterilise it… I remember how the markets mushroomed without planning, and that does have its charms. They get crowded with people, and there's a lot of unorganised activity and not all of it is beautiful and wonderful. But much of it is.[43]

**6 0** Co-caine T-Shirt purchased at Camden Market, 1999 (Museum of London)

# NOTES
## INTRODUCTION

1 Important publications on the culture of city life include :

- M. Auge, *Non-places: Introduction to an Anthropology of Supermodernity*. Verso, London. 1995;
- W. Benjamin, *The Arcades Project*. Belknap, Cambridge, MA. 1999;
- W. Benjamin, *Charles Baudelaire : A Lyric Poet in the Era of High Capitalism*. Verso, London. 1983;
- M. Berman, *All That is Solid Melts Into Air*. Simon & Schuster, New York. 1982;
- I. Borden, J. Kerr, A. Pivaro, J. Rendell (eds), *Strangely Familiar: Narratives of Architecture in the City*. Routledge, London. 1996;
- V. Burgin, *Some Cities*. Reaktion, London. 1996;
- M. de Certeau, *The Practice of Everyday Life*. University of Minnesota Press, Minneapolis. 1998;
- M. Davis: *City of Quartz*. Verso, London. 1991;
- R. Finnegan, *Tales of the City: A Study of Narrative and Urban Life*. Cambridge University Press, Cambridge. 1997;
- D. Frisby and M. Featherstone (eds), *Simmel on Culture*. Sage, London. 1997;
- D. Harvey, *Consciousness and the Urban Experience*. John Hopkins University Press, Baltimore. 1985;
- D. Harvey, *The Condition of Postmodernity*. Blackwell, Oxford. 1989;
- D. Hayden, *The Power of Place*. MIT Press, Cambridge, MA. 1995;
- H. Lefebvre, *Writings on Cities*. Blackwell, Oxford. 1996;
- D. Massey, *Space, Place and Gender*. Polity, Cambridge. 1994;
- M. Miles, T. Hall and I. Borden (eds), *The City Cultures Reader*. Routledge, London. 2000;
- D. Olsen, *The City as a Work of Art*. Yale University Press, New Haven. 1986;
- S. Pile, *The Body and the City*. Routledge, London. 1996;
- J. Raban, *Soft City*. Harvill, London. 1998;
- A. Rifkin, *Street Noises: Parisian Pleasure 1900-1940*. Manchester University Press, Manchester. 1993;
- W. Rybczynski, *City Life*. Scribner, New York. 1995;
- R. Sennett, *Flesh and Stone*. Faber & Faber, London. 1994;
- W. Sharpe and L. Wallock (eds), *Visions of the Modern City*. John Hopkins University Press, Baltimore. 1987;
- N. Thrift, *Spatial Formations*. Sage, London. 1996;
- S. Watson and K. Gibson (eds), *Postmodern Cities and Spaces*. Blackwell, Oxford. 1995;
- J. Wolfreys, *Writing London: The Trace of the Urban Text from Blake to Dickens*. Macmillan, London. 1998;
- S. Zukin, *The Culture of Cities*. Blackwell, Oxford. 1996.

2 Important exceptions include:

- C. Breward, *The Hidden Consumer: Masculinities, Fashion and City Life 1860-1914*. Manchester University Press, Manchester. 1999;
- C. Breward, *Fashion*. Oxford University Press, Oxford. 2003;
- S. Bruzzi and P. Church Gibson (eds), *Fashion Cultures: Theories, Explorations and Analysis*. Routledge, London. 2000;
- N. Green, *Ready to Wear, Ready to Work: A Century of Industry and Immigrants in Paris and New York*. Duke University Press, NC. 1997;
- F. Mort, *Cultures of Consumption: Masculinities and Social Space in Late Twentieth-century Britain*. Routledge, London. 1996;
- L. Nead, Victorian Babylon: *People, Streets and Images in Nineteenth-century London*. Yale University Press, New Haven. 2000;
- M. Ogborn, *Spaces of Modernity: London's Geographies 1680-1780*. Guilford Press, New York. 1998;
- P. Perrot, *Fashioning the Bourgeoisie*. Princeton University Press, Princeton, NJ. 1994;
- E. Rappaport, *Shopping for Pleasure: Women in the Making of London's West End*. Princeton University Press, Princeton, NJ. 2000;
- D. Roche, *The Culture of Clothing*. Cambridge University Press, Cambridge. 1994;
- V. Steele, *Paris Fashion: A Cultural History*. Berg, Oxford. 1998;
- E. Wilson, *Adorned in Dreams: Fashion and Modernity*. Virago, London. 1985;
- E. Wilson, *The Sphinx in the City: Urban Life, the Control of Disorder, and Women*. University of California Press, Berkeley. 1991.

3 Wolfreys, *Writing London*, 7.

4 See J. Entwistle, *The Fashioned Body: Fashion, Dress and Modern Social Theory*. Polity, Cambridge. 2000;
- J. Entwistle and E. Wilson (eds), *Body Dressing*. Berg, Oxford. 2001.

5 Thrift, *Spatial Formations*, 7.

6 De Certeau, *Practice of Everyday Life*, Vol. II, 141.
7 Sennett, *Flesh and Stone*.
8 Steele, *Paris Fashion*; Wilson, *The Sphinx in the City*; and M. Wigley, *White Walls, Designer Dresses*. MIT Press, Boston. 1995.
9 D. Gilbert, 'Urban Outfitting: The City and the Spaces of Fashion Culture', in Bruzzi and Church Gibson (eds), *Fashion Cultures*, 7-24.
10 Gilbert, 'Urban Outfitting', 20.
11 See N. Tarrant, *The Development of Costume*. Routledge, London. 1994;
• L. Taylor, *The Study of Dress History*. Manchester University Press, Manchester. 2002;
• *Fashion Theory* Vol. 2(4), 1998, for discussions of methods relating to the use of clothing as a historical source.
12 See S. Shesgreen (ed.), *The Cries and Hawkers of London: The Engravings of Marcellus Laroon*. Aldershot. 1990;
• H. Mayhew, *London Labour and the London Poor*. Penguin, Harmondsworth. 1985;
• C. Dickens, *Sketches by Boz*. Penguin, Harmondsworth. 1995.
13 In its 'biographical' emphasis, this project draws inspiration from a tradition of historical, creative and sociological writing about London whose content has aimed to define the capital's shifting character through an analysis of the lives and attitudes of its people and its physical, psychological and material environment. Important twentieth-century examples, drawn from the work of academic, journalistic, popular and cult authors include
• F. Madox Ford, *The Soul of London*. J. M. Dent, London. 1995 (1905);
• P. Cohen-Portheim, *The Spirit of London*. Batsford, London. 1935;
• S. E. Rasmussen, *London, the Unique City*. Jonathan Cape, London. 1937;
• R. J. Mitchell and M. D. Leys, *A History of London Life*. Longmans, London. 1958;
• S. Humphries and G. Weightman, *The Making of Modern London 1815-1914*. Sidgwick & Jackson, London. 1983;
• S. Humphries and J. Taylor, *The Making of Modern London 1945-1985*. Sidgwick & Jackson, London. 1986;
• M. Moorcock, *Mother London*. Secker & Warburg, London. 1988;
• P. Wright, *A Journey Through Ruins: The Last Days of London*. Radius, London. 1991;

• R. Porter, *London: A Social History*. Hamish Hamilton, London. 1994;
• I. Sinclair, *Lights Out For the Territory*. Granta, London. 1997;
• S. Inwood, *A History of London*. London. 1998;
• I. Jack (ed.), *London: The Lives of the City*. (Granta 65), Granta, London. 1999;
• P. Ackroyd, *London: The Biography*. Chatto & Windus, London. 2000;
• J. White, *London in the Twentieth Century: A City and its People*. Viking, Harmondsworth. 2001.

14 See M. Kwint, C. Breward and J. Aynsley (eds), *Material Memories: Design & Evocation*. Berg, Oxford. 1999, for discussion of material culture as a memorializing tool.
15 I. De Sola-Morales in S. Whiting (ed.), *Differences*. MIT Press, Boston. 1997. Cited in Wolfreys, *Writing London*, 203.

CHAPTER 1

1 T. Bliss, *Jane Welsh Carlyle: A New Selection of her Letters*. Victor Gollancz, London. 1949, 159.
2 W. Connely, *Count D'Orsay: The Dandy of Dandies*. Cassell & Co., London. 1952, 162.
3 A. Lamington, *In the Days of the Dandies*. Eversleigh Nash, London. 1906, 26-7.
4 Museum of London Accession Number A.9243-4.
5 A. Ribeiro, *The Art of Dress: Fashion in England and France 1750-1820*. Yale University Press, New Haven. 1998, 99.
6 Museum of London Accession Number 87.194.
7 Cpt. Jesse, *The Life of George Brummell Esq.*, Vol. I. John Nimmo, London. 1886, 62-3.
8 Museum of London Accession Number 56.69.
9 A copy of the letter (SR/RBC.7) is held at the Museum of London.
10 Ribeiro, *Art of Dress*, 104-5.
11 R. Porter, *London: A Social History*. Hamish Hamilton, London. 1994, 180.
12 Ibid., 184.
13 See P. McNeil, 'Macaroni Masculinities', *Fashion Theory* 4(4), 2000, 373-405.
14 R. Gronow, *Reminiscences of Captain Gronow*. Smith, Elder & Co., London. 1862, 59.
15 R. Boutet de Monvel, *Beau Brummell and his Times*. Everleigh Nash, London. 1908, 56.
16 Gronow, *Reminiscences*, 62.
17 de Monvel, *Beau Brummell*, 70.
18 Jesse, *George Brummell*, 63.
19 P. Thorold, *The London Rich: The Creation of a Great City from 1666 to the Present*. Viking, London. 1999, 239.

20 M. de Vermont and C. Darnley, *London and Paris or Comparative Sketches*. Longman, London. 1823, 31-2.
21 J. Summerson, *Georgian London*. Pelican, London. 1962, 18-22.
• See also E. McKellar, *The Birth of Modern London: The Development and Design of the City 1660-1720*. Manchester University Press, Manchester. 1999, for a more recent and revised account of the growth of the West End.
22 Summerson, *Georgian London*, 24-5.
23 J. Rendell, 'Industrious Females and Professional Beauties : Or Fine Articles for Sale in the Burlington Arcade.' In I. Borden, J. Kerr, A. Piraro and J. Rendell (eds), *Strangely Familiar: Narratives of Architecture in the City*. Routledge, London. 1996, 36.
• See also J. Rendell, *The Pursuit of Pleasure: Gender, Space and Architecture in Regency London*. Athlone Press, London. 2002, for a further development of Rendell's ideas.
24 G. Walden, *Who's a Dandy?*. Gibson Square Books, London. 2002.
25 Vermont, *London & Paris*, 20-21.
26 H. B. Wheatley, *Bond Street Old and New 1686-1911*. Fine Art Society, London. 1911, 29.
27 'Dear Street' *Country Life*, 1 May 1937.
28 On the face of things the tailors of Savile Row continued to resist overt print-based advertising for the remainder of the nineteenth and twentieth centuries. Aggressive marketing became more closely associated with producers of ready-made menswear and something to be avoided at all costs.
29 R. Walker, *The Savile Row Story*. Prion, London. 1988, 22.
30 F. Whitbourn, *Mr Lock of St James Street*. Heinemann, London. 1971, 60-63.
31 A. Adburgham, *Silver Fork Society: Fashionable Life and Literature from 1814-1840*. Constable, London. 1983, 60.
• See also G. Dart, 'Flash Style: Pierce Egan and Literary London 1820-1828' *History Workshop Journal* 51, Spring 2001, 181-205.
32 P. Egan, *Life in London*. Sherwood, Neely & Jones, London. 1821, 23-4.
33 Ibid., 42.
34 McNeil, 'Macaroni Masculinities'.
• See also M. Ogborn, *Spaces of Modernity: London's Geographies 1680-1780*. Guilford Press, New York. 1998, 133-42.
35 See M. Butler, 'Culture's Medium: The Role of the Review', in S. Curran (ed.), *The Cambridge Companion to British Romanticism*. Cambridge University Press, Cambridge. 1993, 145-6.
36 Anon., *Portraits from Life or Memoirs of a Rambler*. J. Moore, London. 1800, 56.
37 B. Blackmantle, *The English Spy*, Vol I. Sherwood, Gilbert & Piper, London. 1826, 94.
38 Egan, *Life in London*, 139.
39 Ibid., 140.
40 Ibid., 146.
41 P. Mandler, *Aristocratic Government in the Age of Reform: Whigs and Liberals 1830-1852*. Clarendon Press, Oxford. 1990, 46.
42 Ibid., 66-7.
43 Ibid., 16.
44 Adburgham, *Silver Fork*, 127.
45 E. Bulwer Lytton, *Pelham: Or the Adventures of a Gentleman*. Leipzig. 1842, 29.
46 Ibid., 133.
47 Ibid., 129.
48 Gronow, *Reminiscences*, 124.
49 Ibid.,80-7.
50 Anon, *Dandy Bewitched*. London. 1820 (BL 1875 6 30 (51)).
51 Bulwer Lytton, *Pelham*, 180-2.
52 Heath, *Fashion and Folly*. London. 1822 (Guildhall Library: Prints and Drawings).
53 Anon, *The Dandies Ball or High Life in the City*. John Marshall, London. 1819.
54 Egan, *Life in London*, 239.
55 P. Egan (J. Ford (ed.)), *Boxiana or Sketches of Ancient and Modern Pugilism*. Folio Society. 1976, 133.
• See also P. Howe (ed.), *The Best of Hazlitt*. Methuen, London. 1923, 136-155 and
• M. Pointon, 'Pugilism, Painters and National Identity in Early Nineteenth Century England' in D. Chandler, J. Gill, T. Guha and G. Tawadros (eds), *Boxer*. INIVA, London. 1996.
56 Egan, *Boxiana*, 159-60.
57 Thorold, *London Rich*, 125.
58 Blackmantle, *English Spy*, 166.

## CHAPTER 2

1 F. Madox Ford, *The Soul of London*. J.M. Dent, London. 1995 [1905], 48.
2 E. Pugh, *The City of the World: A Book about London and the Londoner*. T. Nelson, London. 1908, 39.
3 T. Burke, *Nights in Town: A London Autobiography*. George Allen & Unwin, London. 1915, 25.
4 P.J. Keating, *The Working Classes in Victorian Fiction*. Routledge & Kegan Paul, London. 1979, 33.
5 See G. Stedman Jones, *Outcast London: A Study in the Relationship between Classes in*

*Victorian Society*. Oxford University Press, Oxford. 1971.

6 I.B. Nadel, 'Gustave Dore: English Art and London Life' in I.B. Nadel and F.S. Schwarzbach (eds), *Victorian Artists and the City: A Collection of Critical Essays*. Pergamon, New York. 1980, 152.

• See also A. Sandison, *Robert Louis Stevenson and the Appearance of Modernism: A Future Feeling*. Macmillan, London. 1996, 224-5.

7 R. Samuel, 'Comers and Goers', in H.J. Dyos and M. Wolff (eds), *The Victorian City: Images and Realities*, Vol. I. Routledge, London. 1999, 125.

8 Ibid., 125.

9 C. Knight, *London*, Vol. III. Virtue & Co., London. 1870, 49-50.

10 M. Williams QC, *Round London*. Macmillan, London. 1896, 74-5.

11 E. Armfeldt, 'Oriental London', in G. Sims (ed.), *Living London*, Vol I. Cassell, London. 1906, 86.

12 Ibid., 81-2.

13 E. Armfeldt, 'Italy in London', in G. Sims (ed.), *Living London*, 183.

14 E. Armfeldt, 'Cosmopolitan London', in G. Sims (ed.), *Living London*, 241.

15 Ibid.

16 Ibid., 247.

17 Burke, *Nights in Town*, 91.

18 J. Schneer, *London 1900: The Imperial Metropolis*. Yale University Press, New Haven, 1999, 113.

19 See C. Tulloch, 'Strawberries and Cream: Dress, Migration and the Quintessence of Englishness', in C. Breward, B. Conekin and C. Cox (eds), *The Englishness of English Dress*. Berg, Oxford. 2002, 61-76.

20 Burke, *Nights in Town*, 350.

21 Museum of London accession number 38.295.

22 G. Sala, *Twice Round the Clock*. Houlston & Wright, London. 1857, 175-182.

23 C. Knight, *London*, Vol. V. Virtue & Co., London. 1870, 896.

24 A. Adburgham, *Shopping in Style*. Thames & Hudson, London. 1979, 122-3.

25 P. Bailey, *Popular Culture and Performance in the Victorian City*. Cambridge University Press, Cambridge. 1998, 200-6.

26 G. Sala, *London Up to Date*. A. & C. Black, London. 1894, 248.

27 G. Mackenzie, *Marylebone: Great City North of Oxford Street*. Macmillan, London. 1972, 93.

28 C. Booth, *Life and Labour of the People in London*, Vol I (reprint). Kelly, New York. 1969, 182.

29 Ibid 187.

30 For a detailed account of working conditions in London's nineteenth-century clothing industries see J. Schmiechen, *Sweated Industries and Sweated Labour: The London Clothing Trades 1860-1914*. University of Illinois Press, Urbana, IL. 1984., and

• C. Walkley, *The Ghost in the Looking Glass: The Victorian Seamstress*. Peter Owen, London. 1981.

31 Museum of London accession number 2000.93a-c.

32 E. T. Cook, *Highways and Byways in London*. Macmillan, London. 1911 (reprint), 294.

33 Ibid., 297.

## CHAPTER 3

1 L. Nead 'From Alleys to Courts: Obscenity and the Mapping of Victorian London' in *New Formations*, 37, 1999.

2 E. Pugh, *The City of the World: A Book about London and the Londoner*. Thomas Nelson & Sons, London. 1908, 19-20.

3 C. Gordon, *Old Time Aldwych, The Kingsway and Neighbourhood*. T. Fisher Unwin, London. 1903, 23.

4 Ibid., 213.

5 'A Description of the Offices of The Strand Magazine', *The Strand Magazine*. IV, July-December 1892, 594-606.

6 J. Hollingshead, *Gaiety Chronicles*. A. Constable, London. 1898, 7-13.

7 W. McQueen Pope, *Gaiety: Theatre of Enchantment*. W. H. Allen, London. 1949, 384.

8 H. Maguire, 'The Architectural Response', in R. Foulkes (ed.), *British Theatre in the 1890s*. Cambridge University Press, Cambridge. 1992, 153.

9 W. McQueen Pope, *Carriages at Eleven: The Story of the Edwardian Theatre*. Hutchinson & Co., London. 1947, 116.

10 N. Jacob, *Me and the Swans*. Wm. Kimber & Co., London. 1963, 41.

11 McQueen Pope, *Carriages*, 119.

12 J. McCarthy, *Charing Cross to St Paul's*. Seeley & Co., London. 1893, 55-7.

13 Ibid., 79.

14 Letter from Kitty Lord's representative Hazel Pethig to the Museum of London, Dress Collection, Museum of London.

15 Programmes for Salone Margherita, Napoli, 1910, Teatro Bellini, 1914 and Ambassadeurs, Paris (undated), Ephemera Collection, Museum of London.

16 Museum of London Accession Number 71.142/5a.

17 Museum of London Accession Number 71.142/6.

18 Museum of London Accession Number 71.142/3a.

19 Museum of London Accession Number 71.142/3b.

20 Museum of London Accession Number 71.142/2c.

21 Museum of London Accession Number 71.142/4a.

22 Museum of London Accession Number 71.142/4c.

23 Museum of London Accession Number 71.142/4d&e.

24 Museum of London Accession Number 71.142/1.

25 M. Booth, *Theatre in the Victorian Age*. Cambridge University Press, Cambridge. 1991, 114-15.

26 M. Booth (ed.), *Victorian Theatrical Trades : Articles from The Stage 1883-1884*. The Society for Theatre Research, London. 1981, 13.

27 Ibid., 14.

28 Ibid., 16.

29 Ibid., 18.

30 Ibid., 19.

31 Ibid., 20-5.

32 Ibid., 1.

33 Ibid., 4.

34 T. Davis, *Actresses as Working Women: Their Social Identity in Victorian Culture*. Routledge, London. 1991, 106-62.

35 J. Douglas, *Adventures in London*. Cassell & Co., London. 1909, 50-2.

36 W. Davenport Adams, *A Book of Burlesque*. Henry & Co., London. 1891, 219.

37 R. Allen, *Horrible Prettiness : Burlesque and American Culture*. University of North Carolina Press, Chapel Hill. 1991, 96.

38 Ibid., 84-7.

39 Ibid., 123.

40 Ibid., 154.

41 B. Reiver, *Is Burlesque Art?* J. Jeffery, London. 1880, 9-10.

42 Allen, *Horrible Prettiness*, 25.

43 Ibid.

44 See P. Stallybrass and A. White, *The Politics and Poetics of Transgression*. Methuen, London. 1986.

45 Allen, *Horrible Prettiness*, 26.

46 Ibid., 107.

47 R. Mander and J. Mitchenson, *Musical Comedy: A Story in Pictures*. Peter Davies, London. 1969, 10.

48 M. Booth, *Victorian Spectacular Theatre*. Routledge, London. 1981, 58.

49 W. Archer, *The Theatrical World of 1894*. Walter Scott, London. 1895, 3-6.

50 Booth, *Spectacular Theatre*, 60.

51 Ibid., 89-90.

52 E. Short, *Fifty Years of Vaudeville*. Eyre & Spottiswoode, London. 1946, 43.

53 Mander and Mitchenson, *Musical Comedy*, 13.

54 Ibid.

55 Archer, *The Theatrical World*, 59-60.

56 Mander and Mitchenson, *Musical Comedy*, 17.

57 Ibid., 18-19.

58 P. Bailey 'Naughty but Nice: Musical Comedy and the Rhetoric of the Girl 1892-1914' in M. Booth and J. Kaplan (eds), *The Edwardian Theatre: Essays in Performance and the Stage*. Cambridge University Press, Cambridge. 1996, 39-40.

• See also E. Rappaport, *Shopping for Pleasure: Women in the Making of London's West End*. Princeton University Press, Princeton. 2000.

59 Bailey, 'Naughty but Nice', 55.

60 M. Borsa, *The English Stage of Today*. John Lane, London. 1908, 7.

61 Ibid., 279.

62 Davis, *Actresses*, 161.

63 C. Collier, *Harlequinade: The Story of my Life*. John Lane, London. 1929, 3-4.

64 Ibid., 60-1.

65 Ibid., 20.

66 Ibid., 69.

67 McQueen Pope, *Gaiety*, 346.

68 Collier, *Harlequinade*, 110.

69 Davis, *Actresses*, 162.

70 S. Dark, *The Marie Tempest Birthday Book*. Stanley Paul, London. 1914, 12.

71 H. Bolitho, *Marie Tempest*. Cobden Sanderson, London. 1936, 89.

72 Ibid., 92.

73 Ibid., 90-91.

74 Ibid., 103.

75 Mrs Aria, *Costume: Fanciful, Historical and Theatrical*. Macmillan, London. 1906, 257-8.

76 Douglas, *Adventures*, 127.

77 Bolitho, *Tempest*, 150.

78 Davis, *Actresses*, 159.

79 Lady Wyndham, *Charles Wyndham and Mary Moore*. Private Printing, London. 1925, 243.

80 Ibid., 242.

81 Ibid., 245.

82 Ibid., 247.

83 Ibid., 242.

84 Lady Duff Gordon, *Discretions and Indiscretions*. Jarrolds, London. 1932, 48.

85 I. Vanbrugh, *To Tell My Story*. Hutchinson & Co., London. 1948, 50.
• M. Etherington Smith and J. Pilcher, *The It Girls*. Hamish Hamilton, London. 1986, 55-87.
• J. Kaplan and S. Stowell, *Theatre and Fashion: Oscar Wilde to the Suffragettes*. Cambridge University Press, Cambridge, 1994.
86 Duff Gordon, *Discretions*, 65.
87 Davis, *Actresses*, 140-3.
88 Borsa, *English Stage*, 5.
89 McQueen Pope, *Gaiety*, 405.

## CHAPTER 4

1 V. Woolf, *Mrs Dalloway*. Penguin, Harmondsworth, 1996, 2-3.
2 Ibid., 9.
3 H. Lee, *Virginia Woolf*. Chatto & Windus. 1996, 552.
4 Woolf, *Dalloway*, 15.
5 A. Light, *Forever England: Femininity, Literature and Conservatism between the Wars*. Routledge, London. 1991, 115.
6 J. Struther, *Mrs Miniver*. Virago, London. 1989, 14.
7 H. Lee, *The Novels of Virginia Woolf*. Methuen, London. 1977, 94.
8 J. B. Priestley, *English Journey*. Heinemann, London. 1934, 401-2.
9 Ibid., 402-3.
10 H. Llewellyn Smith (ed.), *The New Survey of London Life & Labour*, Vol. I. King & Son, London. 1930, 171.
11 Ibid., 191.
12 Ibid., 192-3.
13 C.W. Forester, *Success through Dress*. Duckworth, London. 1925, 62.
14 Ibid., 27.
15 Ibid., 20-1.
16 S. P. Dobbs, *The Clothing Workers of Great Britain*. Routledge, London. 1928, 4.
17 Ibid.,7.
18 Ibid., 70.
19 H. Llewellyn Smith (ed.), *The New Survey of London Life & Labour*, Vol. II. King & Son, London. 1931, 261.
20 Dobbs, *Clothing Workers*, 8, 36.
21 Llewellyn Smith (ed.), *New Survey*, Vol. II, 255.
22 Dobbs, *Clothing Workers*, 77-8.
23 Llewellyn Smith (ed.), *New Survey*, Vol II, 305.
24 Ibid., 272.
25 Ibid., 283.
26 A. Settle, *Clothes Line*. Methuen, London. 1937, 22-3.
27 The Museum of London owns a wedding dress of this type, designed by Hartnell and worn by Mrs Carl Bendix at the Dream of Fair Women Ball held at Claridges Hotel in February 1928. Accession number 39.162a-c.
28 S. Graham, *London Nights*. Hurst & Blackett, London. 1925, 1.
29 J. Schlor, *Nights in the Big City: Paris, Berlin, London 1840-1930*. Reaktion, London. 1998, 269.
30 Graham, *London Nights*, 13-14.
31 Ibid., 195-6.
32 Schlor, *Nights in the Big City*, 172-4.
33 Graham, *London Nights*, 198.
34 J. Richards, *The Age of the Dream Palace: Cinema and Society in Britain 1930-1939*. Routledge & Kegan Paul, London. 1984, 15-33.
35 H. Llewellyn Smith (ed.), *The New Survey of London Life and Labour*, Vol. IX. King & Son, London. 1935, 47.
36 Richards, *Dream Palace*, 209.
37 Ibid., 224.
38 S. Graham, *Twice Round the London Clock and More London Nights*. Ernest Benn, London. 1933, 131-5.
39 Llewellyn Smith (ed.), *New Survey*, Vol. IX, 64-5.
40 Ibid., 51, 77.
41 J. B. Priestley, *Angel Pavement*. William Heinemann, London. 1937, 501-2.
42 M. Garland, *The Indecisive Decade: The World of Fashion and Entertainment in the 30s*. Macdonald & Co., London. 1968, 102-4.
43 T. Benjamin, *London Shops and Shopping*. Herbert Joseph, London. 1934, 189-90.
44 P. Cohen-Portheim, *The Spirit of London*. J. B. Lippincott, Philadelphia. 1930, 41-7.
45 Benjamin, *London Shops*, 190.
46 E. Montizambert, *London Discoveries in Shops and Restaurants*. Women Publishers Ltd., London. 1924, 81.
47 F. Marshall, *London West*. The Studio, London. 1944, 9.
48 Settle, *Clothes Line*, 99.
49 Cohen-Portheim, *Spirit of London*, 41-2.
50 Montizambert, *London Discoveries*, 82.
51 T. Benjamin, *A Shopping Guide to London*. Robert McBride, New York. 1930, 91-2.
52 Montizambert, *London Discoveries*, 43.
53 Ibid.
54 Ibid., 37-40.
55 Cohen-Portheim, *Spirit of London*, 47.
56 Montizambert, *London Discoveries*, 50.
57 Cohen-Portheim, *Spirit of London*, 41.

58 V. Woolf, 'Oxford Street Tide', in *The London Scene*. London, Hogarth Press. 1975, 16-20.
• See also C. Breward, 'In the Eye of the Storm: Oxford Circus and the Fashioning of Modernity', in *Fashion Theory* 4 (1), 2000, 3-26.
59 Montizambert, *London Discoveries*, 7-8.
60 Ibid., 9.
61 Benjamin, *London Shops*, 161.
62 Ibid., 179.
63 Ibid., 95.
64 Ibid., 106.
65 S. Halliday, *Underground to Everywhere: London's Underground Railway in the Life of the Capital*. Sutton, Stroud. 2001.
66 Llewellyn Smith (ed.), *New Survey*, Vol. I,191.
67 O. Green, *Underground Art: London Transport Posters*. Laurence King, London. 1999, 14-15.
68 Ibid., 70.
69 A. Jackson, *Semi-Detached London : Suburban Development, Life and Transport 1900-1939*. Allen & Unwin, London. 1973, 180.
70 L. Raymond, *Guide to Edgware*. The British Publishing Company Ltd., London. 1927, 11-12.
71 *Mill Hill and Edgware*. Service, London. 1934, 2.
72 Ibid., 71.
73 H. Llewellyn Smith (ed.), *The New Survey of London Life and Labour*, Vol. V. King & Son, London. 1933, 163.
74 Ibid., 164-5.
75 D.H. Evans, Mail Order Catalogue and Fashion Supplement. 1939. Guildhall Library. Pam 12379.
76 J. Carey, *The Intellectuals and the Masses*. Faber & Faber, London. 1992.
77 C. Duff (ed.), *Anthropological Report on a London Suburb by Prof. Vladimir Chernichewski*. Grayson & Grayson, London. 1935.
78 N. Humble, *The Feminine Middlebrow Novel, 1920s to 1950*. Oxford University Press, Oxford. 2001, 87-8, 131-2.
79 K.R.G. Browne, *Suburban Days*. Cassell, London. 1928, 211.
80 Settle, *Clothes Line*, 86.

## CHAPTER 5

1 H. Amies, *Just So Far*. Collins, London. 1954, 245.
2 See E. Ehrman 'The Spirit of English Style: Hardy Amies, Royal Dressmaker and International Businessman' in C. Breward, B. Conekin and C. Cox (eds), *The Englishness of English Dress*. Berg, Oxford. 2002, 140-3.
3 The models were interior designer Peter Coats, financier William Ackroyd (who advised Hardy Amies on the habits of the 'county' set), and playboy Mark Gilbey.
4 R. Viscusi, *Max Beerbohm, or the Dandy Dante, Re-reading with Mirrors*. John Hopkins University Press, Baltimore. 1986, 28.
5 Museum of London Accession Numbers 60.30/2, 60.30/6, 60.30/8, 60.30/11.
6 R. Porter, *London: A Social History*. Hamish Hamilton, London. 1994, 344.
7 H. Hopkins, *The New Look: A Social History of the Forties and Fifties*. Secker & Warburg, London. 1964, 427-8.
8 C. MacInnes, *England, Half English: A Polyphoto of the Fifties*. Penguin, Harmondsworth. 1966, 151.
9 T. Fyvel, *The Insecure Offenders: Rebellious Youth in the Welfare State*. Chatto & Windus, London. 1961, 48-51.
10 Ibid., 14-15.
11 D. Hebdige, *Subculture: The Meaning of Style*. Routledge, London. 1979, 51.
12 G. Pearson, *Hooligan: A History of Respectable Fears*. Macmillan, London. 1983, 20-2.
13 H. Williams, *South London*. Robert Hale, London. 1949, 331.
14 Ibid., 320.
15 H. D. Willcock, *Mass Observation Report on Juvenile Delinquency*. Falcon Press, London. 1949, 41.
16 See A. Davies, *Leisure, Gender & Poverty: Working Class Culture in Salford & Manchester*. Open University Press, Buckingham. 1992 and
• L. Ugolini, 'Clothes and the Modern Man in 1930s Oxford', in *Fashion Theory*, 4(4), 2000.
17 Willcock, *Mass Observation*, 50-1.
18 Ibid., 50.
19 Hopkins, *New Look*, 98-9.
20 R. Murphy, *Smash and Grab: Gangsters in the London Underworld 1920-1960*. Faber & Faber, London. 1993, 85.
21 Fyvel, *Insecure Offenders*, 52.
22 MacInnes, *England*, 150.
23 I am grateful for the reminiscences of costume curator Madeleine Ginsburg here.
24 M. Chamberlain, *Growing Up in Lambeth*. Virago, London. 1989, 78-9.
25 D. Sutherland, *Portrait of a Decade: London Life 1945-1955*. Harrap, London. 1988, 49-50.
26 Ibid., 124.
27 F. Marshall, *London West*. The Studio, London. 1944, 58.
28 British Travel and Holiday Association, *Shopping in London*. London. 1953, 27.

29 A. Whife (ed), *The Modern Tailor, Outfitter and Clothier*. Caxton, London. 1949, 8.
30 Ibid., 262.
31 Ibid., 265-71.
32 *Men's Wear*, 25 January 1947, 19.
33 *Men's Wear*, 19 April 1952, 26.
34 *Men's Wear*, 27 September 1952, 18.
35 C. Beaton and K. Tynan, *Persona Grata*. Allan Wingate, London. 1953, 15-16
36 N. Cohn, *Today There Are No Gentlemen*. Weidenfeld & Nicholson, London. 1971, 27.
37 P. Rock & S. Cohen, 'The Teddy Boy' in V. Bogdanor and R. Skidelsky (eds.), *The Age of Affluence 1951-1964*. Macmillan, London. 1970, 291.
38 *Men's Wear*, 3 October 1953, 34.
39 *Men's Wear*, 25 April 1953, 19.
40 *Men's Wear*, 9 January 1954, 18.
41 A. Markham, *Shop Ahoy: Your Shopping and Entertainment Guide to London*. Newman Neame, London. 1959, 61.
42 Sutherland, *Portrait*, 67.
43 F. Mort, 'Mapping Sexual London: The Wolfenden Committee on Homosexual Offences and Prostitution.', *New Formations: Sexual Geographies*. 37. 1999, 92-113.
44 R. Smith, Physique: *The Life of John S. Barrington*. Serpent's Tail, London. 1997.
45 See J. Savage. 'Tainted Love: The Influence of Male Homosexuality and Sexual Divergence on Pop Music and Culture since the War', in A. Tomlinson (ed.), *Consumption, Identity and Style: Marketing, Meanings and the Packaging of Pleasure*. Comedia, London. 1990., and
• S. Napier Bell, *Black Vinyl: White Powder*. Ebury Press, London. 2002.
46 Willcock, *Mass Observation*, 75.
47 D. Farson, *Soho in the Fifties*. Michael Joseph, London. 1987, 151.
48 F. Norman & J. Bernard, *Soho Night and Day*. Secker & Warburg, London. 1966, 14-16.
49 Hebdige, *Subculture*, 51.
50 D. Hobbs, *Doing the Business: Entrepreneurship, the Working Class and Detectives in the East End of London*. Clarendon Press, Oxford. 1988, 122.
51 J. McVicar, *McVicar by Himself*. Arrow, London. 1979, 158.
52 A. Partington, 'The Days of the New Look: Working Class Affluence and the Consumer Culture', in J. Fyrth (ed), *Labour's Promised Land? Culture and Society in Labour Britain 1945-51*. Lawrence & Wishart, London. 1995, 254.
53 MacInnes, *England*.,156.
54 Porter, *London*, 363.

## CHAPTER 6

1 B. Morris, *An Introduction to Mary Quant's London*. London Museum, London. 1973, 29.
2 See C. Booker, *The Neophiliacs: A Study of the Revolution in English Life in the Fifties and Sixties*. Collins, London. 1969.,
• B. Levin, *The Pendulum Years: Britain and the Sixties*. Jonathan Cape, London. 1970, and
• K. Davey, *English Imaginaries*. Lawrence & Wishart, London. 1999.
3 Morris, *Mary Quant's London*, 5.
4 These are summarised in F. and A. Cairncross (eds), *The Legacy of the Golden Age: The 1960s and their Economic Consequences*. Routledge, London. 1992, and
• B. Moore-Gilbert and J. Seed (eds), *Cultural Revolution? The Challenge of the Arts in the 1960s*. Routledge, London. 1992.
5 See also the most significant sociological text on the new consumer society of the late 1950s : M. Abrams, *The Teenage Consumer*. London Press Exchange, London. 1959.
6 C. MacInnes, *England, Half English: A Polyphoto of the Fifties*. Penguin, Harmondsworth. 1966, 153-4.
7 M. Quant, *Quant by Quant*. Cassell, London. 1966, 34.
8 S. Maitland (ed), *Very Heaven: Looking back at the 1960s*. Virago, London. 1988, 36.
9 See K. Wedd, *Creative Quarters: Artist's London Holbein to Hirst*. Merrell, London. 2001.
10 I. Nairn, *Nairn's London*. Penguin, Harmondsworth. 1966, 137-8.
11 L. Deighton (ed), *Len Deighton's London Dossier*. Penguin, Harmondsworth. 1967, 247.
12 G. Melly, *Revolt into Style: The Pop Arts in Britain*. Allen Lane, London. 1970, 145.
13 J. Aitken, *The Young Meteors*. Secker & Warburg, London. 1967, 15.
14 Ibid., 14.
15 Quant, *Quant by Quant*, 35.
16 Ibid 47.
17 Leggatt was a debutante turned model who before her untimely death in Tangiers acted as a muse for Quant and ensured that her clothes enjoyed a currency amongst London's 'smart aristo set'. The enterprising Oldham dressed many of Bazaar's windows before going on to find fame as manager of the Rolling Stones. See A. Loog Oldham, *Stoned*. Secker & Warburg, London. 2000, 91-110, and
• Quant, *Quant by Quant*, 98-9.
18 Quant, *Quant by Quant*, 48-9.
19 Maitland, *Very Heaven*, 37-8.
20 Quant, *Quant by Quant*, 73.

21 P. Denver, *Black Stockings for Chelsea*. Consul Books, London. 1963, 5.

22 Quant, *Quant by Quant*, 74.

23 Professor Elizabeth Wilson notes that in 1955 she took to wearing her grandmother's black lisle stockings to London parties. At one of these her striking leg-wear was noticed by debutante April Brunner who went on to promote the look more widely amongst the Chelsea social set.

24 Quant, *Quant by Quant*, 74.

25 R. Fairley, *A Bomb in the Collection: Fashion with the Lid Off*. Clifton Books, Brighton. 1969, 47-8.

26 Ibid., 45.

27 Ibid., 51.

28 M. Garland 'Mary Quant', in S. Pendergast (ed), *Contemporary Designers*. St James Press, Detroit. 1997, 694-5.

29 Oldham, *Stoned*, 98.

30 Fairley, *Bomb in the Collection*, 53.

31 Small's designs were conservative compared to Quant's. She supplied clothing for Princess Anne.

32 Fairley, *Bomb in the Collection*, 53.

33 Ibid., 58.

34 Melly, *Revolt into Style*, 147.

35 Ibid.

36 Oldham, *Stoned*, 93.

37 Aitken, *Young Meteors*, 18.

• See also J. S. Hyde Harris and G. Smith, *1966 and All That*. Trefoil, London. 1986,

• J. Lobenthal, *Radical Rags: Fashions of the Sixties*. Abrams, New York. 1990, and

• M. Fogg, *Boutique: A '60s Cultural Phenomenon*. Mitchell Beazley, London. 2003., for retrospective accounts of boutique culture in the 1960s.

38 Aitken, *Young Meteors*, 20.

39 Ibid.

40 Deighton, *London Dossier*, 202.

41 Aitken, *Young Meteors*, 20. Wedge's sober appearance echoed the American 'Modern Jazz' look championed by Andrew Oldham from the late fifties. Angus McGill, men's fashion writer for the Evening Standard, described Oldham as sleek and elegant in his 'school shirt, which was grey, a tie and jacket.' Oldham, *Stoned*, 76-81.

42 Aitken, *Young Meteors*, 22.

43 Deighton, *London Dossier*, 30.

44 Ibid.

45 J. Green, *All Dressed Up: The Sixties and the Counter Culture*. Pimlico, London. 1999, 80-1.

46 See A. O'Neill, 'John Stephen : A Carnaby Street Presentation of Masculinity 1957-1975', in *Fashion Theory* 4(4), 2000. 502-3.

47 Aitken, *Young Meteors*, 24.

48 Green, *Dressed Up*, 80.

49 K. Dallas, *Swinging London: A Guide to Where the Action is*. Stanmore Press, London. 1967, 38.

50 Aitken, *Young Meteors*, 24.

51 S. Sontag, *Against Interpretation and Other Essays*. Eyre & Spottiswoode, London. 1967.

52 Booker, *Neophiliacs*, 295.

53 Ibid., 308.

54 Ibid., 273-4.

55 G. Debord, *La Societe du Spectacle*. Buchet/Chantel, Paris. 1967, and

• H.M. MacLuhan and Q. Fiore, *The Medium is the Massage*. Harmondsworth, Penguin. 1967.

56 Booker, *Neophiliacs*, 18.

57 Green, *Dressed Up*, 72.

58 *Time*, 15 April 1966, 11.

59 This strategy lampooned the current popularity of British films set in or based on London's swinging scene such as *Tom Jones* (1963) - an adaptation of Fielding's novel which drew parallels between the earthy élan of eighteenth-century English society and contemporary permissiveness, *Darling* (1965) - the morality tale of a young model's life starring Julie Christie, and *The Knack* (1965) - a comedy of sexual awakening starring Michael Crawford and Rita Tushingham. Other films in production during 1966 which drew on the same material included *Smashing Time*, *Morgan - A Suitable Case for Treatment*, *Here We Go Round the Mulberry Bush* and *Blow-Up*.

60 *Time*, 15 April 1966, 41.

61 *Time*, 22 April 1966.

62 *Time*, 29 April 1966.

63 *Time*, 6 May 1966, 9.

64 For examples of the desire of those on the Left to accommodate the contradictions of Swinging London see Marxist activist David Widgery's feelings of fascination and repulsion towards the Chelsea myth as expressed in his early articles for the counter-cultural magazine *Oz* and remembered in

• J. Green, *Days in the Life: Voices from the English Underground 1961-1971*. Pimlico, London. 1998, 147, and

• feminist pioneer Sheila Rowbotham's personal account of her enjoyment of the new fashions in S. Rowbotham, *Promise of a Dream: Remembering the Sixties*. Allen Lane, London. 2000, 118-134.

65 Moore-Gilbert and Seed (eds), *Cultural Revolution?* 3.
66 Levin, *Pendulum Years*, 186-7.
67 B. Martin cited in J. Richards 'New Waves and Old Myths : British Cinema in the 1960s', in Moore-Gilbert and Seed (eds), *Cultural Revolution?* 233.
68 Rowbotham, *Promise*, 118.
69 Green, *Dressed Up*, 76.
70 MacInnes, *England*, 153.
71 Melly, *Revolt*, 153.
72 Maitland, *Very Heaven*, 23-4.
73 Booker, *Neophiliacs*, 26.
74 'Pop Eye', *London Life*. 25 December 1965, 16.
75 'Spoil Yourself', *London Life*. 25 Dec 1965, 22-5.
76 Maitland, *Very Heaven*, 215.
77 Green, *Dressed Up*, 81.
78 For further discussion of the shift in fashion photography from the statuesque elegance promoted in the 1950s to the mobile and expressive tenor of 1960s imagery see B. Rogers and V. Williams, *Look at Me: Fashion and Photography in Britain 1960-1999*. British Council, London. 1999., and
• M. Harrison, *Appearances: Fashion Photography since 1945*. London. 1991.
79 H. Radner 'On the Move : Fashion photography and the Single Girl in the 1960s', in S. Bruzzi and P. Church Gibson (eds), *Fashion Cultures: Theories, Explorations and Analysis*. Routledge, London. 2000. 128.
80 P. Juliana Smith "You Don't Have to Say You Love Me' : The Camp Masquerade of Dusty Springfield', in P. Juliana Smith (ed) *The Queer Sixties*. Routledge, New York. 1999, 106.
81 Radner, *On the Move*, 130.
82 Juliana Smith, *Queer Sixties*, 112.
83 Aitken, *Young Meteors*, 34.
84 Maitland, *Very Heaven*, 215.
85 Museum of London Accession Number 91.35.
86 Museum of London Accession Number 72.17. This item was purchased (for personal use) by mail-order from a Biba catalogue by museum curator Naomi Tarrant.
87 Maitland, *Very Heaven*, 36.
88 Ibid., 39.
89 B. Hulanicki, *From A to Biba*. Hutchinson, London. 1983, 75-6.
90 Aitken, *Young Meteors*, 17-18. Aitken's reference to 'mahogany wardrobes' here is probably mistaken. The fittings of the Grocer's shop were retained and these cupboards were actually the original display cabinets. (I am grateful to Elizabeth Wilson for this observation.)

91 Aitken, *Young Meteors*, 18.
92 Hulanicki, *A to Biba*, 98.
93 Mail-order supported the foundation of Biba in 1964 and was re-introduced on a more ambitious scale in 1968.
94 Aitken, *Young Meteors*, 18.
95 Hulanicki, A to Biba, 79.
96 Aitken, Young Meteors, 19.
97 See M. McCurrie and E. Grimshaw (eds), *Shop in London*. Specialist Features, London. 1972, 23-4., and
• *The London Fashion Guide*. Farrol Kahn, London. 1975, 136., for pointed descriptions of Biba's excesses at the end of its run.
98 Maitland, *Very Heaven*, 39.
99 Hulanicki, *A to Biba*, 98.
100 *Biba - The Label: The Lifestyle: The Look*. Newcastle, Tyne & Wear Museums. 1993, 11.

## CHAPTER 7

1 M. Kohn, 'Market Force', *Observer*, 14 January 1990.
2 Bruce Robinson's film *Withnail and I*, starring Richard E. Grant and Paul McGann as struggling young actors renting a sordid flat in the Camden of the late 1960s, was released in 1987. The distinctive sartorial and verbal styles of its protagonists earned the film a cult following among British students.
3 M. Ginsberg, 'Rags to Riches: The Second-Hand Clothes Trade 1700-1978', *Costume* 14. 1980, 121-35.
4 See C. Breward, *The Hidden Consumer: Masculinities, Fashion and City Life 1860-1914*. Manchester University Press, Manchester. 1999, 122-7, for examples of nineteenth-century writing on second-hand markets.
5 M. Benedetta, *The Street Markets of London*. John Miles, London. 1936, 155-59.
6 J. White, *London in the Twentieth Century: A City and its People*. Viking, Harmondsworth. 2001, 252-3.
7 J. Brown, *I had a Pitch on the Stones*. Nicholson & Watson, London. 1946, 11.
8 Ibid., 98-9.
9 Ibid.., 115-6.
10 Cited in J. Richardson, *Camden Town and Primrose Hill Past*. Historical Publications, London. 1991, 119-21.
• See also G. Tindall, *The Fields Beneath*. Temple Smith, London. 1977, 205-7.
11 K. Wedd, *Artists' London: Holbein to Hirst*. Merrell, London. 2001, 108.
12 J. Whitehead, *The Growth of Camden Town 1800-2000*. Jack Whitehead, London. 1999, 121-3.

13 Ibid., 126-31.

14 D. Thomson, *In Camden Town*. Penguin, Harmondsworth. 1985, 14.

15 M. Boxer, *The Times We Live In*. Jonathan Cape, London. 1978, 51-2.

16 Ibid., 8.

17 M. Gray, *London's Rock Landmarks*. Omnibus Press, London. 1985, 13.

18 N. Tomalin, 'Camden's Treasure Box' 1973. Camden Libraries Local History Collection.

19 T. Christensen, *Neighbourhood Survival: The Struggle for Covent Garden's Future*. Prism Press, Dorchester. 1979.

20 J. Raban, *Soft City*. Hamish Hamilton, London. 1974, 101-2.

21 A. Scanlon, *Those Tourists Are Money: The Rock n Roll Guide to Camden*. Tristia, London. 1997, 97.

22 Thomson, *Camden Town*, 115.

23 Scanlon, *Those Tourists*, 138.

24 K. Perlmutter, *London Street Markets*. Wildwood House, London. 1983, 73-4.

25 *City Limits*. 6-12 August, 1982.

26 London Borough of Camden, Development Control Sub Committee. 18 February 1986.

27 Camden Public Relations News. 24 September 1993.

28 London Borough of Camden, Planning and Transport (North East Area) Sub Committee. 23 July 1987.

29 V. Toulouse, 'The Common Market'. *i-D* 'The Political Issue' October 1989, 70.

30 A. McRobbie, 'Second Hand Dresses and the Rag Market', in A. McRobbie, (ed.), *Zoot Suits and Second Hand Dresses*. Macmillan, London. 1989, 32-3.

31 Ibid., 32.

32 C. McDowell, *Jean-Paul Gaultier*. Cassell & Co., London. 2000, 50.

33 P. Mauries (ed.), *Pieces of a Pattern: Lacroix by Lacroix*. Thames & Hudson, London. 1992, 79-80.

34 McRobbie, 'Second Hand', 39.

35 A. Carpenter, 'Body Map Bust Out' , *Ms London*, 8 July 1985, 10.

36 A. McGill, 'Mapping a Way Ahead' *London Evening Standard*, 14 March 1984, 21-4.

37 N. Jeal, 'Body Map', *Observer*, 12 June 1988, 35.

38 Carpenter, 'Body Map Bust Out', 10.

39 T. Blanchard, 'Body Map', *Independent* 'Weekend', 9 June 1994.

40 T. Kingswell, *Red or Dead: The Good, the Bad and the Ugly*. Thames & Hudson, London. 1998, 10.

41 'Wayne Hemmingway', *UCL People Alumni Magazine*, Spring 2001, 8.

42 C. Evans, 'Fashion Stranger than Fiction: Shelley Fox' in C. Breward, B. Conekin and C. Cox (eds), *The Englishness of English Dress*. Berg, Oxford. 2002, 191.

43 *Guardian* Space Magazine. 9 April 1999.

# BIBLIOGRAPHY
## ARCHIVAL SOURCES

Camden Libraries, London.
    Local History Collection
City of Westminster Local Archives Centre,
    London.
    Photographic Collection
Guildhall Library, London.
    Trade Card Collection
London College of Fashion, London.
    Emap Archive
Museum of London, London.
    Dress Collection
    Ephemera Collection
National Archive of Art and Design, London.
National Monuments Record, London.
    Photographic Collection
Yale University, New Haven.
    Center for British Art, Prints & Drawings
    Collection

## NEWSPAPERS AND PERIODICALS

Blitz
Camden Public Relations News
City Limits
Country Life
Drapers Record
i-D
London Life
Men's Wear
Ms London
Oz Magazine
The Daily Mail
The English Spy
The Face
The Fred
The Guardian
The Independent
The London Evening Standard
The Observer
The Strand Magazine
Square Peg
Time
Time Out
UCL People Alumni Magazine

## PRIMARY SOURCES

Abrams, M., The Teenage Consumer. London Press
    Exchange, London. 1959.
Aitken, J., The Young Meteors. Secker & Warburg,
    London. 1967.
Amies, H., Just So Far. Collins, London. 1954.

Anon, Dandy Bewitched. London.
    1820 (BL 1875 6 30 (51)).
Anon, The Dandies Ball or High Life in the City.
    John Marshall, London. 1819.
Anon., 'A Description of the Offices of The Strand
    Magazine', The Strand Magazine, Vol. IV. July-
    December 1892.
Anon., 'Dear Street', Country Life, 1 May 1937.
Anon., Mill Hill and Edgware. Service, London.
    1934.
Anon., Portraits from Life or Memoirs of a Rambler.
    J. Moore, London. 1800.
Anon., The London Fashion Guide. Farrol Kahn,
    London. 1975.
Archer, W., The Theatrical World of 1894. Walter
    Scott, London. 1895.
Aria, Mrs, Costume: Fanciful, Historical and
    Theatrical. Macmillan, London. 1906.
Armfeldt, E., 'Cosmopolitan London', in G. Sims
    (ed.), Living London, Vol. I. Cassell, London.
    1906.
Armfeldt, E., 'Italy in London', in G. Sims (ed.),
    Living London, Vol. I. Cassell, London. 1906.
Armfeldt, E., 'Oriental London', in G. Sims (ed.),
    Living London, Vol. I. Cassell, London. 1906.
Beaton, C. and K. Tynan, Persona Grata. Allan
    Wingate, London. 1953.
Benedetta, M., The Street Markets of London. John
    Miles, London. 1936.
Benjamin, T., A Shopping Guide to London. Robert
    McBride, New York. 1930.
Benjamin, T., London Shops and Shopping. Herbert
    Joseph, London. 1934.
Blackmantle, B., The English Spy, Vol I.
    Sherwood, Gilbert & Piper, London. 1826.
Blanchard, T., 'Body Map', Independent
    'Weekend', 9 June 1994.
Bolitho, H., Marie Tempest. Cobden Sanderson,
    London. 1936.
Booth, C., Life and Labour of the People in
    London, Vol. I. Kelly, New York. 1969.
Borsa, M., The English Stage of Today. John Lane,
    London. 1908.
British Travel and Holiday Association, Shopping
    in London. London. 1953.
Brown, J., I had a Pitch on the Stones. Nicholson
    & Watson, London. 1946.
Browne, K.R.G., Suburban Days. Cassell, London.
    1928.
Bulwer Lytton, E., Pelham: Or the Adventures of a
    Gentleman. Leipzig. 1842.
Burke, T., Nights in Town: A London
    Autobiography. George Allen & Unwin,
    London. 1915.
Camden Public Relations News. 24 September
    1993.

Carpenter, A., 'Body Map Bust Out', *Ms London*, 8 July 1985.

*City Limits*. 6-12 August, 1982.

Cohen-Portheim, P., *The Spirit of London*. J. B. Lippincott, Philadelphia. 1930.

Collier, C., *Harlequinade: The Story of my Life*. John Lane, London. 1929.

Cook, E. T., *Highways and Byways in London*. Macmillan, London. 1911.

D. H. Evans, *Mail Order Catalogue and Fashion Supplement*. 1939. Guildhall Library. Pam 12379.

Dallas, K., *Swinging London: A Guide to Where the Action Is*. Stanmore Press, London. 1967.

Dark, S., *The Marie Tempest Birthday Book*. Stanley Paul, London. 1914.

Davenport Adams, W., *A Book of Burlesque*. Henry & Co., London. 1891.

Deighton, L. (ed.), *Len Deighton's London Dossier*. Penguin, Harmondsworth. 1967.

Denver, P., *Black Stockings for Chelsea*. Consul Books, London. 1963.

Dobbs, S.P., *The Clothing Workers of Great Britain*. Routledge, London. 1928.

Douglas, J., *Adventures in London*. Cassell & Co., London. 1909.

Duff Gordon, Lady, *Discretions and Indiscretions*. Jarrolds, London. 1932.

Duff, C. (ed.), *Anthropological Report on a London Suburb by Prof. Vladimir Chernichewski*. Grayson & Grayson, London. 1935.

Egan, P. (J. Ford (ed.)), *Boxiana or Sketches of Ancient and Modern Pugilism*. Folio Society. 1976.

Egan, P., *Life in London*. Sherwood, Neely & Jones, London. 1821.

Fairley, R., *A Bomb in the Collection: Fashion with the Lid off*. Clifton Books, Brighton. 1969.

Ford, F. Madox, *The Soul of London*. J.M. Dent, London. 1995 [1904].

Forester, C.W., *Success through Dress*. Duckworth, London. 1925.

Fyvel, T., *The Insecure Offenders: Rebellious Youth in the Welfare State*. Chatto & Windus, London. 1961.

Gordon, C., *Old Time Aldwych, The Kingsway and Neighbourhood*. T. Fisher Unwin, London. 1903.

Graham, S., *London Nights*. Hurst & Blackett, London. 1925.

Graham, S., *Twice Round the London Clock and More London Nights*. Ernest Benn, London. 1933.

Gronow, R., *Reminiscences of Captain Gronow*. Smith, Elder & Co., London. 1862.

Heath, *Fashion and Folly*. London. 1822. (Guildhall Library: Prints and Drawings).

Hollingshead, J., *Gaiety Chronicles*. A. Constable, London. 1898.

Jeal, N., 'Body Map', *Observer*, 12 June 1988.

Knight, C., *London*, Vol. III. Virtue & Co., London. 1870.

Knight, C., *London*, Vol. V. Virtue & Co., London. 1870.

Kohn, M., 'Market Force', *Observer*, 14 January 1990.

Lamington, A., *In the Days of the Dandies*. Eversleigh Nash, London. 1906.

Llewellyn Smith, H. (ed.), *The New Survey of London Life and Labour*, Vol. I. King & Son, London. 1930.

Llewellyn Smith, H. (ed.), *The New Survey of London Life and Labour*, Vol. II. King & Son, London. 1931.

Llewellyn Smith, H. (ed.), *The New Survey of London Life and Labour*, Vol. IX. King & Son, London. 1935.

Llewellyn Smith, H. (ed.), *The New Survey of London Life and Labour*, Vol. V. King & Son, London. 1933.

London Borough of Camden, Development Control Sub Committee. 18 February 1986.

London Borough of Camden, Planning and Transport (North East Area) Sub Committee. 23 July 1987.

*London Life*. 25 December 1965.

Markham, A., *Shop Ahoy: Your Shopping and Entertainment Guide to London*. Newman Neame, London. 1959.

Marshall, F., *London West*. The Studio, London. 1944.

McCarthy, J., *Charing Cross to St Paul's*. Seeley & Co., London. 1893.

McCurrie, M., and E. Grimshaw (eds.), *Shop in London*. Specialist Features, London. 1972.

McGill, A., 'Mapping a Way Ahead', *London Evening Standard*, 14 March 1984.

*Men's Wear*, 19 April 1952.

*Men's Wear*, 25 April 1953.

*Men's Wear*, 25 January 1947.

*Men's Wear*, 9 January 1954.

*Men's Wear*, 3 October 1953.

*Men's Wear*, 27 September 1952.

Montizambert, E., *London Discoveries in Shops and Restaurants*. Women Publishers Ltd., London. 1924.

Nairn, I., *Nairn's London*. Penguin, Harmondsworth. 1966.

Norman, F., and J. Bernard, *Soho Night and Day*. Secker & Warburg, London. 1966.

Priestley, J.B., *Angel Pavement*.
William Heinemann, London. 1937.
Priestley, J.B., *English Journey*.
William Heinemann, London. 1934.
Programmes for Salone Margherita, Napoli, 1910,
Teatro Bellini, 1914 and Ambassadeurs, Paris
(undated), Ephemera Collection, Museum of
London.
Pugh, E., *The City of the World: A Book about
London and the Londoner*.
Thomas Nelson & Sons, London. 1908.
Quant, M., *Quant by Quant*. Cassell, London.
1966.
Raymond, L., *Guide to Edgware*. The British
Publishing Company Ltd., London. 1927.
Reiver, B., *Is Burlesque Art ?* J. Jeffery, London.
1880.
Sala, G., *London Up to Date*. A. & C. Black,
London. 1894.
Sala, G., *Twice Round the Clock*.
Houlston & Wright, London. 1857.
Settle, A., *Clothes Line*. Methuen, London. 1937.
*The Guardian Space Magazine*. 9 April 1999.
*Time*. 29 April 1966.
*Time*. 6 May 6 1966.
*Time*. 15 April 1966.
*Time*. 22 April 1966.
Tomalin, N., 'Camden's Treasure Box' 1973.
Camden Libraries Local History Collection.
Toulouse, V., 'The Common Market', *i-D*
'The Political Issue', October 1989.
*UCL People Alumni Magazine*, Spring 2001.
Vanbrugh, I., *To Tell My Story*. Hutchinson & Co.,
London. 1948.
Vermont, M. de., and C. Darnley, *London & Paris or
Comparative Sketches*. Longman, London.
1823.
Wheatley, H.B., *Bond Street Old and New
1686-1911*. Fine Art Society, London. 1911.
Whife, A. (ed.), *The Modern Tailor, Outfitter and
Clothier*. Caxton, London. 1949.
Willcock, H. D., *Mass Observation Report on
Juvenile Delinquency*. Falcon Press, London.
1949.
Williams QC, M., *Round London*. Macmillan,
London. 1896.
Williams, H., *South London*. Robert Hale, London.
1949.
Wray, M., *The Women's Outerwear Industry*.
Duckworth, London. 1957.
Wyndham, Lady, *Charles Wyndham and Mary
Moore*. Private Printing, London. 1925.

## SECONDARY SOURCES

Ackroyd, P., *London: The Biography*.
Chatto & Windus, London. 2000.
Adburgham, A., *Shopping in Style*.
Thames & Hudson, London. 1979.
Adburgham, A., *Silver Fork Society: Fashionable
Life and Literature from 1814-1840*.
Constable, London. 1983.
Allen, R., *Horrible Prettiness: Burlesque and
American Culture*. University of North Carolina
Press, Chapel Hill. 1991.
Auge, M., *Non-places: Introduction to an
Anthropology of Supermodernity*.
Verso, London. 1995.
Bailey, P., 'Naughty but Nice: Musical Comedy
and the Rhetoric of the Girl 1892-1914' in
M. Booth and J. Kaplan eds., *The Edwardian
Theatre: Essays in Performance and the Stage*.
Cambridge University Press, Cambridge. 1996.
Bailey, P., *Popular Culture and Performance in the
Victorian City*. Cambridge University Press,
Cambridge. 1998.
Benjamin, W., *Charles Baudelaire: A Lyric Poet in
the Era of High Capitalism*. Verso, London.
1983.
Benjamin, W., *The Arcades Project*. Belknap,
Cambridge, MA. 1999.
Berman, M., *All That is Solid Melts Into Air*.
Simon & Schuster, New York. 1982.
Bliss, T., *Jane Welsh Carlyle: A New Selection of
her Letters*. Victor Gollancz, London. 1949.
Booker, C., *The Neophiliacs: A Study of the
Revolution in English Life in the Fifties and
Sixties*. Collins, London. 1969.
Booth, M. (ed.), *Victorian Theatrical Trades:
Articles from The Stage 1883-1884*. The
Society for Theatre Research, London . 1981.
Booth, M., *Theatre in the Victorian Age*.
Cambridge University Press, Cambridge. 1991.
Booth, M., *Victorian Spectacular Theatre*.
Routledge, London. 1981.
Bordern, I., J. Kerr, A. Pivaro, J. Rendell (eds.),
*Strangely Familiar: Narratives of Architecture in
the City*. Routledge, London. 1996.
Boutet de Monvel, R., *Beau Brummell and his
Times*. Everleigh Nash, London. 1908.
Boxer, M., *The Times We Live In*. Jonathan Cape,
London. 1978.
Breward, C., 'In the Eye of the Storm: Oxford
Circus and the Fashioning of Modernity',
*Fashion Theory* 4(1), 2000.
Breward, C., *Fashion*. Oxford University Press,
Oxford. 2003.
Breward, C., *The Hidden Consumer: Masculinities,
Fashion and City Life 1860-1914*. Manchester
University Press, Manchester. 1999.

Bruzzi, S., and P. Church Gibson (eds), *Fashion Cultures: Theories, Explorations and Analysis*. Routledge, London. 2000.

Burgin, V., *Some Cities*. Reaktion, London. 1996.

Butler, M., 'Culture's Medium: The Role of the Review' in S. Curran (ed.), *The Cambridge Companion to British Romanticism*. Cambridge University Press, Cambridge. 1993.

Cairncross, F. and A. Cairncross (eds), *The Legacy of the Golden Age: The 1960s and their Economic Consequences*. Routledge, London. 1992.

Carey, J., *The Intellectuals and the Masses*. Faber & Faber, London. 1992.

Chamberlain, M., *Growing Up in Lambeth*. Virago, London. 1989.

Christensen, T., *Neighbourhood Survival: The Struggle for Covent Garden's Future*. Prism Press, Dorchester. 1979.

Cohn, N., *Today There Are No Gentlemen*. Weidenfeld & Nicholson, London. 1971.

Connely, W., *Count D'Orsay: The Dandy of Dandies*. Cassell & Co., London. 1952.

Dart, G., 'Flash Style : Pierce Egan and Literary London 1820-1828', *History Workshop Journal* 51, Spring 2001.

Davey, K., *English Imaginaries*. Lawrence & Wishart, London. 1999.

Davies, A., *Leisure, Gender and Poverty: Working Class Culture in Salford and Manchester*. Open University Press, Buckingham. 1992.

Davis, M., *City of Quartz*. Verso, London. 1991.

Davis, T., *Actresses as Working Women: Their Social Identity in Victorian Culture*. Routledge, London. 1991.

De Certeau, M., *The Practice of Everyday Life*. University of Minnesota Press, Minneapolis. 1998.

Debord, G., *La Societe du Spectacle*. Buchet/Chantel, Paris. 1967.

Dickens, C., *Sketches by Boz*. Penguin, Harmondsworth. 1995.

Ehrman, E., 'The Spirit of English Style: Hardy Amies, Royal Dressmaker and International Businessman', in C. Breward, B. Conekin and C. Cox (eds.), *The Englishness of English Dress*. Berg, Oxford. 2002.

Entwistle, J., and E. Wilson (eds.), *Body Dressing*. Berg, Oxford. 2001.

Entwistle, J., *The Fashioned Body: Fashion, Dress and Modern Social Theory*. Polity, Cambridge. 2000.

Etherington Smith, M., and J. Pilcher, *The It Girls*. Hamish Hamilton, London. 1986.

Evans, C., 'Fashion Stranger than Fiction: Shelley Fox', in C. Breward, B. Conekin and C. Cox (eds), *The Englishness of English Dress*. Berg, Oxford. 2002.

Farson, D., *Soho in the Fifties*. Michael Joseph, London. 1987.

*Fashion Theory*, Vol. 2(4), 1998.

Finnegan, R., *Tales of the City: A Study of Narrative and Urban Life*. Cambridge University Press, Cambridge. 1997.

Fogg, M., *Boutique: A '60s Cultural Phenomenon*. Mitchell Beazley, London. 2003.

Frisby, D., and M. Featherstone (eds.), *Simmel on Culture*. Sage, London. 1997.

Garland, M., *The Indecisive Decade: The World of Fashion and Entertainment in the 30s*. Macdonald & Co., London. 1968.

Gilbert, D., 'Urban Outfitting : The City and the Spaces of Fashion Culture', in S. Bruzzi and P. Church Gibson (eds), *Fashion Cultures*. Routledge, London. 1999.

Ginsberg, M., 'Rags to Riches: The Second-Hand Clothes Trade 1700-1978', *Costume* 14. 1980.

Gray, M., *London's Rock Landmarks*. Omnibus Press, London. 1985.

Green, J., *All Dressed Up: The Sixties and the Counter Culture*. Pimlico, London. 1999.

Green, J., *Days in the Life: Voices from the English Underground 1961-1971*. Pimlico, London. 1998.

Green, N., *Ready to Wear, Ready to Work: A Century of Industry and Immigrants in Paris & New York*. Duke University Press, NC. 1997.

Green, O., *Underground Art: London Transport Posters*. Laurence King, London. 1999.

Halliday, S., *Underground to Everywhere: London's Underground Railway in the Life of the Capital*. Sutton, Stroud. 2001.

Harrison, M., *Appearances: Fashion Photography since 1945*. London. 1991.

Harvey, D., *Consciousness and the Urban Experience*. John Hopkins University Press, Baltimore. 1985.

Harvey, D., *The Condition of Postmodernity*. Blackwell, Oxford. 1989.

Hayden, D., *The Power of Place*. MIT Press, Cambridge, MA. 1995.

Hebdige, D., *Subculture: The Meaning of Style*. Routledge, London. 1979.

Hobbs, D., *Doing the Business: Entrepreneurship, the Working Class and Detectives in the East End of London*. Clarendon Press, Oxford. 1988.

Hopkins, H., *The New Look: A Social History of the Forties and Fifties*. Secker & Warburg, London. 1964.

Howe, P. (ed.), *The Best of Hazlitt*. Methuen, London. 1923.

Hulanicki, B., *From A to Biba*. Hutchinson, London. 1983.

Humble, N., *The Feminine Middlebrow Novel, 1920s to 1950*. Oxford University Press, Oxford. 2001.

Humphries, S., and G. Weightman, *The Making of Modern London 1815-1914*. Sidgwick & Jackson, London. 1983.

Humphries, S., and J. Taylor, *The Making of Modern London 1945-1985*. Sidgwick & Jackson, London. 1986.

Hyde Harris, J.S., and G. Smith, *1966 and All That*. Trefoil, London. 1986.

Inwood, S., *A History of London*. London, 1998.

Jack, I. (ed.), *London: The Lives of the City (Granta 65)*, Granta, London. 1999.

Jackson, A., *Semi-detached London: Suburban Development, Life and Transport 1900-1939*. Allen & Unwin, London. 1973.

Jacob, N., *Me and the Swans*. Wm. Kimber & Co., London. 1963.

Jesse, Cpt., *The Life of George Brummell Esq.*, Vol. I. John Nimmo, London. 1886.

Juliana Smith, P. (ed.) *The Queer Sixties*. Routledge, New York. 1999.

Kaplan, J., and S. Stowell, *Theatre and Fashion: Oscar Wilde to the Suffragettes*. Cambridge University Press, Cambridge. 1994.

Keating, P. J., *The Working Classes in Victorian Fiction*. Routledge & Kegan Paul, London. 1979.

Kingswell, T., *Red or Dead: The Good, the Bad and the Ugly*. Thames & Hudson, London. 1998.

Kwint, M., C. Breward and J. Aynsley (eds), *Material Memories: Design and Evocation*. Berg, Oxford. 1999.

Lee, H., *The Novels of Virginia Woolf*. Methuen, London. 1977.

Lee, H., *Virginia Woolf*. Chatto & Windus. 1996.

Lefebvre, H., *Writings on Cities*. Blackwell, Oxford. 1996.

Levin, B., *The Pendulum Years: Britain and the Sixties*. Jonathan Cape, London. 1970.

Light, A., *Forever England: Femininity, Literature and Conservatism between the Wars*. Routledge, London. 1991.

Lobenthal, J., *Radical Rags: Fashions of the Sixties*. Abrams, New York. 1990.

Loog Oldham, A., *Stoned*. Secker & Warburg, London. 2000.

MacInnes, C., *England, Half English: A Polyphoto of the Fifties*. Penguin, Harmondsworth. 1966.

Mackenzie, G., *Marylebone: Great City North of Oxford Street*. Macmillan, London. 1972.

MacLuhan, H. M., and Q. Fiore, *The Medium is the Massage*. Harmondsworth, Penguin. 1967.

Maguire, H., 'The Architectural Response', in R. Foulkes (ed.), *British Theatre in the 1890s*. Cambridge University Press, Cambridge. 1992.

Maitland, S. (ed.), *Very Heaven: Looking Back at the 1960s*. Virago, London. 1988.

Mander, R., and J. Mitchenson, *Musical Comedy: A Story in Pictures*. Peter Davies, London. 1969.

Mandler, P., *Aristocratic Government in the Age of Reform: Whigs and Liberals 1830-1852*. Clarendon Press, Oxford. 1990.

Massey, D., *Space, Place and Gender*. Polity, Cambridge. 1994.

Mauries, P. (ed.), *Pieces of a Pattern: Lacroix by Lacroix*. Thames & Hudson, London. 1992.

Mayhew, H., *London Labour and the London Poor*. Penguin, Harmondsworth. 1985.

McDowell, C., *Jean-Paul Gaultier*. Cassell & Co., London. 2000.

McKellar, E., *The Birth of Modern London: The Development and Design of the City 1660-1720*. Manchester University Press, Manchester. 1999.

McNeil, P., 'Macaroni Masculinities', in *Fashion Theory* 4(4), 2000.

McQueen Pope, W., *Gaiety: Theatre of Enchantment*. W. H. Allen, London. 1949.

McQueen Pope, W.., *Carriages at Eleven: The Story of the Edwardian Theatre*. Hutchinson & Co., London. 1947.

McRobbie, A. (ed.), *Zoot Suits and Second Hand Dresses*. Macmillan, London. 1989.

McVicar, J., *McVicar by Himself*. Arrow, London. 1979.

Melly, G., *Revolt into Style: The Pop Arts in Britain*. Allen Lane, London. 1970.

Miles, M., T. Hall and I. Borden (eds), *The City Cultures Reader*. Routledge, London. 2000.

Mitchell, R.J., and M.D. Leys, *A History of London Life*. Longmans, London. 1958.

Moorcock, M., *Mother London*. Secker & Warburg, London. 1988.

Moore-Gilbert, B., and J. Seed (eds), *Cultural Revolution? The Challenge of the Arts in the 1960s*. Routledge, London. 1992.

Morris, B., *An Introduction to Mary Quant's London*. London Museum, London. 1973.

Mort, F., 'Mapping Sexual London: The Wolfenden Committee on Homosexual Offences and Prostitution.', *New Formations: Sexual Geographies*. 37, 1999.

Mort, F., *Cultures of Consumption: Masculinities and Social Space in Late Twentieth-Century Britain*. Routledge, London. 1996.

Murphy, R., *Smash and Grab: Gangsters in the London Underworld 1920-1960*. Faber & Faber, London. 1993.

Nadel, I. B., 'Gustave Dore: English Art and London Life', in I. B. Nadel & F. S. Schwarzbach (eds.), *Victorian Artists and the City: A Collection of Critical Essays*. Pergamon, New York. 1980.

Napier Bell, S., *Black Vinyl: White Powder*. Ebury Press, London. 2002.

Nead, L., 'From Alleys to Courts: Obscenity and the Mapping of Victorian London', *New Formations: Sexual Geographies*. 37, 1999.

Nead, L., *Victorian Babylon: People, Streets and Images in Nineteenth-Century London*. Yale University Press, New Haven. 2000.

O'Neill, A., 'John Stephen : A Carnaby Street Presentation of Masculinity 1957-1975' *Fashion Theory* 4(4), 2000.

Ogborn, M., *Spaces of Modernity: London's Geographies 1680-1780*. Guilford Press, New York. 1998.

Olsen, D., *The City as a Work of Art*. Yale University Press, New Haven. 1986.

Partington, A., 'The Days of the New Look: Working Class Affluence and the Consumer Culture' in J. Fyrth (ed.), *Labour's Promised Land? Culture and Society in Labour Britain 1945-51*. Lawrence & Wishart, London. 1995.

Pearson, G., *Hooligan: A History of Respectable Fears*. Macmillan, London. 1983.

Pendergast, S. (ed.), *Contemporary Designers*. St James Press, Detroit. 1997.

Perlmutter, K., *London Street Markets*. Wildwood House, London. 1983.

Perrot, P., *Fashioning the Bourgeoisie*. Princeton University Press, NJ. 1994.

Pile, S., *The Body and the City*. Routledge, London. 1996.

Pointon, M., 'Pugilism, Painters and National Identity in Early Nineteenth Century England' in D. Chandler, J. Gill, T. Guha and G. Tawadros (eds), *Boxer*. INIVA, London. 1996.

Porter, R., *London: A Social History*. Hamish Hamilton, London. 1994.

Raban, J., *Soft City*. Hamish Hamilton, London. 1974.

Rappaport, E., *Shopping for Pleasure: Women in the Making of London's West End*. Princeton University Press, Princeton, NJ. 2000.

Rasmussen, S. E., *London, the Unique City*. Jonathan Cape, London. 1937.

Rendell, J., 'Industrious Females and Professional Beauties: Or Fine Articles for Sale in the Burlington Arcade.' In I. Borden, J. Kerr,

A. Piraro and J. Rendell (eds), *Strangely Familiar: Narratives of Architecture in the City*. Routledge, London. 1996.

Rendell, J., *The Pursuit of Pleasure: Gender, Space and Architecture in Regency London*. Athlone Press, London. 2002.

Ribeiro, A., *The Art of Dress: Fashion in England and France 1750-1820*. Yale, New Haven. 1998.

Richards, J., *The Age of the Dream Palace: Cinema and Society in Britain 1930-1939*. Routledge & Kegan Paul, London. 1984.

Richardson, J., *Camden Town and Primrose Hill Past*. Historical Publications, London. 1991.

Rifkin, A., *Street Noises: Parisian Pleasure 1900-1940*. Manchester University Press, Manchester. 1993.

Roche, D., *The Culture of Clothing*. Cambridge University Press, Cambridge. 1994.

Rock, P., and S. Cohen, 'The Teddy Boy' in V. Bogdanor and R. Skidelsky (eds), *The Age of Affluence 1951-1964*. Macmillan, London. 1970.

Rogers, B., and V. Williams, *Look at Me: Fashion and Photography in Britain 1960-1999*. British Council, London. 1999.

Rowbotham, S., *Promise of a Dream: Remembering the Sixties*. Allen Lane, London. 2000.

Rybczynski, W., *City Life*. Scribner, New York. 1995.

Samuel, R., 'Comers and Goers' in H. J. Dyos and M. Wolff (eds), *The Victorian City: Images and Realities*, Vol. I. Routledge, London. 1999.

Sandison, A., *Robert Louis Stevenson and the Appearance of Modernism: A Future Feeling*. Macmillan, London. 1996.

Savage. J., 'Tainted Love: The Influence of Male Homosexuality and Sexual Divergence on Pop Music and Culture since the War' in A. Tomlinson (ed.), *Consumption, Identity and Style: Marketing, Meanings and the Packaging of Pleasure*. Comedia, London. 1990.

Scanlon, A., *Those Tourists Are Money: The Rock n Roll Guide to Camden*. Tristia, London. 1997.

Schlor, J., *Nights in the Big City: Paris, Berlin, London 1840-1930*. Reaktion, London. 1998.

Schmiechen, J., *Sweated Industries and Sweated Labour: The London Clothing Trades 1860-1914*. University of Illinois Press, Urbana, IL. 1984.

Schneer, J., *London 1900: The Imperial Metropolis*. Yale University Press, New Haven, 1999.

Sennett, R., *Flesh and Stone*. Faber & Faber, London. 1994.

Sharpe, W., and L. Wallock (eds.), *Visions of the Modern City*. John Hopkins University Press, Baltimore. 1987.

Shesgreen, S., (ed.), *The Cries and Hawkers of London: The Engravings of Marcellus Laroon*. Aldershot. 1990.

Short, E., *Fifty Years of Vaudeville*. Eyre & Spottiswoode, London. 1946.

Sinclair, I., *Lights Out For the Territory*. Granta, London. 1997.

Smith, R., *Physique: The Life of John S. Barrington*. Serpent's Tail, London. 1997.

Sontag, S., *Against Interpretation and Other Essays*. Eyre & Spottiswoode, London. 1967.

Stallybrass, P., and A. White, *The Politics and Poetics of Transgression*. Methuen, London. 1986.

Stedman Jones, G., *Outcast London: A Study in the Relationship between Classes in Victorian Society*. Oxford University Press, Oxford. 1971.

Steele, V., *Paris Fashion: A Cultural History*. Berg, Oxford. 1998.

Struther, J., *Mrs Miniver*. Virago, London. 1989.

Summerson, J., *Georgian London*. Pelican, London. 1962.

Sutherland, D., *Portrait of a Decade: London Life 1945-1955*. Harrap, London. 1988.

Tarrant, N., *The Development of Costume*. Routledge, London. 1994.

Taylor, L., *The Study of Dress History*. Manchester University Press, Manchester. 2002.

Thomson, D., *In Camden Town*. Penguin, Harmondsworth. 1985.

Thorold, P., *The London Rich: The Creation of a Great City from 1666 to the Present*. Viking, London. 1999.

Thrift, N., *Spatial Formations*. Sage, London. 1996.

Tindall, G., *The Fields Beneath*. Temple Smith, London. 1977.

Tulloch, C., 'Strawberries and Cream : Dress, Migration and the Quintessence of Englishness', in C. Breward, B. Conekin and C. Cox (eds), *The Englishness of English Dress*. Berg, Oxford. 2002.

Tyne & Wear Museums. *Biba - The Label: The Lifestyle: The Look*. Newcastle, Tyne & Wear Museums. 1993.

Ugolini, L., 'Clothes and the Modern Man in 1930s Oxford', *Fashion Theory*, 4(4), 2000.

Viscusi, R., *Max Beerbohm, or the Dandy Dante, Re-reading with Mirrors*. John Hopkins University Press, Baltimore. 1986.

Walden, G., *Who's a Dandy?* Gibson Square Books, London. 2002.

Walker, R., *The Savile Row Story*. Prion, London. 1988.

Walkley, C., *The Ghost in the Looking Glass: The Victorian Seamstress*. Peter Owen, London. 1981.

Watson, S., and K. Gibson (eds), *Postmodern Cities and Spaces*. Blackwell, Oxford. 1995.

Wolfreys, J., *Writing London: The Trace of the Urban Text from Blake to Dickens*. Macmillan, London. 1998.

Wedd, K., *Artist's London: Holbein to Hirst*. Merrell, London. 2001.

Whitbourn, F., *Mr Lock of St James Street*. Heinemann, London. 1971.

White, J., *London in the Twentieth Century: A City and its People*. Viking, Harmondsworth. 2001.

Whitehead, J., *The Growth of Camden Town 1800-2000*. Jack Whitehead, London. 1999.

Whiting, S. (ed.), *Differences*. MIT Press, Boston. 1997.

Wigley, M., *White Walls, Designer Dresses*. MIT Press, Boston. 1995.

Wilson, E., *Adorned in Dreams: Fashion and Modernity*. Virago, London. 1985.

Wilson, E., *The Sphinx in the City: Urban Life, the Control of Disorder and Women*. University of California Press, Berkeley. 1991.

Woolf, V., *Mrs Dalloway*. Penguin, Harmondsworth, 1996.

Woolf, V., *The London Scene*. London, Hogarth Press. 1975.

Wright, P., *A Journey Through Ruins: The Last Days of London*. Radius, London. 1991.

York, P., *Style Wars*. Sidgwick & Jackson, London. 1980.

Zukin, S., *The Culture of Cities*. Blackwell, Oxford. 1996.

# INDEX